The Political Economy of Progress

OXFORD STUDIES IN THE HISTORY OF ECONOMICS

Series Editor: Steven G. Medema, University of Colorado, Denver

This series publishes leading-edge scholarship by historians of economics and social science, drawing upon approaches from intellectual history, the history of ideas, and the history of the natural and social sciences. It embraces the history of economic thinking from ancient times to the present, the evolution of the discipline itself, the relationship of economics to other fields of inquiry, and the diffusion of economic ideas within the discipline and to the policy realm and broader publics. This enlarged scope affords the possibility of looking anew at the intellectual, social, and professional forces that have surrounded and conditioned economics' continued development.

The Political Economy of Progress

John Stuart Mill and Modern Radicalism

Joseph Persky

OXFORD
UNIVERSITY PRESS

OXFORD
UNIVERSITY PRESS

Oxford University Press is a department of the University of Oxford. It furthers the University's objective of excellence in research, scholarship, and education by publishing worldwide. Oxford is a registered trade mark of Oxford University Press in the UK and certain other countries.

Published in the United States of America by Oxford University Press
198 Madison Avenue, New York, NY 10016, United States of America.

CIP data is on file at the Library of Congress
ISBN 978-0-19-046063-1

To Victoria,
We are well met.

CONTENTS

ACKNOWLEDGMENTS

Various parts of this work have benefited greatly from comments by colleagues. A warm acknowledgment goes to the regular members of the informal Chicago History of Economics group: John Berdell, Steve Engelmann, Sam Fleischacker, and Deirdre McCloskey. I have gained much from their insightful discussions of several chapters. Core chapters have also benefited from comments by participants in the last several History of Economics Society annual meetings, including Charalampos Konstantinidis and Margaret Schabas. Two chapters here reflect the substantial input of Tim Taylor, who puts in yeoman service as the managing editor of the *Journal of Economic Perspectives* and institutional guardian of the Retrospectives feature there. The entire manuscript has been carefully read by Steve Medema, who went well beyond the duties of a series editor in helping me digest various arguments, including several with which he surely doesn't agree. And, thanks to Scott Parris who, as economics editor for Oxford University Press, allowed me—indeed, encouraged me—to move past Mill as a nineteenth-century figure and to consider his continuing influence in modern political economy and political philosophy.

Five of the following chapters are based on earlier publications, although in several cases with substantial rethinking. Chapter 7, "Poverty, the Poor Laws, and the Family," draws on "Classical Family Values: Ending the Poor Laws as They Knew Them," in the *Journal of Economic Perspectives* 11, no. 1 (1997). Chapter 3 on Bentham first appeared as "From Usury to Interest," also in the *Journal of Economic Perspectives* 21, no. 1 (2007). Chapter 4, "Utilitarian Perspectives on Private Property," was published with a somewhat different thesis as "On the Thinness of Utilitarian Defenses of Private Property," in the *Journal of the History of Economic Thought* 32, no. 1 (2010). Chapter 12, "Rawls and the Means of Production," grows out of "Rawls's Thin (Millean) Defense of Private Property," in *Utilitas* 22, no. 2 (2010). Finally, chapter 13, "Radical Luck," first saw the light of day as "*Utilitarianism* and Luck," in *History of Political Economy* 45, no. 2 (2013).

This seems an appropriate spot to also acknowledge the members of the Chicago Political Economy Group (http://www.cpegonline.org/) not so much for any specific comments on the present manuscript as for their keeping me honest about my own broader Millean radicalism. And for much the same reasons, the University of Illinois at Chicago United Faculty (http://uicunitedfaculty.org/), the gestation of which paralleled and often complicated the writing of this book. I like to think Mill would have approved our efforts to gain a cooperative voice in our workplace.

Finally, I thank the current and past faculty of the Economics Department at the University of Illinois at Chicago. Over forty years, with more graciousness than is shown in many economics departments, they have tolerated and I hope made some use of my continuing absorption in intellectual history.

PROLOGUE: MODERN RADICALISM AND MILL

This book is about John Stuart Mill and his political economy of progress. Mill's approach to progress married radical reform and serious social science. As such, it marked the beginning of a long Anglo-American tradition. A rereading of Mill along these lines will, it is hoped, prove of interest to those who respect him for his contributions to philosophy and/or economics, but find his move toward radicalism confusing at best and reprehensible at worst. For this audience I will make the case that Mill's radical thought is the coherent and compelling product of his utilitarian position.

But there is another, perhaps more favored audience for the present work. These readers are sure of their sympathies to modern radicalism, but they think of Mill (if they think of Mill at all) as only marginally relevant to the expansion of radicalism from the late nineteenth century to the present. My hope is that a reading of Mill as a radical can prove especially valuable to such modern radicals, who have adopted much of Mill's concern with equality and justice, but have lost his progressive optimism—and especially his optimism with respect to fundamental institutional change in people's work lives. Let me start, then, with a sketch of this favored audience.

With the end of World War II, awash in the disillusionment generated by totalitarian regimes, liberals in Western Europe and the United States reopened a debate on the nature of the just society. Over the years, liberalism had come to include a wide range of people and ideas. Throughout this volume, the terms "liberal" and "liberalism" are taken in their broadest possible meanings. A "liberal" is committed to guaranteeing the intellectual and religious freedoms of individuals, government through the active consent of the governed, and meaningful opportunities for (in the Declaration of Independence's most felicitous phrase) the pursuit of happiness. In the postwar years the discussion focused very much on how best to interpret and facilitate this last liberal tenet.[1]

1. Given the breadth of this definition, which is meant to include everyone from libertarians to democratic socialists, one might reasonably ask who is not included

Perhaps not surprisingly, one side of this debate reasserted classical arguments in favor of laissez-faire capitalism.[2] Some of the most persuasive advocates of such a position were drawn from the economics profession—professors like Milton Friedman and F. A. Hayek, who in turn received considerable support from the traditional business community. In their view, a system of laissez-faire capitalism best achieved liberal goals. Such a system allowed individuals the greatest possible freedom in running their lives. In this neoliberal reading, a right to the pursuit of happiness was best served and most fully embodied in a civil right to private property and contract.[3] At a philosophical level, the argument (made most prominently by Isaiah Berlin) asserted that there was no way to reconcile this classical liberal idea of "freedom from" with efforts to expand "freedoms to."

For the most part, liberal economists and political scientists of the midcentury avoided this position of the right and instead gravitated to the political center. Echoing progressive themes from the prewar years, they advocated for the role of the technocrat and expert in both government and business. They emphasized problem solving over ideology. A new

under the liberal tent. Both in the past and the present, the answer is many people. A considerable majority of the world's population live in countries with governments that fail to fully enforce liberal democratic values. (For attempts at quantification, see Economist Intelligence Unit [2015]). For sure, advocates of various types of authoritarian states cannot possibly meet the standard. These would include fascists of the right like the Nazis and of the left like the Chinese communists. Those who justify single-party rule or dictatorial powers by charismatic leaders certainly aren't liberal. Similarly, proponents of theocracy are not liberals. At one time conservatives supporting tradition and monarchal power would not qualify as liberals, but in countries that have accepted democratic principles it is unusual for conservatives (who by definition oppose change) not to also be liberals. However, reactionaries, such as racists or homophobes in the United States, fail the liberal test. As argued below, the ongoing liberal debate is not so much about politics as about political economy—i.e., what type of economic system best matches the purposes of liberalism.

2. By "laissez-faire capitalism" I mean a mode of production in which private firms hire individual workers in a labor market and are free to seek profits both domestically and internationally in largely unregulated markets. For the most part the economics of "classical liberals"—i.e., "classical political economy"—saw in laissez-faire capitalism an attractive set of institutional structures. Of course, capitalism can take other forms—e.g., mercantile capitalism, authoritarian or fascist capitalism, and welfare-state capitalism.

3. The term "neoliberal" has been used in any number of ways, including as a political epithet. For this book, it is meant only to refer to that resurgence of classical liberal thinking characterized by the works of economists such as Friedman and Hayek. It is useful to keep in mind that serious advocates of the broad policies of neoliberalism often allow for (even major) exceptions justifying government interference or regulation. Moreover, they appreciate that there never (and certainly not in nineteenth-century Britain) has been a pure laissez-faire capitalist economy.

appreciation of macroeconomics promised a relatively nonintrusive set of tools capable of guaranteeing prosperity. While the center accepted big government, it viewed large corporations as the efficient engines of the economy. For these pragmatists, liberal goals including the pursuit of happiness were best realized in the context of maintaining macro-prosperity and growth.

To the left of the pragmatists were the liberals who had been won over to the logic of trade unionism and the welfare state. While relatively few American economists fell into this group (a possible exception being J. K. Galbraith), the backbone of the welfarist liberal camp was made up of the labor unions. The unions and their allies were considerably stronger in Western Europe than in the United States. And in Europe they mixed their liberalism with echoes of social democracy. The labor liberals fought to include working-class representation in the halls of power as a countervailing force to large capital. In this role they were often ready to tax and (in Europe) nationalize the wealth of the corporations and very rich. For the labor liberals the individual's pursuit of happiness was best forwarded by such broad institutional changes that aimed to temper the power and control of the most wealthy.

Often allied with the labor liberals was a fourth grouping, a distinctly radical grouping. These left liberals insisted that a right to the pursuit of happiness must entail more than a general prosperity or nationalized industries. For them, equality required more than opportunities seizable by only the most energetic and aggressive. In the radical view, justice and fairness in a wealthy society can only be achieved when meaningful paths to self-definition and participation are available to all, including the least advantaged. These are the radicals who make up the favored audience of the present book. Strongly influenced by the young Marx's theory of alienation and Martin Luther King's tactics of nonviolent resistance, modern radicals in America actively supported the civil rights movement, union democratization, anti-Vietnam War efforts, and an emerging feminist movement. At the intellectual level, modern radicalism has crystallized in the political left-liberal philosophy of John Rawls.

Four observations may help to clarify this impressionistic description of modern radicalism and its place in the liberal tent. First, modern radicalism in the United States and Western Europe has been reformist and not revolutionary. The word *radical* is open to any number of associations. In many contexts, *radical* is combined with *revolutionary*. There is nothing inappropriate with such usage. Radical revolutionaries as opposed to opportunistic revolutionaries base their revolutions on a radical analysis. Such an analysis claims to identify root questions that can only be addressed by revolutionary means. But in post-World War II Western Europe and the United States, the persuasiveness of the radical revolutionary argument has been minimal. Against this background most modern radicals have been advocates of major reform and not revolution.

Second, for the purposes undertaken here, modern radicals are best viewed as the left wing of liberalism.[4] Modern radicals have consistently struggled to construct broader liberal coalitions with the purpose of drawing in supporters of the welfare-state liberals of the center and on occasion even libertarians of the right. The American civil rights movement is perhaps the most powerful example of this effort to coalesce liberal sensibilities. As a practical matter, modern radicals have generally supported trade unions and welfare-state reforms, but always with reservations. Radicals view such programs as vital and necessary for the bridge they can provide to a deeper set of institutional changes. The mix has generated some success in Western Europe, but in the United States modern radicals have remained vague, maddeningly vague, about what form such changes are eventually to take. With an approving nod to the social democracies of Scandinavia and the Netherlands, with elusive references to the "greening of America," with a hazy sympathy for the Third World, modern radicals in the United States have failed to outline a clear plan for broader institutional change.

Third, it is important to recognize the considerable influence of Marxism on modern radicals. Marx's theory of alienation has a strong appeal to modern radicals. Modern radicals also share a materialist outlook with Marxists. At many levels of discourse, the two groups maintain a set of assumptions and observations that generate a considerable give and take. In a range of labor parties of Western Europe, modern radicals have drawn heavily on Marxist categories and analysis. That said, the main body of modern radicals in both the United States and Western Europe have been frightened by the history of revolutionary Marxism as lived out in the Soviet Union and China. The revelations of the 1950s concerning the Stalinist excesses and the unfolding of China's Cultural Revolution cannot be rationalized in any sort of liberal ideology. While some radicals have attempted to do so, their defenses, like libertarian defenses of dictatorial regimes in Latin America, ring of a hollow self-deception. Most modern radicals are caught between a dissatisfaction with many of the

4. If the expression weren't so awkward, I would be tempted to use "rad-libs" instead of "modern radicals" throughout this book.

institutions of modern capitalism and a fear of the totalitarian character of the two most powerful Marxist regimes. Despite much talk of a "third way," modern radicalism has failed to crystallize a clear alternative to the dominance of capitalist relations in production.

Fourth, in recent years some of the best energy of modern radicals has been devoted to intellectual activity, and especially political philosophy. Starting with John Rawls, modern radicals have constructed a new and exciting moral philosophy. This new philosophy represents a major reconsideration of the liberal canon. Like any philosophic effort, modern radicalism has deep roots. Those roots reach down below Marx, the socialists and the communists, all the way down to the early nineteenth century. Those roots are fed by many streams of thought from that time and even earlier. Philosophers such as Rawls, Peter Singer, Amartya Sen, and the Marxist G. A. Cohen have drawn on and utilized that pre-Marxian radical liberalism. In doing so, however, they have often paid only passing attention to the political economy on which that early radicalism was built. The result has been a less than full explanation of the promise of material progress. In particular, the radical philosophers have provided little guidance as to the major institutional reforms consistent with their broad political agendas. Nor has modern radical political economy offered significant help in this key enterprise.[5]

At the intellectual level, the term "modern radicalism" is best thought of as referring to these radical philosophers with their emphasis on justice; at the practical level, it can be taken as pointing toward the radical activists who have sought to inform their own work with serious moral philosophy of this stripe. The present book aims to explore the connections of this type of modern radicalism to the utilitarian radicalism of John Stuart Mill.

The proposed archeological expedition is of some interest in its own right. Tracing the intricacies and connections of intellectual history stimulates our curiosity and broadens our vision. The reader should be warned that there is a good deal of such meandering in the material that follows. But the effort also has a more explicit ideological purpose. Mill's attempt to comprehend the promise of material progress growing out of

5. Of course, there are exceptions. The political economy literature on worker ownership and profit sharing is acknowledged briefly in chapter 9. That said, it should be noted that in recent years radical economists have seemed reluctant to consider their deep connections to Mill and his political economy. For example, Duncan Foley in his recent overview of the history of economic thought, *Adam's Fallacy* (2006), doesn't even mention Mill or Mill's radical agenda.

the industrial revolution encouraged him to bring together his radical utilitarian egalitarianism and his understanding of the political economy of accumulation. At the philosophical level this synthesis produced an evolutionary theory of justice, while at the economic level it generated a truly radical program of institutional reform. Key to that program was Mill's conviction that the laissez-faire capitalism of his day, while playing an immensely useful role in spurring accumulation, would ultimately be replaced by an economy built on a more cooperative base.[6] Mill's radical agenda was imbued with an analysis of material progress. The ideological concern of the present work is that modern radicals, disillusioned with the bureaucratic centralism of twentieth-century communism, have failed to elaborate a material ideology of progress, a plausible utilitarian blueprint of fundamental institutional change. In the context of the continuing debates within modern liberalism, the lack of such a blueprint has left radicals at a great disadvantage; indeed, it has reduced our best arguments to moral exhortations. It is hard to fathom or take seriously a reformist radicalism that looks for a meaningful development of justice in the future without projecting a logic and a program for how and why material production will, over time, be reorganized along more democratic and humanly fulfilling lines.

I will not attempt to prove this fundamental radical/materialist tenet. But I do claim that we can gain insight into its power by studying Mill's political economy of progress. Most likely, the details of Mill's vision of a more cooperative society do not translate directly into solutions to our present problems. But a rereading of the history of Mill's foundational radicalism points up the coherence and energy a radical reform agenda derives if it builds on such a material blueprint. Mill stands at a critical point in the development of radical thought. He gathers together a range of radical themes from the past, deepens their analytical foundations, and sets in motion a serious modern radicalism. Drawing on the Enlightenment, popular radicalism, and utilitarian insights, Mill constructed a political economy of progress that pointed toward an economy freed from an obsession with profits, open to democratic principles, focused on meeting

6. It should be noted that Mill does not use the term "capitalism." He does use the term "capitalist." More significantly, he focuses considerable attention on the relation between the "class of employers" and the "class of the employed." This relationship lies at the very heart of Marx's understanding of the capitalist mode of production. For Mill as well as for Marx, it is from this alienated relationship that profits arise and accumulation proceeds. Under the circumstances it seems fair to refer to Mill's attitudes toward or analysis of "capitalism," or more specifically "laissez-faire capitalism." For a more extensive comparison between Mill and Marx, see chapter 10.

real human needs, and increasingly capable of providing meaningful work. In such a context, justice becomes coherent and reforms consequential. Despite his ambivalences, there are lessons in Mill's approach worth absorbing, lessons of deep relevance to modern radicalism.

Much of the present work can be viewed as a contribution to the ongoing reconsideration of Mill's radicalism. Claeys (2013) has presented a particularly cogent version of the argument for viewing Mill as a serious radical. Claeys's treatment is a valuable addition to a literature emerging in the areas of political philosophy and the history of philosophy. That literature is primarily concerned with the tension between Mill's emphasis on liberty and his willingness to support the expansion of community and governmental powers. To a large extent the focus of these works is to reconcile the radical Mill with the Mill of *On Liberty*. The focus here is a largely complementary one: to reconcile the radical Mill with Mill's broad endorsement of laissez-faire capitalism. In exploring both problems, it is more or less natural to turn to Mill's utilitarian egalitarianism and his understanding of progress to find a consistent base for his radicalism. These themes are just as central to Mill's radical political economy as to his radical political philosophy. And, of course, both approaches draw heavily for examples on Mill's practical reform agenda.

A SKETCH

After a close association with this project for several years, the basic steps in the argument strike me as straightforward and compelling. But for those who need a bit of encouragement to set off on a journey claiming to link John Stuart Mill, author of *On Liberty* and champion of nineteenth-century liberalism, with modern radicalism (or for those who are just appreciative of a simple roadmap), here is a précis of the argument to be found in the subsequent chapters.

There was radical thought, much radical thought, before Mill. Mill's basic contribution is to provide a serious foundation for that body of thought, a foundation consistent with political economy and explicit as to its standards for evaluating policy. His ideas do not emerge de novo, but take as raw materials a range of radical themes from the eighteenth century and even earlier. To appreciate what he added, we do well to review at least a smattering of that radical history.

The radical wing of Enlightenment thought bequeathed three critical visions to the nineteenth century. The first was an ultra-egalitarian outlook on human nature and potential, a conviction that in some operational sense people are fundamentally similar to one another. The second was a reading of the past that saw it as characterized by progress and a reading of the future that promised even more rapid gains. The third, a proto-utilitarian dictum, held that societies broadly, and governments more narrowly, were best judged by the extent to which they achieved the greatest happiness of the greatest number.

Toward the end of the Enlightenment, in the last half of the eighteenth century, the emergence of the field of political economy marked a heightened interest in the material conditions of society, an interest to be further stimulated by the industrial revolution. The French physiocrat school and Adam Smith were both influenced by contemporary Enlightenment thought, including the three key premises noted above. However, these early economists did not appreciate the scale of the economic changes taking place, nor did they anticipate any fundamental alterations in what Marx would come to call the mode of production.

These pioneers focused on constructing an analytical base for political economy. When politically active, they applied the arguments of their new science to supporting traditional liberal reforms. In very much this spirit, the utilitarian polymath Jeremy Bentham early in his career put forward a triumphalist liberal position in support of laissez-faire capitalism. Despite his deep commitment to an egalitarian view of human nature, Bentham's apology argued that laissez-faire capitalism generated the best possible outcomes for the mass of people.

Meanwhile, the Reverend Robert Malthus incorporated into political economy his theory of population. That theory directly attacked the progressive optimism of the Enlightenment philosophes and especially the work of Condorcet. The implications of Malthus's theory were further formalized by David Ricardo's impressive proto-models of the capitalist economy.

It was at this juncture that John Stuart Mill, heir to the political economy of his father James Mill, the utilitarian liberalism of Jeremy Bentham, and the new analytics of David Ricardo, began to put together a set of arguments that we can recognize today as radical. Although Mill remained committed to many traditional liberal concepts, within his liberalism he steadily moved toward a more radical outlook—one that aspired to a much wider sharing of the economy's bounty, one that anticipated a major reorganization of the economy's structure over time. Like the later work of Marx, but unlike much of the Enlightenment literature that inspired both, the core of Mill's theory attempted an analytical formalism. That theory saw the accumulation of capital set in motion by the industrial revolution as providing the basis for a new mode of production. For Mill, laissez-faire capitalism was an efficient—indeed, necessary—stage in that process. Ultimately, however, it was not in itself the end state of progress. Mill anticipated that the economy was moving toward a stationary state capable of supporting a far more egalitarian society. Mill argued that this new stationary state might achieve the utilitarian goal of the greatest happiness of the greatest number. But this outcome was only possible, according to Mill, if the working classes and their allies in the middle classes were able to bring about fundamental institutional reforms.

Mill proposed a lengthening list of institutional changes to be implemented through legislation. But most critically, Mill held that the working classes through their own initiatives must achieve two goals: the control of population growth and the establishment of workers' cooperatives. Mill had always emphasized the Malthusian theme of worker self-control. Over time, he became more and more committed to a radical transition in the employment relationship. Although not inevitable, the material progress under way in the nineteenth century made these developments possible and even likely.

In effect, Mill's approach to progress anticipated much of Marx's historical materialism. Both Marx and Mill were working from the same classical economic base. While Marx was to remain almost vituperative in his discussions of Mill, it is not difficult to make an argument that sees much of Mill in Marx. But, of course, Mill was committed to avoiding a highly centralized economy and to working through reform, not revolution.

Mill's themes were explicitly adopted by the radicals of the late nineteenth and early twentieth century. Most notably, the Fabians of Great Britain took the radical Mill as their champion and analytical economics as their tool. While the strong Fabian commitment to nationalization was at odds with Mill's concerns, their continued support of structural reforms bolstered by political economy had a distinctly Millean cast.

Closer to the present, clear echoes of Mill's radicalism can be found in Rawls's approach to justice. But modern radicals like Rawls offer relatively little in the way of an institutional blueprint for a new economy. This lacuna threatens the entire logic of the modern radical project. Whereas Mill anticipates that workers will be able to govern their own labor in a cooperative setting, the modern radicals put forward no clear description of the productive relations toward which working and middle classes might aspire. Nor do modern radicals describe any forces active in the economy that give any sense of necessity to their reform agenda. Recent philosophical debates about luck can be largely reconciled if our future promises meaningful material progress in the context of more democratic economic institutions.

The claim, then, is that Mill's political economy of progress is both relevant and exemplary. Like Mill's agenda, modern reform to be persuasive needs a material base on which to be founded. The story to be told here describes Mill's increasingly radical effort to fashion a coherent framework for reform from the diverse elements of late eighteenth-century and early nineteenth-century radical thought. Mill's final product was far from perfect. It shows at points Mill's deep ambivalences. But for all that, it possesses a coherence that modern radicalism often lacks. Rereading Mill cannot in itself generate a radical program fully suitable to today's world, but it does underscore the deep connection between realizing equality and achieving the most fundamental institutional reforms.

PART I

The Utilitarian Reading of Accumulation

CHAPTER 1

Antecedents

The nineteenth-century British utilitarians inherited the new discipline of political economy from Adam Smith and his encyclopedic researches summarized in the *Wealth of Nations*. Smith's insights had emphasized the "obvious and simple system of natural liberty" as the best guide to social policy. Smith had seen that system as the base for achieving the wealth of the nation. And he had roughly identified the expansion of that wealth with the general prosperity of the population at large.[1] The utilitarians brought to this suggestive discourse a more sharply defined principle of justice: the greatest happiness of the greatest number.[2] Jeremy Bentham, the insightful, prolific, and eccentric founder of British utilitarianism, famously claimed to have discovered this principle in the philosophy of Smith's good friend David Hume. Such a reading of Hume is open to considerable doubt. Bentham's principle is much more easily derived from the philosophes of the French Enlightenment,[3] despite similarities to Scottish thought. Bentham, himself, acknowledged the intellectual dilettante and philosophe Claude Adrien Helvetius as a major influence. In any event, Smith had certainly not formally worked the utilitarian principle into his system. This was the utilitarian challenge to be taken up by John Stuart Mill.

1. Smith ([1776] 1976, 687–688, and 96). For an ambitious and sympathetic overview of Smith's project, see Evensky (2005).

2. For the origins and early history of the utilitarian coda, see Shackleton (1972), as well as the discussion in the next chapter.

3. The French philosophes may have been inspired by Hutcheson, Smith's instructor (Shackleton 1972).

One line of argument that easily suggested itself to some utilitarians was to assert that Smith's system of natural liberty was fully sufficient to meet the utilitarian standard. In this view, a system of laissez-faire capitalism, achieved through the progress of liberty and built on free markets, private property, and the wage relationship, did about as well as possible for the great majority of people. This was essentially a traditional or even triumphalist liberal position. Most notably among utilitarians, Bentham early put this line forward. Indeed, on one occasion he did so in direct opposition to Smith.

This traditional or classical liberal position pervaded much of early nineteenth-century utilitarianism. Later in the century it bequeathed a set of themes to the neoclassical economic school, despite numerous theoretical differences.[4] More recently, it has shown considerable resilience, echoing down through the years and reemerging in support of the neoliberal ideology of the present day. But these liberal apologetics have not been the only utilitarian themes.[5] Indeed, the history of utilitarianism would be quite dull if all it produced was a version of triumphal liberalism. While early nineteenth-century utilitarians devoted much attention to the codification of traditional liberalism, John Stuart Mill developed a set of increasingly radical themes. These themes like utilitarianism more generally took as their starting point an egalitarian psychology. They were built on a confidence in the promise of progress, and particularly on the possibilities created by extensive capital accumulation. They put forward a range of major reforms aimed at sharing the benefits of growing productivity more widely. These themes included land reform, restrictions on inheritance, and access to education. They also included the extension of the franchise. They embraced the granting of civil rights to national minorities, blacks, and women. They extended to reproductive rights. And perhaps most fundamentally, they included the possibility of reorganizing production in cooperative enterprises. In the end, John Stuart Mill claimed that much of the economic system created by the industrial revolution would be only transitional in nature. His conviction was that the economy that replaced laissez-faire capitalism would not only expand the material base but also make possible meaningful personal growth for the largest share of the population.

4. The classical liberal view feeds directly into the work of Alfred Marshall, often regarded as the founder of modern economics.

5. Here and throughout this volume the terms "apologetics" and "apology" are not meant to convey disparagement but, rather, to suggest serious efforts to defend institutions and arrangements that on the surface may appear less than optimal.

Admittedly these radical themes were developed parallel to a more traditional liberal utilitarianism. At many points the two sets of ideas overlap and intertwine. Indeed, Mill's own radical position developed in a somewhat ambivalent manner. That ambivalence stretched across both analytics and policy. The tension between these two liberalisms remains relevant because of the widespread influence of neoliberalism. Exploring J. S. Mill's radical utilitarian thought—its origins, theoretical underpinnings, successes and failures—can, it is hoped, shed light on the debate that continues to characterize the relation between classical liberal and radical ideologies. That debate hinges on the radical interpretation of the promise of progress: the rapidity of its timing, the breadth of its material dimensions, the character of its political and moral impacts, the ability of society to facilitate and ameliorate the process, the potential contributions of the social sciences, and the extent to which progress will (and should) recast the fundamental institutions of capitalism. That debate hinges on the claim that only radical change can ultimately achieve the most basic aims of utilitarian liberalism.

At the same time Mill's radicalism stands in contrast to more revolutionary solutions. Utilitarians do not rule these out on the basis of any aversion to revolution per se. Mill is sympathetic to both the American and French revolutions. But, Mill asserts that, in the context of mid-nineteenth-century Britain, the revolutionary solution fails the utilitarian test. Progress and the achievements of the industrial revolution are not spent, but ongoing. Rather than improving the happiness of the greatest number, an egalitarian revolution will make matters worse, reduce general welfare, and leave society in chaos. What is required is not revolution, but meaningful reforms to abet and speed the pace of progress.

Despite his ambivalence, Mill presents the foundational argument for modern radical reform. That argument postulates that progress is at work. Material conditions are developing and changing the consciousness and expectations of the great mass of the population. The job is to define and accelerate those institutional changes that point toward a more just society.

THREE RADICAL STREAMS

Obviously Mill's radicalism did not emerge full blown out of a vacuum. Rather, it drew on at least three intertwining lines of thought and action: the radical faction of the eighteenth-century Enlightenment, the popular radicals of the late eighteenth century British reform movement that eventually fed the Chartist struggles of the 1830s, and most immediately the utilitarian philosophical radicals including their Parliamentary allies in the first half of the nineteenth century.[6]

Recently, Jonathan Israel (2011a, 2011b) has drawn attention to a fundamental split between the traditional liberal and the radical streams of thought in eighteenth-century Enlightenment philosophy. Israel assigns Montaigne, as well as the political economists Smith, Hume, and Turgot, to the former. He places Spinoza and Diderot, along with the proto-utilitarians Helvetius, Condorcet, and Godwin, with the latter. If we take the "liberal Enlightenment" to encompass those who emphasized liberty under a rule of law, then, at the risk of oversimplifying, we can use the "radical Enlightenment" to refer to those who, denying the justness of the current order, advocated changes to make equality more meaningful for the great mass of people. In this spirit, the traditional liberal Enlightenment can lay an obvious claim to inspiring J. S. Mill, the author of *On Liberty*. But more important for the purposes here, Mill also developed a radical argument, one rooted in the radical Enlightenment.

The radical Enlightenment was materialist in its philosophy, egalitarian in its morality, and utilitarian in its policy. Most centrally, radical writers saw human progress, guided by reason, as both possible and likely. Many looked forward to the coming of a utopian society. The radicals disparaged traditional institutions that couldn't be justified by reason. If the radical Enlightenment was vague (or even pusillanimous) in its political economy, it was explicit in its support of republican and democratic restructuring. All told the Enlightenment radicals envisioned a fundamental break with the status quo, a break that would allow progress to accelerate.

While some historians have described the Enlightenment as essentially an intellectual phenomenon with little political significance in the short run, Israel has bolstered the claim that the radical Enlightenment laid the very foundation for the upheavals of the French Revolution (Israel 2011b). In much the same way, radical Enlightenment writers (including Paine and Godwin from England) had widespread influence in the popular movement for radical reform in Britain. The popular radicals, drawn largely from the artisan class, began their organizing around Parliamentary reform, seen as central to achieving democracy and meaningful change.

6. A somewhat different classification of British radicals can be found in M. Roberts (2009). In addition to popular and philosophical radicals, Roberts includes the "Manchester School" free-traders (for example, Richard Cobden), and radical evangelical moral reformers (most notably the abolitionist William Wilberforce).

The British popular radicals were spurred to activity by the examples of the American and French revolutions. They drew on middle-class and artisan elements concerned to maintain their roles in a rapidly changing economy and dissatisfied with their lack of access to an antique political system. As emphasized by Craig Calhoun (2012) these British radicals in many respects sought to maintain, rebuild, or reimagine what they viewed as traditional society. In these efforts they were not infrequently at odds with changes that other classes might perceive as progress.

One of the most extreme of the British popular radicals was Thomas Spence, who starting in the 1770s advocated fundamental land reform, universal suffrage, and a primitive safety net. More typical, Major John Cartwright, elder brother of Edmund Cartwright, the inventor of the steam power loom, pushed for universal male suffrage and Parliamentary reform. Cartwright had refused to serve in British forces in the American Revolution and was much taken with the democratic developments of the colonies. His Society for Constitutional Information gave way to the London Corresponding Society (LCS). The latter in the heady days of the 1790s was the political home of an entire generation of new popular radicals, including Francis Place who later became close friends with the utilitarians including Bentham and the Mills (Miles 1988; Place 1972).

Popular radicalism spread in the wake of the Napoleonic wars and the increasing impact of the industrial revolution. Hard times led to heightened protest. The key demand remained Parliamentary reform. In 1819 the Patriotic Union Society called a mass rally for Manchester's St. Peter's Field. They invited Henry Hunt, a radical orator, to address the rally. Hunt openly espoused the extension of the franchise and other aspects of Parliamentary reform. The rally sparked an overreaction by the authorities and ended in what became known as the Peterloo massacre. It was followed by a broad political repression. Hunt served more than two years in prison (Thompson 1984).

There is a clear line from these efforts at Parliamentary reform to the rise of Chartism in the late 1830s. Disappointed, if not disillusioned, by the very limited expansion of the franchise achieved through the Reform Act of 1832, popular radicals including Feargus O'Connor, founder of the radical Yorkshire paper *Northern Star*, turned to massive petitions in support of universal male suffrage. The Chartists eventually embraced a range of radical themes, including unionization and land reform. The movement also flirted with elements of violence, although open insurrection was generally rejected by Chartists (Thompson 1984).

Drawing on Enlightenment radical themes and against the background of the expansion of popular radicalism of the 1820s and '30s, the utilitarian followers of Bentham called themselves "philosophical radicals." J. S. Mill in his autobiography used this label to identify his group within the London Debating Society, active in the mid-1820s.[7] Somewhat embarrassed, he acknowledged that the Enlightenment philosophes were the model for the radical utilitarians.[8] There can be little doubt that Mill adopted the term in his autobiography and elsewhere in contradistinction to many of the followers of popular radicalism. In 1838 Mill, in a letter to Albany Fonblanque, defended and clarified the use of the term by the *London Review*, the journal he edited in the late 1830s. There he emphasized that the *Review* "gave the name to the thinking radicals generally, to distinguish them from the demagogic radicals such as Wakley, & from the historical radicals of the Cartwright school, & from the division of property radicals if there be any" (Mill 1963, 369–371).[9]

The reference to the "division of property radicals" echoes Jeremy Bentham's cautious defense of his radical reform bill of 1819.[10] Bentham's bill identified the radical utilitarians with efforts at meaningful Parliamentary reform based on the logic of democratic representation. Bentham had the next year, in the wake of the repression following the Peterloo massacre, written but not published a defense, "Radicalism Not Dangerous" (Bentham [1819] 1962). The central point of that defense was to argue that the radical reform of Parliament would not, indeed could not, lead to the "*subversion of the rights of property*" (italics Bentham's). Bentham demonstrated to his own satisfaction that an equal division of property is a practical impossibility. Once started, there would be no halfway point. The logic of redistribution required attempting a fully equal division. If attempted it would destroy efficiency, encourage sloth, and spread poverty. He draws the conclusion that since a successful division is

7. In the early draft of his *Autobiography*, Mill asserts that this phrase described his group "as we thought ourselves." This afterthought is dropped from the published manuscript (Mill [1873] 1981, 132). Chief among the philosophic radicals were John Roebuck, Charles Austin, Charles Buller, George Grote, and his wife Harriet Grote. J. S. Mill was the major organizer of the group, his father was the senior personage, while Bentham remained at some distance. For an excellent history of the political activities of philosophic radicals see Hamburger (1965).

8. "What we (or rather a phantom substituted in the place of us) were sometimes, by a ridiculous exaggeration, called by others, namely a "school," some of us for a time really hoped and aspired to be. The French philosophes of the eighteenth century were the example we sought to imitate, and we hoped to accomplish no less results" (Mill [1873] 1981, 111).

9. Wakley was a Radical Member of Parliament, supporter of Chartism, and a founder of the medical journal *Lancet*.

10. And Bentham's discussion in his tract against the levelers in the *Principles of the Civil Code* (Bentham [1838] 1962).

impossible, a democratic government would not attempt a division at all. He then goes on to cite the case of American democracy which after forty years had produced no effort to destroy private property.

Bentham's argument reflected his own conviction that the institutions of private property and the market economy meet the utilitarian test. We will return to this defense. But whatever the strength or weaknesses of the logic, the argument clearly shows Bentham's concern with distinguishing his own form of philosophical radicalism from more aggressive radical movements.

And in this vein, it cannot be questioned that John Stuart Mill also saw philosophical radicalism as essentially an outgrowth of liberalism itself. For Mill, the radicalism the Benthamites had put forward in the 1820s in the *Westminster Review* "was the only attempt which had been made to give principles and philosophy to the Liberalism which was growing into importance" (Mill [1873] 1981, 132). The point is emphasized in Elie Halevy's (1955) landmark and well-reasoned study, *The Growth of Philosophic Radicalism*. Halevy in covering "The Birth of Radicalism" sees both Bentham and James Mill as advancing a "Radical theory of the representative regime" that "interpreted in this way, tended to be assimilated to the thesis of traditional English Liberalism" (264). Halevy labels the incipient Radical Party based on utilitarian principles as a party of "'intellectual' or 'Philosophical Radicals'" not to be confused with "the revolutionaries, robbers and incendiaries—disciples of Spence . . . who struck terror into aristocrats and bourgeois" (264).

There is little doubt that Bentham and Mill in the 1820s subscribed to a narrow definition of their radicalism. But it should be noted that in the Benthamite camp there were representatives of a more radical position. Most important among these was William Thompson, devoted utilitarian, Ricardian socialist, and advocate of Owenite schemes of cooperation. Thompson was also the author of a book on the rights of women.[11]

EGALITARIANISM AND PROGRESS

Where the young Mill subscribed to the cautious philosophical radicalism outlined by Bentham, as he matured he increasingly drew on elements of

11. *Appeal of One Half the Human Race, Women, Against the Pretensions of the Other Half, Men, to Retain Them in Political, and thence in Civil and Domestic Slavery.* This volume ([1825] 1970) anticipated much of Mill's later argument in the *Subjection of Women* ([1869] 1984). In his *Autobiography,* Mill acknowledged Thompson's work, although with little detail. See Lowenthal [1911] 1972, 16.

British popular radicalism, as well as the agenda of more radical utilitarians like Thompson. We will return to consider the development of these policy proposals in Part II, which discusses Mill's advocacy of the extension of the franchise, land reform, limitations on inheritance, expansion of education, and ultimately workers' cooperatives. Mill moved from his philosophical radicalism toward this set of more aggressive structural reforms, anchored in popular radical traditions. Characteristically, Mill attempted to derive his reform proposals from the analytics of his utilitarianism and political economy. So it seems the best course to postpone a discussion of the Millean reform program until after those analytics are developed in the next several chapters.

Before setting off on those explorations, we do well to devote some attention to two overarching motifs Mill inherited from the radical Enlightenment: egalitarianism and progress. Both of these motifs gain resonance as Mill moved toward the left. Both pervade his mature writings in political economy, starting at least with his *Principles* of 1848. Both are worth introducing in the context Mill would have first absorbed them.

Helvetius and Egalitarianism

Mill's worldview assumes an extreme version of egalitarianism inherited directly from the Enlightenment. In our modern social Darwinian world, it is a serious challenge to grasp fully the egalitarian ethos generated by the philosophes. And the word *equality* has been so trivialized amid the falseness of modern politics that it is easy for us to hear in it little more than a slogan. But the assertion of equality was for the radical egalitarians no less than the assertion of the soul for the Christian theologian. Building on Locke's tabula rasa, the radical champions, Diderot and most notably Helvetius, constructed a sociology of deep equality. Given modern cynicism, some attention to the Enlightenment discovery of equality is in order.

In his own day, Helvetius was criticized for a lack of subtlety and originality. Voltaire claimed that all of Helvetius's ideas had been borrowed from Diderot. Some questioned Helvetius's commitment to philosophy.[12]

12. A widely circulated story due to the counterrevolutionary intellectual Jean-Francois de La Harpe held that the young and handsome Claude Adrien Helvetius was only attracted to scholarly pursuits when he observed the attention lavished by "a circle of women" on the older and much less imposing Pierre Louis Maupertuis, a French mathematician, geographer, and sometime philosopher. According to La Harpe, "Helvetius was struck by the glamour and the pleasures of a scholar, a man of letters, might owe to his celebrity; he resolved at that moment to acquire them for himself" (quoted in Turnovsky 2010, 77).

Be that as it may, Helvetius's writings have the virtues of simplicity and directness. It is not easy to miss his point. Helvetius propounded a completely egalitarian materialism. This position was certainly unexpected, coming as it did from this eighteenth-century courtier, the son of a court physician and husband to the wealthy Anne-Catherine de Ligniville. But unexpected or not, it was stated with a ruthless clarity. Marx, one generally quite willing to find fault, praised Helvetius unstintingly. Indeed, when Marx commented briefly on Bentham's utilitarian philosophy, he dismissed it as eccentric, bombastic, and derivative from Helvetius's more engaging and articulate treatment. In fairness, Bentham himself credited Helvetius with stimulating his utilitarian position.[13] And central to that position was Helvetius's almost absolute view of equality among humans. If this idea was hardly original with Helvetius, he certainly laid it out in a bold and striking manner.

Helvetius takes as a fundamental axiom that most all humans have the same basic capacity to reason. Differences among people are, then, the result of their education in the broadest sense. He doesn't hold this position as a metaphor. He holds it as a concrete reality. Given his overall materialist outlook on the world, he asserts that all people—Newton *and* the agricultural laborer—are endowed with fundamentally the same mental capacities. The greatest part of the difference between these two lies not in their inherent intelligence but, rather, in their nurture and education.

While this notion strikes many today as implausible, Helvetius was quite serious. Consider, for example, his argument as he attempted to explain the uncommonness of genius. Why, Helvetius asks, are there so few Descartes or Corneilles? He considers a country like France of 16 million "persons endued with the most happy disposition of mind." In a curiously French manner, Helvetius immediately insists that only those 800 thousand residents of Paris are likely to experience a rich enough environment to bring forth genius.[14] Now since women are systematically kept from formal education, we are down to 400 thousand. Take out children and those more or less forced into employment, that leave them little time for thinking, and we have maybe six thousand. Of these perhaps six hundred are "animated with the desire of instruction." Only three hundred then possess the warmth necessary to incubate great ideas, and

13. Bentham also credited Hume as a major influence, but that is far more problematic. See Shackleton (1972).

14. "Country talents are always condemned to obscurity; and . . . the muses so fond of woods, meadows and fountains would be no better than country lasses, if they did not from time to time breathe the air of great cities" (Helvetius [1758] 1807, 339). I think Marx is right that Helvetius writes far more pleasantly than Bentham.

only a hundred have the constancy and patience required. But both the warmth of passion and patience are products of environment. And again just fifty will have actually kept focus "insensible to love and ambition." These loves and ambitions themselves grow up in response to stimuli individuals' experience. Finally, reverses of fortune, accidents, and death further reduce the number to just about what we observe in practice: the Descartes and Corneilles.

Both logic and history, according to Helvetius, demonstrate the fundamental equality of men's reason. "The great inequality of mind observable in mankind, therefore, only depends on the educations they receive and the unknown and varied circumstances in which they are placed" (Helvetius [1758] 1807, 337).

The radical implications of Helvetius's clearly stated egalitarianism did not go unnoticed. Somewhat surprisingly Helvetius had actually submitted his manuscript to the official censors.[15] At first publication was allowed, but soon the radicalism of the work became clear. After the publication of *De l'Esprit* in 1758, Helvetius was attacked by the Church, although the churchmen were more concerned with his atheism than his egalitarianism. The book was burned in Paris. These harassments continued despite Helvetius's previous role as a tax farmer-general and his then current status as *maitre d'hotel* and confidant of the queen. It is reported he had even read portions of his manuscript to the king himself (Turnovsky 2010). Of course, other less protected radicals including Diderot had been treated much worse. In the end, Helvetius lost his position in the royal court. "And while some contemporaries were actually surprised by the leniency with which he was treated—for instance, he was saved from imprisonment or exile by the intervention of important court allies such as Madame Pompadour and the duc de Choiseul—Helvetius was shaken enough by the episode never again to publish" (Turnovsky 2010, 71).

There is a striking irony that Helvetius, the courtier, one-time farmer-general, and rural aristocrat should provide the clearest statement of eighteenth-century egalitarianism. It is ironic that according to Diderot this most extreme of egalitarians was in constant tension with the impoverished poachers and trespassers of his country estate. In his own home, the great egalitarian was "the unhappiest of men . . . surrounded by peasants and by neighbours who hate him. They break the windows of his mansion; they ravage his property at night; they cut his trees and break down

15. The following summary of the publication history of *De l'Esprit* draws heavily on Turnovsky (2010, 70–99).

his fences." Apparently the "border of his woods was peopled with the unfortunate wretches who had been driven from their homes into pitiful hovels." Helvetius, although "pusillanimous," insisted on rigorously prosecuting poachers (Diderot, *Voyage a Bourbonne,* 344, as quoted in Morley 1886, 130–131).

But whatever the irony, it was Helvetius who put the egalitarian case most directly. And it is reasonable to credit Helvetius with channeling egalitarianism into political economy. Of course, the more conservative elements of the Enlightenment were not about to embrace this radicalism. In France, Turgot would have no part of it. He described *De l'Esprit* as "a book of philosophy without logic, literature without taste, and morality without goodness," (Morley 1886, 142). The pragmatic Turgot felt that Helvetius had gone too far in his criticism of despotism and his provocation of the powers that be.

Hume's evaluation of Helvetius was only mildly more positive. As early as 1748, Hume had indicated his view that men at root were, if not equal, quite similar. He also had suggested that what most differentiated men were their educations and not native differences. In "Of the Original Contract" he wrote, "When we consider how nearly equal all men are in their bodily force, and even in their mental powers and faculties, till cultivated by education; we must necessarily allow, that nothing but their own consent could, at first, associate them together, and subject them to any authority"([1748] 1826, 291). Thus, it is not surprising that Hume was invited by Helvetius to translate *De l'Esprit* into English—an invitation he apparently declined. Presumably, Hume thought Helvetius had gone too far. With something less than full enthusiasm, Hume in 1759, shortly after the publication of *De l'Esprit*, recommended it to Smith. According to Morley, Hume "wrote to Adam Smith that it was worth reading, not for its philosophy, which he did not highly value, but for its agreeable composition," (Morley 1886, 134).

With Adam Smith it would seem Helvetius found a more receptive reader. It is impossible not to see the similarity between Helvetius's discussion in *De l'Esprit* and Smith's own famous treatment of the "vanity of the philosophers":

> The difference between the most dissimilar characters, between a philosopher and a common street porter, for example, seems to arise not so much from nature, as from habit, custom, and education. When they came into the world, and for the first six or eight years of their existence, they were, perhaps, very much alike, and neither their parents nor play—fellows could perceive any remarkable difference. About that age, or soon after, they come to be employed

> in very different occupations. The difference of talents comes then to be taken notice of, and widens by degrees, till at last the vanity of the philosopher is willing to acknowledge scarce any resemblance. (Smith [1776] 1976, 28–29)

This deeply egalitarian idea is central to Smith's entire scheme. It forms the very base of his theory of the division of labor. It is the division of labor made possible by the "disposition to truck, barter, and exchange" that provides the "difference of employment" upon which arises "any great difference of talents" (Smith [1776] 1976, 29).

Smith's egalitarian position is quite consistent with that of Helvetius and the radical philosophes.[16] We know that Hume had given Helvetius a backhanded recommendation. But Smith seemed to think better of the work. In 1763, Smith wrote to Hume, then in Paris. Hume was enjoying something of an unexpected triumph in the French capital. Smith congratulated his friend on well-deserved recognition. He also asked Hume to "make my Compliments to all the men of Genius in France who do me the honour to know anything about me: But above all to Mr. Helvetius whether he should know anything about me or not." Smith also instructed Hume to make clear to Helvetius that Smith had not had the opportunity to read *De l'Esprit* before publishing *The Theory of Moral Sentiments*. If he had, he would have included an "account of it among the other systems of Philosophy" (Smith 1987, 414).

Despite these comments, Smith never included Helvetius in his major revisions of a *Theory of Moral Sentiments*. In 1764–65 he did meet Helvetius in Paris. But by that time the "vanity of the philosopher" passage had already been included in an early draft of the *Wealth of Nations* (1763) that Smith had prepared (Smith [1776] 1976, 29n13).

All things considered, it seems Smith's egalitarianism in his discussion of philosophers and street porters goes beyond the position of Hume. For Hume, egalitarianism was less central to his worldview. Smith may have found Helvetius and the other radical philosophes more congenial in part because their ideas of egalitarianism fit well with his own theories of the division of labor.

As noted earlier, Jonathan Israel categorizes both Hume and Smith with the members of the conservative Enlightenment.[17] This call may or may

16. But it should be noted that while both Smith and Helvetius argued for an almost complete ex-ante egalitarianism, and both looked forward to an increasing living standard for the mass of the population, neither suggested that such a position required anything close to an ex-post equality in material conditions.

17. However, Sam Fleischacker (2016) argues that Smith is more reasonably viewed as a liberal, if not a radical.

not be correct. But in either case, the fact that these mainstream moral philosophers, destined to be heroes of traditional liberalism, used language only slightly more moderate than that of Helvetius himself strongly points up how deeply both an egalitarian outlook and a respect for education and nurture had penetrated into early political economy.

By the 1780s, when Bentham begins to put together the utilitarian position, virtually all the serious moral philosophy he would have read took the initial equality of men (but probably not women) as a given. We know Bentham read Helvetius, Hume, and Smith. In the works of the first he could hardly have avoided the idea. In the works of Hume and Smith he would see little to argue the opposite. Rather than a break with eighteenth-century thought, Bentham's assertion of full equality was simply an endorsement of a central tenet of that century's moral philosophy.

Bentham was to claim the absence of any contradiction between his views on an essential equality and his endorsement of a triumphal liberalism. However, to reconcile these beliefs took a considerable effort.[18] Over time, Mill would come to question such rationalizations. Mill, accepting the radical Enlightenment conception of equality, was first to express ambivalence over the triumphal liberal ideology, and then largely to desert it. If the philosopher and street porter were brothers under the skin (indeed, virtually identical twins), how could an egalitarian not take umbrage at the vast inequality that characterized their material positions? While traditional liberalism spoke eloquently for the spread of personal liberty, the freedom of the marketplace, and political participation, it seemed almost mute in the face of the depressing inequality of the new industrial economy. Mill increasingly judged his program in terms of its ability to realize a more complete equality.

Condorcet and Progress

The motif of progress constitutes the second foundational contribution of the Enlightenment to radical utilitarianism.[19] Enlightenment writers had been eloquent in their celebration of the promise of progress. But they were maddeningly vague as to exactly how, if at all, progress was to resolve the extreme inequalities of the market economy. Progress for the philosophes consisted of a hodgepodge of advances in arts, sciences,

18. Chapters 3 and 4 explore these efforts.

19. While this section focuses on the theme of progress the utilitarians inherited from the French *philosophes*, it should be noted that a case can be made that

morals, and material conditions. For them progress was closely linked to the Enlightenment view that reason, if allowed scope, could not only stimulate artistic and scientific pursuits but also enhance the moral, organizational, and material condition of society.[20] This broad sentiment pervades the work of the Encyclopedists.

The main argument was laid down by Turgot in the mid-eighteenth century.[21] But it was at the end of the century in the chaos of the Revolutionary Terror that the radical promise of progress was most forcefully invoked. Condorcet's famous essay *Outlines of an Historical View of the Progress of the Human Mind* ([1794] 1802) presented a powerful vision.

It is difficult to imagine a more dramatic moment. Having originally sided with the liberal Girondists, Condorcet had been pulled by the logic of the French Revolution toward more and more radical political positions. Yet he was not willing to ally with Robespierre's Montagnards, the extremist faction of the Revolution moving quickly into the implementation of the Terror. He differed with them in particular over the form of the new constitution, an area in which he might reasonably have been considered an expert. The resulting indictment sent him into hiding. It was in the midst of this persecution in 1794 that Condorcet set himself the task of summarizing the Enlightenment understanding of progress. It would be easy to understand how in his position Condorcet might have taken a pessimistic view of the future. But instead, he constructed a virtual paean to the unlimited possibilities of progress. Within the year he was to be arrested. He died under mysterious circumstances two days after being taken into custody.

Nicolas de Condorcet brought together the radical Enlightenment position. He connects reason with progress at every level. Characteristically, Condorcet suggests "nature has connected, by a chain which cannot be broken, truth, happiness, and virtue" ([1794] 1802, 233). The continued improvement of our understanding lays a foundation for social happiness

eighteenth-century British writers such as Godwin and Priestly also anticipated and influenced the utilitarian understanding of progress (Spadafora 1990, 398–401).

20. As J. B. Bury put it many years ago, "The idea of the progress of knowledge had created the idea of social Progress and remained its foundation" (1920, 120).

21. Condorcet was clearly influenced by Turgot. But it should be noted that not all Enlightenment writers endorsed progress. Quesnay and the physiocrats had envisioned an essentially static economy with only modest technological changes. On this point see Vardi (2012, 275–276). (See, however, Meek [1963, 293–294] for a reading of the physiocrats that interprets their model as addressing an essentially "'dynamic' problem.") More generally, Vardi's insightful study emphasizes the recurrent physiocratic invocation of an illiberal repression of self-interest in favor of an almost "religious program."

from which virtue can spring. Condorcet anticipates no limit on either our knowledge or the improvement of the species that knowledge makes possible. As long as the earth exists, humans will improve.

While reason makes material sciences productive, it also renders the social sciences useful. In considering political organization, rational reflection points toward majority rule[22] subject to the protection of individual liberty. And, according to Condorcet, the new science of political economy extends these insights to the practical business of organizing the activities of the economy. Here the influences of Turgot and Smith are obvious. Despite the complexities of an emerging global economy, Condorcet holds, "we still perceive, by a general law of the moral world, the efforts of each individual for himself conducing to the good of the whole, and, notwithstanding the open conflict of inimical interests, the public welfare requiring that each should understand his own interest, and be able to pursue it freely and uncontrolled" ([1794] 1802, 236).

Condorcet suggestively weaves laissez-faire into the fabric of the progressive dispensation of reason:

> Hence it appears to be one of the rights of man that he should employ his faculties, dispose of his wealth, and provide for his wants in whatever manner he shall think best. The general interest of the society, so far from restraining him in this respect, forbids, on the contrary, every such attempt; and in this department of public administration, the care of securing to every man the rights which he derives from nature, is the only sound policy, the only control which the general will can exercise over the individuals of the community. (236–237)

The freedom of the market is no less than a human right, justified in turn by its ability to advance the general interest of the society.

Condorcet's endorsement of laissez-faire as an instrument of progress is triumphal and close to absolute,[23] but painfully short on specifics. The progress achievable through laissez-faire in combination with an enlightened democratic form of government will, according to Condorcet, bring

22. Condorcet had virtually invented the logical analysis of voting systems, their strengths and limitations.

23. Still, following the physiocratic position, he does leave room for a government financed by the "superogatory value" generated from "the growth of every year" over and above the remuneration of the labor "of which this growth is the fruit" and the portion used to "supply the stock which is to secure an equal and more abundant growth in time to come." Taxing this unearned income presumably injures no individual's rights ([1794] 1802, 238).

about an increasing equality of outcomes. While not as extreme in his egalitarianism as Helvetius, Condorcet was convinced that the major sources of economic inequality were inequality in inherited wealth, the vagaries of working lifetimes, and inequality in education. The first of these would be greatly reduced by the new freer economic system. "It is easy to prove that fortunes naturally tend to equality," writes Condorcet, if "positive law had not introduced factitious means of amassing and perpetuating them" (329). As to working lifetimes, Condorcet saw the promise of actuarial calculations (a field to which he had also made major contributions) for providing a much enhanced security to the elderly and modest capital stocks to the young. And Condorcet is confident that once scholars have carefully considered the problem, the amount of education required for an engaged life will prove relatively modest: "but a few years of infancy, and, in subsequent life, only some occasional hours of leisure" (333).

Condorcet's confidence in the underlying current of progress provides a powerful, almost unconditional, optimism to his buoyant forecasts of a better future. But Condorcet, like other Enlightenment writers, left the argument surprisingly vague. Mill was enthralled by Condorcet's vision. He very much wanted to share in Condorcet's enthusiasm. But Mill was to become less and less sure of the triumphal liberalism with which Condorcet identified his progress. The course of progress had yet to be fully articulated. Increasingly Mill was to see that course in terms of popular struggle, working-class struggle.

THE MALTHUSIAN COUNTERPOINT

Inheriting Helvetius's egalitarianism and Condorcet's broad optimism concerning the promise of progress, Mill had to pick up these themes in a much changed environment. The development of political economy required a tighter and more analytical framework for serious social argument. Indeed, Mill's reform project consisted in anchoring his utilitarian radicalism in the rigorous soil of political economy. And that soil had become anything but hospitable to radical reform. The pessimistic, but brilliant writings of the anti-Condorcet, the Reverend Robert Malthus, could not be ignored.

The Enlightenment worldview suffuses John Stuart Mill's radicalism. But a deep Malthusian countercurrent almost equally informs Mill's work. Much of the tension in Mill's political economy has its source in the persuasive and pessimistic arguments of Malthus. Malthus had published his famous *Essay on the Principles of Population* only three years after

Condorcet's *Outlines*. But Malthus's attack on progress was both pointed and profound. In context, it completely reshaped the challenge facing Mill's radical utilitarian project.

Malthus had explicitly addressed his essay to the progress envisioned by Condorcet.[24] Malthus sincerely regretted and repeatedly attempted to ameliorate the pessimism that was enmeshed in his view of population. He also sincerely respected Condorcet (Winch 1996).[25] Yet, Malthus argued, Condorcet had fundamentally failed to appreciate the limitation to human improvement inherent in the omnipresent threat of population pressures.[26]

In his *Outlines*, Condorcet had asserted that population growth presented no serious limit to the progress he envisioned. Condorcet explicitly asked "Whether the number of inhabitants in the universe at length exceeding the means of existence, there will not result a continual decay of happiness and population, and a progress towards barbarism, or at least a sort of oscillation between good and evil?" Condorcet answered in the negative. First, the improvement of science would probably be so great as to avoid the problem all together. Second, an enlightened population will come to realize "the duties they . . . [are] under relative to propagation . . . consist not in the question of giving existence to a greater number of beings, but *happiness*." They will then seek "the general welfare of the human species; of the society in which they live; of the family to which they are attached; and not the puerile idea of encumbering the earth with useless and wretched mortals" (129). From the context it is not clear whether Condorcet is here referring to some variant of what Malthus would call moral restraint, or to the possibilities of birth control. In either case, Condorcet is convinced that progress is not limited by uncontrollable population growth.

24. The full title of Malthus's first essay was *An Essay on the Principle of Population, as it affects the future Improvement of Society, with Remarks on the Speculations of Mr. Godwin, M. Condorcet, and Other Writers*. Donald Winch (1996, 47) suggests that had he lived, Condorcet would have been a "worthier opponent of Malthus" than Godwin proved to be.

25. "Mr. Condorcet's *Esquisse d'un tableau historique des progrès de l'esprit humain* was written, it is said, under the pressure of that cruel proscription which terminated in his death. . . . [I]t is a singular instance of the attachment of a man to principles, which every day's experience was so fatally for himself contradicting. . . . [The terror] must have been such a tremendous shock to his ideas of the necessary and inevitable progress of the human mind, that nothing but the firmest conviction of the truth of his principles, in spite of all appearances, could have withstood" (Malthus 1826, 2:3).

26. Condorcet wrote in 1794, while Malthus's first essay on population was published in 1798 and was itself meant to answer Condorcet's arguments, as well as those of Godwin.

Where Condorcet held out an optimistic forecast, Malthus saw grave and persistent threats. Malthus would have nothing of Condorcet's conjecture that technological change could reasonably allow for expected population growth. Working with statistics and a smattering of mathematics (e.g., geometric and arithmetic series), Malthus painted a dire picture of an unrelenting expansion of population overwhelming any plausible technical progress. And when it came to Condorcet's assurances as to a possible social and behavioral response, Malthus was scathing. He concluded that Condorcet "alludes, either to a promiscuous concubinage, which would prevent breeding, or to something else as unnatural." Presumably Malthus here was referring to birth control. Malthus then argued "To remove the difficulty in this way, will, surely, in the opinion of most men, be to destroy that virtue, and purity of manners, which the advocates of equality, and of the perfectibility of man, profess to be the end and object of their views" (Malthus [1798] 1970, 124).

For John Stuart Mill, the emerging radical utilitarian, Malthus's essay was powerfully unsettling. It added depth to themes already present in Smith. Anticipating a major argument of classical economics, Smith had foreseen declining profit rates leading to a stationary economy. In Smith's view such stagnation was particularly threatening to the working classes. For reasons Smith never fully explained, he thought workers did best when the economy was expanding whereas a stationary state implied stagnation and poverty. This theme was soon to become a centerpiece of the Ricardian argument. For Ricardo, Smith's fall in profit rates was inexorably driven by Malthusian population pressures. The Malthusian-Ricardian development of political economy created a new problematic for radical thought. How, given this depressing logic of the new political economy, were the Enlightenment promises of egalitarianism and progress to be realized?

J. S. MILL AND THE RADICAL UTILITARIAN PROJECT

Here, then, is the intellectual environment in which John Stuart Mill began moving toward a more radical reformism. In the spirit of Helvetius and Condorcet, fortified by the political economy of Smith, but accepting the centrality of Malthus's population calculus and Ricardo's falling rate of profit, Mill over time constructed a new radical utilitarianism. This utilitarian theory must make clear where the industrial revolution was heading, how those developments were impacting the greatest number, and what if any political changes and policy interventions were required to guarantee the greatest happiness.

The analytical heart of J. S. Mill's emerging radical utilitarian project was to use the new tools of political economy to provide a theoretical and empirical explanation of the material dynamics of progress. In doing so, those same tools promised to identify key economic reforms capable of accelerating the very pace of progress. The radical position asserted the necessity of enhancing the steady effects of time with the prodding of serious reform. Ambivalent with respect to economic liberalism, J. S. Mill maintained a cautious, but hopeful, stance with respect to progress. Progress held the promise of resolving the tensions generated by the liberal economy and the industrial revolution.

J. S. Mill took his fundamental motifs from the writings of the Enlightenment. But he became sure that triumphal liberalism was inadequate to achieve the Enlightenment promise of equality. And he had to acknowledge that the optimism and vagueness of the Enlightenment promise of progress had been seriously undermined by classical political economy: Malthus's population theory and the Ricardian model. Awed by the ongoing accumulation of capital, totally skeptical of any revolutionary schemes, but sure of his egalitarian precepts, John Stuart Mill projected a new utilitarian radicalism. Rooted in social science, Mill's utilitarian radicalism accepted, however reluctantly, the need for time. Time, not revolution, was to be the effective medium for material and social progress. Rooted in social science, Mill's utilitarian radicalism committed itself to serious egalitarian reform—reform designed to facilitate the workings of progress and the crucial development of human potentials. More than the dreams of the Enlightenment, more than the plans of revolutionaries, Mill's utilitarian radicalism remains the effective starting point for modern radicalism.

A NOTE ON MILL'S CONSISTENCY AND HIS THEORY OF PROGRESS

There can be no doubt that John Stuart Mill in the 1820s and early 1830s largely limited his advocacy of reform to little more than an expansion of the franchise coupled to free markets. But just as surely, over time he developed a broader and far more radical agenda. Reflecting his deep eighteenth-century commitment to egalitarianism and his observation of the material progress launched by the industrial revolution, he built up claims for the greatest happiness of the greatest number. By 1848, in the *Principles of Political Economy* (and even more clearly in the 1852 revision, much influenced by the French Revolution of 1848), he weaved these fundamentals deep into the theoretic discussion. In that work he took positions supporting several popular radical proposals, including land reform and inheritance. Most notably, in the *Principles* he began to look forward to a major transition from capitalist labor markets to worker cooperatives.

Mill's radical programmatics can seem almost at odds with the liberal framework of much of his analysis even after 1852. The question is whether a reconciliation of these tendencies within a coherent radical utilitarianism is possible. An easy way around the question is to offer the simplest and most obvious answer: Mill was notoriously and hopelessly inconsistent. Drawn this way and that by the ideas and events of his times, stretching over more than fifty years of intellectual and political debate, Mill touched base with one and then another stream of thought, some traditional, some liberal, and some radical. It is not outrageous to argue that Mill failed to offer a serious synthesis of this potpourri.[27] The story of Mill's depression and rebellion against his father are common knowledge recounted dramatically in his autobiography. Overwhelmed by the strain of a controlling father, excited by romantic visions, emotionally committed to a fashionably radical wife, Mill was hardly a candidate for well-reasoned consistency.[28] In accepting this ramble for what it was, we can perhaps avoid an arch academic mistake—that is, to demand consistency where consistency doesn't exist. Even J. S. Mill (at least in his romantic periods) might have endorsed Emerson's famous warning: "A foolish consistency is the hobgoblin of little minds, adored by little statesmen and philosophers and divines."

Alternatively, a number of scholars have argued that Mill moved over time from a traditional liberal to a radical position fundamentally at odds with his earlier liberalism. These efforts have often taken a critical tone. For example, F. A. Hayek has offered an interpretation. In Hayek's view, Mill under the influence of Harriet Taylor developed into a "radical rationalist" favoring continental socialist ideas over traditional British liberalism.[29] The upshot in Hayek's view was far from attractive.

A variant on this theme is presented by Himmelfarb (1974,) who sees Mill's apostasy as early as 1831 in his series of articles entitled the "Spirit of the Age." Himmelfarb sees those writings, strongly influenced by the

27. As Robert Lekachman wrote some years ago, "Mill's position could scarcely strike anyone in the 1950's as consistent" (1959, quoted in Schwartz [1972], 244).
28. For a workable biography of J. S. Mill's life, which however doesn't emphasize Mill's political economy, see Reeves (2007).
29. For a discussion of Hayek's views, see Légé (2008) and Caldwell (2008).

Saint-Simonians, as fundamentally illiberal and elitist.[30] A softer version of the Himmelfarb thesis can be found in Hamburger (1999), who argues that while Mill freed himself from the most authoritarian versions of the Saint-Simonian creed and Auguste Comte's religiosity, he still mixed his emphasis on liberty with an acknowledgment of a need for social control, even to the point of endorsing a "religion of Humanity."

In a similar vein, Pedro Schwartz argues that Mill's "New Political Economy" represented little theoretical advance on Ricardo, focusing instead on the "Future Society." Schwartz emphasizes the continuing appeal of Mill's vision of "a society of equal, free and just individuals, politically and economically self-governing." However, Schwartz accuses Mill of giving in to a Utopian vision at odds with the "true nature of capitalism" (Schwartz 1972, 240).

The claim that Mill had essentially deserted liberalism as he aged comes rather easily to classic liberals who sense that Mill and the utilitarians more generally had been too completely taken over by a continental radicalism that threatened the very heart of British liberalism. These commentators are often suspicious that the radical utilitarians had allowed an undermining of the core liberal vision.

Some truths undoubtedly reside in these descriptions of J. S. Mill. But they fail to appreciate the extent to which the mature Mill was himself aware of the tensions in his position—the extent to which he was self-consciously ambivalent with respect to traditional liberalism. Lekachman might see J. S. Mill as simply inconsistent. Hayek might see J. S. Mill as seduced by radical ideas, slipping toward some version of an alien socialism. But a more sympathetic reading of J. S. Mill suggests that by mid-nineteenth century his utilitarian radicalism reflected a deep ambivalence toward traditional liberalism in general and laissez-faire capitalism in particular. This ambivalence expresses itself in Mill's thoughtful sensitivity to both the positives and the negatives generated by the growth of the capitalist economy in the years after the industrial revolution.

Traditional liberalism made appealing universal claims. But when viewed from a radical perspective in the here and now of the mid-nineteenth century, the triumphal liberal endorsement of laissez-faire capitalism seemed to leave unaddressed the egalitarian principles generated in the Enlightenment. The growth of the economy left the great bulk of the population with neither prosperity nor meaningful community.

30. Himmelfarb's position is well discussed by O'Rourke (2001, 23–33). O'Rourke presents a convincing rebuttal that emphasizes Mill's continuing commitment to the liberal value of individuality.

Mill was strongly attracted to classical liberal values, even as he took umbrage at the social turmoil the laissez-faire capitalist economy created. The result was an ambivalence that fundamentally informed his increasingly radical understanding of the industrial revolution.

Certainly the easiest response to ambivalence is to turn to apologetics. In this case, accepting the ideology of liberal triumphalism provides a path out. Apologetics are a serious response to the discomfiture of ambivalence. And indeed, this was the course of the more cautious utilitarians, most notably the young Bentham. Early in his career, J. S. Mill did engage in apology. But as he matured, he followed a more nuanced path. Already well defined by the middle of the nineteenth century, this path addressed ambivalence by seeking a resolution, not in the immediate present but, rather, over the indefinite future. A commitment to progress acknowledges the darkness harbored in the present, even as it promises a bright future.

Ambivalent over laissez-faire capitalism, J. S. Mill increasingly invoked the promise of progress as a bridge to a more attractive economy and society. Time can provide the material base for such a society. Time can facilitate the maturation of the working classes and the expansion of a middle class committed to social progress. If the current liberal industrial system can reasonably be expected to lead over time to a much more egalitarian economy—indeed, if laissez-faire capitalism provides the quickest and most reliable means of ushering in such an egalitarian economy—then a radical endorsement of much of the status quo becomes not only defensible but also essential to the achievement of the greatest happiness of the greatest number.

The radical Mill came to see the new capitalist projectors empowered by the industrial revolution as the sources of growth and promise, even as they exhibit the most primitive forms of greed. The accelerated accumulation of capital at the heart of the industrial revolution lays out the path of progress, even though in the short run it seems to benefit only the wealthiest. The centerpiece of Mill's response to his own ambivalence is a new more fully articulated investigation of progress. Only meaningful progress can reconcile the liberal economy of the industrial revolution with the egalitarian prospect of the Enlightenment.

As Mill surveyed and enriched the new science of political economy he could not fully resolve the deep uncertainty concerning the future course of the industrial revolution. At his most optimistic, Mill saw in the accumulation of capital an efficient engine of progress for the great mass of workers. But at other times Mill feared such progress might fail to materialize, leaving the greater part of the population in subsistence conditions.

In this context, the consequences of rapid capital accumulation became the fundamental theoretical question facing the radical John Stuart Mill. As will be discussed in chapter 5, he was never fully able to answer this central question. The resulting uncertainties surrounding the course and consequences of future accumulation raised doubts over the egalitarian promise of progress. But in his most optimistic interpretation Mill looked forward to a full-scale transformation of the productive economy.

Mill's effort to achieve a reconciliation of ambivalence through the assertion of the promise of progress attempts to build on a social science capable of making convincing predictions concerning the future. Without such a base, radical utilitarianism reduces to optimistic wishfulness at best or pusillanimous procrastination at worse. Hence, the deep need to develop and make use of the social sciences. John Stuart Mill can reasonably be considered the first of the modern line of radical reformers[31] who, rejecting the efficacy of revolutionary change, look forward to a progress built on economic growth, social development, and interventions made possible by the effective application of social science. A sympathetic critique of Mill's radicalism in its historical context, the course proposed for this volume, can offer a base from which to reaffirm our modern understanding of radicalism, even while cautioning us against a too easy faith in progress and social science.

31. Or at least the first in the Anglo-American tradition.

CHAPTER 2

The Greatest Happiness of the Greatest Number

British utilitarian thought emerged in the late eighteenth and early nineteenth centuries as an effort to formalize the key insights of the eighteenth-century French and Scottish Enlightenments. Though traditional liberal and radical utilitarians were to debate loudly the policy implications, they entered the debates with an agreement on the yardstick to be used. That social system was best, that public policy was best, which yielded the greatest happiness for the greatest number. The credo, derived from Enlightenment thinkers in the eighteenth century, provided the definition of utilitarian consequentialism and distinguished the utilitarian position from all other schools. Yet for the most part the history of the utilitarian normative standard was not one of wild-eyed radicalism, but of apologetics.

Today, in some rough-and-ready sense the utilitarian credo still stands as the chief practicable guideline for modern social policy. Putting aside implausible classroom exercises, embarrassing glorifications of natural rights, and far-fetched interpretations of hypothetical contracts, most of us today do not even question this standard.[1] We use it to evaluate an

1. It is not my purpose here to provide a defense for the utilitarian standard vis-à-vis alternatives, but only to observe its ubiquity. There may be a few genuine doubters, mostly in philosophy departments, but for the rest of us, including not a few Iranian theocrats and U.S. politicians spouting natural-law doctrines, the bottom line is whether the system works, whether it delivers what the majority of the people want.

economic system, a penal code, or a social custom.[2] But the utilitarian credo with its emphasis on consequences is a modern invention, an invention of the Enlightenment. Like any deep idea, it has from the start been subject to a range of interpretations. Our understanding of Mill's utilitarian radicalism must necessarily depend on an appreciation of how he ultimately redesigned the instrument he took up in the basic credo—how he reshaped it from apologetics to radical critique.

FROM VIRTUE TO SOCIAL SCIENCE

The most often cited first source for the utilitarian credo is Francis Hutcheson, academic mentor to Adam Smith and David Hume, and a key founder of the Scottish Enlightenment. And the phrase is certainly there. In his *An Inquiry into the Original of our Ideas of Beauty and Virtue* ([1725] 2004), Hutcheson offers a fundamental judgment: "that Action is best, which procures the greatest Happiness for the greatest Numbers; and that, worst, which, in like manner, occasions Misery" (125).

Any number of scholars and pundits have pointed out the ambiguity lying at the heart of this famous expression of what was to become the utilitarian creed. "The greatest happiness of the greatest number" gives us no hint as to how to balance an increase or diminishment in the level of good achieved for each person affected against a diminishment or increase in the number of persons affected. If an action increases the good per affected person by 10 percent, but reduces the number so affected by 5 percent, should it be counted better or worse than the status quo? The creed gives us no guideline.

Curiously, Hutcheson actually avoided this logical problem in his first statement of the principle. At the beginning of the sentence that introduces the famous phrase, Hutcheson wrote, "in equal Degrees of Happiness, expected to proceed from the Action, the Virtue is in proportion to the Number of Persons to whom the Happiness shall extend; . . . and in equal Numbers, the Virtue is as the Quantity of the Happiness, or natural Good," (125). At least at the start, all Hutcheson is saying is that holding constant the level of per capita happiness increasing numbers adds to the moral worth of an action and that holding constant the number of people affected increasing the average happiness adds to the moral worth.

2. Economists might object that formal project and policy evaluations are carried out using cost-benefit analysis, a methodology that most often doesn't include the type of distributional concerns contained in the utilitarian credo. However, as a practical matter, cost-benefit studies are only one input into a larger evaluative process that inevitably asks how the project or policy affects "the greatest number."

Now, from this easily defended proposition the transition to the final more ambiguous statement of "greatest happiness of the greatest number" seems less than obvious. Yet, Hutcheson himself is not to blame for our confusion. He seems to have had a clear idea in mind. For him, the social utility is simply the sum of all individual utilities. In this context, the "Virtue" of an action can be reckoned by the "compound Ratio of the Quantity of Good, and Number of Enjoyers"—that is, the level of the good per person times the number of people affected, (125).[3]

Hutcheson's formulation seems on this first reading to be quite egalitarian. Yet he does make a telling qualification to his rule when he states, "the Dignity, or moral Importance of Persons, may compensate Numbers." All people are equal, but some are more equal than others.

If Hutcheson wasn't a full egalitarian, neither was he a full consequentialist. His notion of a virtuous action required that it be motivated in a benevolent manner. Actions of great good to others lose their moral standing if pursued for private gains. The moral sense Hutcheson projected onto persons required this condition. Such a moral sense responds to the benevolent actions of others and encourages imitation. For Hutcheson, a benevolent action that fails to generate the desired result is still virtuous. An action with substantial positive consequences loses its moral and virtuous quality if it flows from self-love. The greatest-happiness metric is meant only to direct benevolent choices and not in itself to serve as the definition of merit.

The moral sense with which Hutcheson endows us is the direct ancestor of Adam Smith's impartial spectator, that superego with which we more or less continually judge ourselves. And Smith in many ways comes close to the utilitarian position. Yet, he never explicitly suggests basing judgments on the greatest-happiness principle. Although Smith in the *Wealth of Nations* clearly takes as his own standard for the welfare of a nation the consumption possibilities open to its great mass of working people, and he repeatedly judges legislation and public decisions by a proto-utilitarian yardstick, he avoided repeating Hutcheson's dictum.

Hutcheson, Smith's mentor, is reasonably credited with inventing the greatest-happiness principle. Smith's self-proclaimed acolyte Bentham[4] was to make that principle famous. Yet the direct chain from Hutcheson

3. Hutcheson uses the term "compound Ratio," which should in modern usage apply only to the product of two ratios. However, the reading presented here has it as the product of two numbers, only the first of which could be considered a ratio—i.e., the average good. However, this seems the only way to make sense of the text.

4. Although never formally a student of Smith, Bentham always cited Smith as the source of his political economy. Bentham's *Defence of Usury* was written as a set of letters to Smith. See chapter 3 for a discussion of Bentham's relation to Smith.

to Bentham is, in effect, broken by Smith's reluctance to explicitly advocate the greatest-happiness principle.

It might have been just an overlooked opportunity. Smith, after all, does not cite or quote many people, even his great friend David Hume. Alternatively, Smith may have been sensitive to the criticisms Hutcheson received for attempting a pseudo-quantitative calculation.[5] I would speculate the reason lies deeper. Smith's central point in the *Wealth of Nations* is that society benefits the most from agents' attempts to do no more than maximize their own wealth. At the end of the famous passage on the invisible hand, Smith wrote of the narrow wealth maximizer who "By pursuing his own interest . . . frequently promotes that of the society more effectually than when he really intends to promote it."

For Hutcheson the good generated by such self-serving motivations doesn't qualify at all for his benefit calculation. Self-interest for Hutcheson is at best neutral. The book in which he first introduced the greatest-happiness principle was written explicitly to defend the moral sense of the Earl of Shaftesbury against those such as Bernard Mandeville, who in his *Fable of the Bees* saw good arising from self-interest. The title page from Hutcheson's first edition makes the point quite clear:

> An Inquiry into the Original of Our Ideas of
> Beauty and Virtue;
> In Two Treatises.
>
> In which the principles of the late Earl of Shaftesbury are Explain'd and Defended, against the Author of the *Fable of the Bees:* and the Ideas of Moral Good and Evil are establish'd, according to the Sentiments of the Antient Moralists. With an Attempt to introduce a Mathematical Calculation in Subjects of Morality.[6]

Smith, Hutcheson's student, must surely have been aware of these purposes. And most probably he identified the greatest-happiness principle with one side of an argument that he himself was attempting to straddle.

In any event, Smith's eschewing of the greatest-happiness formulation meant that Bentham's usage came from other sources. Shackleton

5. See Shackleton (1972).

6. See Hutcheson ([1725] 2004) and discussion of the opposition of Shaftesbury and Mandeville in the introduction to that volume by Wolfgang Leidhold. The "Mathematical Calculation in Subjects of Morality" refers to the greatest happiness principle. The criticisms of this portion of the text may have led Hutcheson to withdraw the subtitle in later editions.

tells us that Hutcheson was translated into French in 1749 (1972, 1469). Shackleton also relates that in 1755, Maupertuis (recall the supposed object of Helvetius's envy) developed a rule for legislators: "a number of men being assembled, to achieve for them the greatest sum of happiness possible."[7] Now this is not exactly Hutcheson's formulation, nor Bentham's. But what is of particular interest here is the focus on public policy. It seems fair to label this extension a French contribution. Both Diderot and Helvetius wrote of the general interest, not to speak of Rousseau's more famous *volonté générale*. But none of these repeats the Hutcheson's formula.

The story comes together with the Italian jurist Cesare Beccaria. Beccaria, like the French, is looking for a rule not so much of general morals as of legislation. Thus in his famous *Essay on Crimes and Punishments,* he writes that laws too often reflect "the passions of a few" rather than "the greatest happiness of the greatest number." Shackleton notes that the Italian original is better translated "the greatest happiness of the majority," which is hardly the same thing as either Hutcheson's original phrase or Bentham's dictum. Be that as it may, the first English translation of Beccaria (1767) reads "the greatest happiness of the greatest number." And Shackleton concludes, "There can be no reasonable doubt that it was the English version of *Dei delitti dell pene* which put the phrase 'the greatest happiness of the greatest number' before the eyes of Bentham"[8] (1972, 1474).

In his first use of the credo in his *Fragment on Government*, Bentham makes a quite general statement: "It is the greatest happiness of the greatest number that is the measure of right and wrong." Looking back on this first foray, Bentham later in his life held that the *Fragment* "undertook to set up . . . the greatest happiness of the greatest number, in the character of the proper, and only proper and defensible, end of government; as the only standard by which any apt judgment could be formed on the propriety of any measure, or of the conduct of any person, occupied in making opposition, or giving support to it" (Bentham [1828] 1962, 242). From this reminiscence it might seem that the principle was meant like those of Maupertuis and Beccaria to apply exclusively to the evaluation of government actions. But if Bentham sees the public arena as the primary sphere for the use of the dictum, he like utilitarians after him carved out

7. Original quoted in French by Shackleton (1972, 1469), translated by the author.

8. Shackleton (in my opinion convincingly) concludes this despite Bentham's much edited reminiscence on the origin of the phrase. That piece suggests Bentham got the expression from Joseph Priestly (Shackleton 1972).

a broader claim. The "principle of utility" according to Bentham was "the standard of right and wrong in the field of Morality in general."

Harkening back to Hutcheson's guide to personal virtue, nineteenth-century utilitarians including Mill at times seemed to require mankind to develop almost saint-like constitutions. A moral philosophy of this type can only end bemoaning most of human activity as less than virtuous. Perhaps for this reason the history of utilitarianism is replete with efforts to soften these strong claims on individuals. For example, proponents of *rule utilitarianism* can be read as demanding only a submission to guidelines that are well aligned with utilitarian principles. This standard seems less demanding than that of *act utilitarianism*, which requires a full utilitarian calculation for virtually every choice by an individual. Scholars have long debated whether Mill was an act utilitarian or a rule utilitarian. Wendy Donner (Donner and Fumerton 2009, ch. 3) argues that Mill was essentially a rule utilitarian because he advocated a version of a moral code. However, David Brink (2013, 84–98) makes a strong case that Mill, while acknowledging the practicality of secondary rules, was essentially an act utilitarian because for him the full calculation of utility was required to judge the ultimate value of following a rule.[9] Whatever his true position, Mill on occasion could fall back into an almost platitudinous moralizing.

For present purposes—that is, the tracing of the radical content of utilitarian thought—these issues of utilitarian morality are of only secondary interest. Yes, utilitarians including Mill wished to see something of a moral reawakening, but that hardly distinguishes them from any number of nineteenth-century moralists. Putting aside such Victorian forays, the focus here is instead on the utilitarian effort to fashion the greatest happiness principle into a normative standard for public policy and social science. From this perspective, the utilitarian challenge was to bring the Benthamite principle to bear on all of political economy. Not so much deserting as holding in abeyance evaluations of individual virtue, the best of utilitarian thinking set itself the task of empowering social science in

9. Also see Wiggins (2006, 150–155) for a discussion of Mill's relation to the act/rule distinction. Another way out of the dilemma notes that most of us in our daily decisions have little impact on anyone but our closest family and friends. In that sphere, the greatest-happiness principle may be quite workable, and especially so for those who aspire to be "nice guys." If our world is small enough, being a utilitarian is not that difficult. The modesty of the position works well for many of us, looking for a low-stakes path to achieving utilitarian virtue. If I understand him correctly, this seems to be the view of the modern utilitarian Hare (1981). But consider in this light the compelling arguments by Singer (1972) in favor of taking a broader, "global village" view in considering our utilitarian responsibilities.

the interest of the greatest number. Ultimately the goal was to develop a social science capable of reckoning the complex consequences of public policies in the past and of forecasting the likely outcomes of public actions in the future.

THE GREATEST NUMBER

Viewed in a constructive light, the history of utilitarian thought is essentially the record of the continuing effort to move from aspiration to practice, from ideological speculation to social science. Perhaps the first challenge faced by such efforts was to resolve the much-commented-on ambiguities in the credo itself. Bentham's statement is powerful and appealing in its egalitarianism. Yet, like most epigrammatic propositions, it lacks precision. The social science called for by the utilitarian credo must define both "greatest happiness" and "greatest number." Perhaps not surprisingly, the early utilitarians failed to reach a clear consensus on either. But the history of their ruminations suggests much about the radicalism implicit in the new dictum.

In early utilitarian exercises, the "greatest number" was variously interpreted as the majority, the laboring classes, recipients of earned income (the laboring classes plus the middle classes), or the entire population. The utilitarian invocation of the greatest number suggested universal claims inspired by Enlightenment thought. But it was difficult for the utilitarians nurtured in the class analysis of the new political economy[10] to fully avoid the obvious fact that the working classes represented by far the greatest number of the population.

A focus on a simple numerical majority grows out of the philosophical and mathematical work of Nicolas de Condorcet. Condorcet had set himself the challenge of operationalizing Rousseau's *volonté générale*, or "general will," through democratic voting. For all his proto-utilitarian understanding, Condorcet attributed an almost mystical quality to majority rule. And at root he envisioned the institution of democratic voting more in terms of protecting natural rights than in terms of constructing positive legislation. In his *Outlines* he wrote glowingly of the Ninth Epoch leading up to the French Revolution, a period in which "Philosophy . . . obtained an influence on the thinking class of men, and these on the people and their

10. Classical economists from Smith forward divided the economy into laborers, capitalists, and landowners.

governments." The result was "a revolution in the entire mass of certain nations, and gave thereby a secure pledge of the general revolution one day to follow that shall embrace the whole human species." And at the heart of this enlightened revolution was the realization that the maintenance of individual "rights was the only object of political union." Majority rule was the means for guaranteeing basic rights. "The will of the majority is the only principle which can be followed by all, without infringing upon the common equality" (Condorcet [1794] 1802, 155).

Bentham and James Mill rejected the rights-based approach to the significance of the majority. Instead, as John Stuart Mill reported in his autobiography, James Mill advanced "democratic suffrage the principal article of his political creed, not on the ground of liberty, Rights of Man, or any of the phrases, more or less significant, by which, up to that time, democracy had usually been defended, but as the most essential of 'securities for good government'" (Mill [1873] 1981, 109). While James Mill thought that men over forty provided a broad enough base for the suffrage (an opinion with which John Stuart strongly disagreed), it is not immediately clear that he or Bentham identified their proposed extension of the franchise as corresponding to the "greatest number" of the utilitarian credo. In fact, in James Mill's famous *Britannica* essay, "Government" (1825, 21–23), he seems to suggest that the franchise might be extended to any fraction greater than a majority of adult males (for example, on the basis of a property requirement) and still maintain the central purpose of guaranteeing the identity of the interest of all and the interest of that electorate.

Apart from questions of how best to shape the electorate, the early utilitarians at times seemed to identify the greatest number with the laboring classes, or even the poorer elements. The notion of judging the success of the national economy by the conditions of its working poor certainly had antecedents in Adam Smith. Smith strongly endorsed the "progressive state" when a "society is advancing to the further acquisition, rather than when it has acquired its full complement of riches." According to Smith it was only in such a state "that the condition of the labouring poor, of the great body of the people, seems to be the happiest and the most comfortable" (Smith [1776] 1976, 87). Smith was very fond of the expression "the great body of the people." It appears throughout the *Wealth of Nations*.[11] But in this passage he explicitly suggests that "the great body of the people" consists of "the labouring poor." Smith goes on to comment with approval that workers fared best in countries (like North America)

11. Some 36 times, to be exact.

that were experiencing rapid growth. This progressive state is "cheerful" and "hearty." By contrast "the stationary is dull" and "the declining, melancholy." He leaves the distinct impression that conditions in North America were to be preferred to those in of England, even though England had accumulated a higher level of static wealth (87–88).

Smith's viewpoint was consistent with the numerical importance of the laboring classes in late eighteenth- and early nineteenth-century England. Estimates by Lindert (1986) for 1810 show that if we define the upper classes as households headed by those with titles ("gentlemen and up") and merchants (including most financiers and industrialists), we have only 2.7 percent of all households. Generously defining the middle classes as professionals, farmers, and shopkeepers adds 14.8 percent of households. This leaves the laboring classes defined as yeomen, husbandmen, those in the industrial trades and building trades, laborers, paupers, and others, accounting for 82.5 percent.

The early utilitarians must have been aware of the broad outlines of the social structure; still, they stopped short of explicitly identifying the greatest number with the working classes. Like Smith, Bentham was very much concerned with the welfare of rural and urban workers, yet he never explicitly equated the "greatest number" to the working classes. Where Marx and Engels were to announce without reservation the identity of the working classes with the "immense majority," the early utilitarians for all their talk of the "greatest number" failed to fully clarify who is to be included in the calculation of benefits.

Of course, the utilitarians were more than willing to scorn the landed aristocracy who reaped where they had never sown. The new industrialists were often described as progressive, although lacking in elements of morality. In the triumphal liberal argument, the economic freedoms of the new class were defended by the utilities they gave rise to, rather than by the happiness of the industrialists themselves. The utilitarians' treatment of the middle classes was generally more sympathetic. The middle classes no longer in fear of immediate discomfort had time and energy for education, culture, and a range of broader interests. At their best, the middle classes stood as exemplars to the working classes. For the utilitarians, unlike Marx, middle-class incomes were "earned incomes" and not portions of the economic surplus. And in any event, there would be little to be gained by the working classes if they were to expropriate the wealth of the relatively small and only modestly prosperous middle classes.

Suffice it to say that the precise fit between the "greatest number" and the classes of the economy was never fully defined by the early utilitarians. The Benthamite credo allowed for a considerable elasticity. But at the same time, it set the stage for more radical interpretations. Radical utilitarians did not have to be revolutionaries to identify the "greatest number" with the overwhelming numerical preponderance of the early nineteenth-century British working class. In the reading advanced in later chapters, just such a view eventually motivated John Stuart Mill to write his famous chapter on the future of the laboring classes.

THE GREATEST HAPPINESS

If early utilitarian attempts to define the greatest number evince a substantial ambiguity, early utilitarian attempts to clarify the possibilities of the greatest happiness border on apologetics. Despite their embrace of the credo's egalitarian core, the early utilitarians were far from optimistic as to what might reasonably be accomplished for (or perhaps by) the greatest number. Drawing on only the broadest elements of a liberal ideology, the first utilitarian efforts yielded surprisingly conservative conclusions.

The proto-utilitarian Helvetius provides a good example. Helvetius, of course, came from an extremely well-off family and by all accounts enjoyed a luxurious if not decadent lifestyle. And as described in chapter 1, Helvetius was a complete egalitarian, asserting that all of us start out with essentially the same machinery. Against this background Helvetius turned to the question of what happiness the greatest number can expect. He started off with a conservative assertion: "There is no society in which all the members can be equally rich and powerful" ([1772] 1969, 2:198). If, as the "majority of mankind" maintains, equal happiness requires all to be "equally rich and powerful," then equality of happiness is unobtainable. Yet Helvetius held out a modest hope for the greatest number. If "every citizen has some property, is in a certain degree of ease, and can by seven or eight hours labour, abundantly supply his own wants, they are then all as happy as can be" (198). When the worker eats well he is "content." For the bulk of mankind, "Good cheer is that to which we have been accustomed."[12] It is the "busy man" who is the "happy man." And the "opulent idler" far from being happy is constantly confronted with boredom and discontent. And in the end "*The rich cannot dine twice*" (206).

12. Helvetius at this point adds a charming footnote on the cultural relativism of tastes. He cites a French cook who puzzles over how in England with its "hundred different religions" there is but one sauce for meat, while in France with its one religion "there is no meat that we do not eat with a hundred different sorts of sauce" ([1772] 1969, 200).

Helvetius insists that some minimum material conditions are necessary to achieve a happy state. And he asserts that virtually all nations are plagued by imperfect law and a "too unequal partition of their riches." His concrete suggestion, however, remains vague at best.[13] He opined that even modest redistributions can't be effectively achieved at a stroke, but only through "continual and insensible alterations." Over time if "the laws . . . assign some property to every individual they would snatch the poor from the horror of indigence, and the rich from the misery of discontent and render them both more happy" (207–208). As he expanded on this theme he focused almost exclusively on the miseries of discontent that surround the rich and left undeveloped the mechanisms that might achieve the redistribution at which he hinted.

A similar apologetics can be seen in the utilitarian writings of William Paley (1743–1805). Paley, like Helvetius, subscribed to the utilitarian credo, had little insight into political economy, and projected little hope for redistribution as a source of happiness. William Paley, the arch-deacon of Carlisle, famously developed the theological argument of design. The complex interworkings of the cosmos, like the fine precision of a watch, offer a proof of the necessity of an original design. The complexity of the structure argues for a designer possessed of no less than infinite wisdom and power. Paley extended the argument to moral philosophy, maintaining that God had designed the world in such a manner that our means are well adapted to the achievement of human happiness.

Paley was a man of considerable intelligence, and in his student days he had been recognized as such at Cambridge. He was a serious opponent to slavery. He was sensitive to the struggles of the working poor. On more than one occasion he suffered real personal losses for his championing of Enlightenment ideas within a religious context. Yet with respect to the material conditions of the great mass of workers, he advanced an ideology of apologetics. As a churchman he developed a moral philosophy consistent with the precepts of the conservative Enlightenment.

The author of *Principles of Moral and Political Philosophy*, first published in 1785, Paley could reasonably be identified as a co-developer with Bentham of the principles of utilitarianism. Paley's own formulation of the central guiding principle very much echoes Hutcheson. For Paley "Virtue is 'the

13. In fairness to Helvetius and other commentators of the eighteenth and nineteenth centuries, the mechanics of even modest redistributions at the time must have appeared far from straightforward. For example, income taxes, the backbone of much modern redistribution, were virtually unfeasible before the expansion of civil services and the improvement of public accounting practices.

doing good to mankind, in obedience to the will of God, and for the sake of everlasting happiness.'" This formulation and Paley's book more generally were destined to become the accepted wisdom of establishment intellectual thought in the early nineteenth century. More widely read and far more praised than Bentham's ungainly prose, Paley's careful, humane conservatism found a place for utilitarian precepts in an establishment context.

Paley's religious version of utilitarianism solves the incentive problem neatly by promising "everlasting happiness" as the reward of virtue. Such happiness should easily tip the scales in just about all calculations. And while Paley was reluctant to offer an estimate of how much virtue will achieve this reward, he was confident that any reasonable person should see the way to right action. Paley anticipated twentieth-century utilitarians in his emphasis on applying the utilitarian rule in the circle of family and friends where individuals can actually make a greater difference. But as he extended the circle, the argument becomes, if not weaker, more opaque and more apologetic of the existing order.

On the economic side, he made a stab at justifying private property in rather vague consequentialist terms: "[E]ven the poorest and the worst provided, in countries where property and the consequences of property prevail, are in a better situation, with respect to food, raiment, houses, and what are called the necessaries of life, than any are in places where most things remain in common" ([1785] 2002, 65–66). As a moral proposition such a conservative conclusion defends an institution that Paley acknowledged as the source of much human unhappiness. It asserts the need to weigh good against evil, but falls back on little more than a conventional wisdom.[14] It almost painfully begs for a social science that could offer more substantial analytic and empirical support or critique.

Similarly, when Paley came to defend the highly uneven representation provided by the House of Commons in his day, he put forth a consequentialist argument, but only as a weak rationalization of the status quo. In good utilitarian style, Paley sought to judge the Parliament not by abstract natural rights but by the conformity of its decisions to his version of the greatest-happiness principle. He implausibly concluded that the system of election then in place was capable of producing a House of Commons with a keen sense of the national good. He went on to warn against too quick reforms.[15]

14. We will return to this defense and radical utilitarian views of private property in chapter 4.

15. However, it should be noted that Paley looked at the "experiment" then taking shape in America as potentially promising.

Paley was undoubtedly sincere in his beliefs, but his conservative version of utilitarianism became an easy apologetic for the conventional wisdom of the time. This type of less-than-rigorous Panglossian optimism was to remain a persistent threat to more radical utilitarian thought both in the nineteenth century and up to the present.

The anchoring of apologetics in egalitarian premises characterized early utilitarianism. Even Paley was not willing to give up his powerful egalitarian parables.[16] He fully subscribed to the egalitarian starting point. In much the same way, Bentham combined his fundamental egalitarianism with a distinctly limited view of the possible happiness of the greatest number. Like Paley and more completely than Helvetius, Bentham ruled out from the start any substantive redistribution. He clearly stood ready to tolerate massive inequalities.

Bentham early on had broken down the "happiness of body politic" into four "subordinate objects":

> Subsistence
> Abundance
> Equality
> Security

The purposes of the state are "to provide for subsistence; to secure abundance; to befriend equality; to maintain security" (Bentham [1838] 1962, 302). As Bentham admitted, "This division does not possess all the clearness and precision which could be desired." In the *Civil Code*, Bentham did not actually endorse an explicit goal for the greatest happiness. Rather, he presented an introductory exploration of the contributions of each subordinate object to the happiness of the body politic.[17] As Bentham recognized, considerable tension exists among these four heads.

Bentham's commitment to equality is grounded on reason. His key analytic concept today would be called diminishing marginal utility of wealth or income. Bentham couldn't be clearer:

> Place on one side one thousand labourers, having enough to live upon, and a little to spare: place on the other side . . . a well apportioned prince, he himself as rich as all these labourers together. It is probable that his happiness will

16. Most specifically he advanced a famous "parable of the pigeons" that asserted pigeons would never allow a privileged few to eat to excess while the bulk of the flock starved.

17. In the next chapter we return to Bentham's more complete endorsement of Smith's obvious and simple system of natural liberty.

> be greater than the medium happiness of each of them, but not equal to the sum-total of all their little masses of happiness. . . . If the mass of his happiness should be found ten times, or even five times greater, this would still be much. (305)

Bentham had no doubt that the simple sum of utilities or happinesses is the appropriate metric for social choice. Like Paley, Bentham was fully committed to egalitarianism. Almost by syllogism we expect a radical egalitarian solution. But that was not the direction Bentham took. Instead, he held up against equality the goal of security.[18] Security provided by "the laws" is the very bedrock of private property and the foundation for civilization. "This inestimable good is the distinctive mark of civilization: it is entirely the work of the laws. Without law there is no security; consequently no abundance, nor even certain subsistence. And the only equality which can exist in such a condition, is the equality of misery" (307).

Bentham acknowledged, "[T]he laws ought to do for subsistence many things which they ought not to permit to be done for abundance" (302). Yet it is security, not subsistence or equality that lies at the core of his understanding of the greatest good. It is security that allows progress in subsistence. When the four goals conflict, Bentham argued, "subsistence and security rise together to the same height: abundance and equality are manifestly of an inferior order." Equality where it exists must depend on security; abundance grows on subsistence. "The two first ends are like life itself: the two last are the ornaments of life." And between these two, security and subsistence, "the most important object is security. . . . [C]ommand cultivation; you will have done nothing: but secure to the cultivator the fruits of his labour, and you most probably have done enough." Equality for all its appeal "ought not to be favoured, except in cases in which it does not injure security" (303).

And to drive home the point, he saved his greatest scorn for the "Levelling System." Such a system was necessarily "destructive both of security and of wealth." Echoing Hume, Bentham argued that any effort to begin redistributions in favor of equality must undermine the entire bulwark of security. There is no stopping point down that road. "[I]f any line had been drawn, or were to be attempted to be drawn, the attempt would not so much as palliate, much less remedy the evil: and that to the imputation of error it would only add the reproach of inconsistency and dereliction of principle" (362).

18. For a discussion of Bentham's counterpoising equality and security, see Ryan (1984, 100–102).

The conclusion is painfully blunt, hardly sweetened as in the case of Helvetius. Lest we have any doubt, "Inequality is the natural condition of mankind. Subjection is the natural state of man. It is the state into which he is born: it is the state in which he always has been born, and always will be, so long as man is man. . . . Absolute equality is absolutely impossible" (361). The subsistence of the poor can only be guaranteed by the security and opulence of the rich. In fashioning his apology, Bentham had virtually lost sight of the commitment to equality, the original inclusion of equality among the four basic "subordinate objects" of the "happiness of the body politic." All people gain, he was saying, from the fundamental guarantee of security that undergirds progress. If the rich gain more, that is the necessary price for the more modest gains achieved by the greatest number. Such is the greatest happiness that can be promised and delivered to the greatest number.

TOWARD A POLITICAL ECONOMY OF PROGRESS

The greatest-happiness principle provides a major advance in liberal thought, because it moves all social, political, and economic evaluation from dubious principles of natural rights and natural laws to the bedrock of civil rights and consequentialism. Allowing for all the difficulties in defining both the greatest happiness and the greatest number, we still today judge our governments by the extent to which they seem seriously to accept the utilitarian challenge. We judge our economic institutions by the extent to which they facilitate the utilitarian purpose.

The great contribution of the early utilitarians lies in their willingness to hold up their political and economic principles to this most demanding yardstick. And if many of these utilitarians reached traditional liberal conclusions, they did so not by some deus ex machina of natural law, but by attempting to justify those conclusions through an apologetic theodicy.[19] Whatever their final positions, this commitment represented an act of deep—indeed, radical—intellectual courage, a courage that forever shifted the terms of political and economic discourse.

As the nineteenth century opened, political economy became an obvious focal point for those espousing the utilitarian standard. Adam Smith's new science had set out to explore the wealth of nations, but quickly enough

19. Here we limit our attention to liberal theories of policy. The Tory conservatives needed neither natural law nor utilitarian calculation, but only a vague faith in the rightness of the British Constitution to justify their rationalizations of the status quo.

Smith had turned his audience's attention to the material conditions of the largest share of the population. Smith, while broadly sympathetic to the mass of the working poor, reached the conclusion that their welfare could only be improved as the result of high levels of private investment guided by market prices. Malthus, of course, painted a darker picture of what might be accomplished even under the best of circumstances.

The problem was to determine what options remained for improvement or progress as judged by the utilitarian standard. The challenge became one of squaring the commitment to the greatest happiness of the greatest number with a deepening understanding of the realities of political economy. Using the tools of the new discipline, the triumphal liberal argument found room in the utilitarian standard to accommodate a broad apology for inequality. But John Stuart Mill, with his radical understanding of political economy, was to insist that the utilitarian credo required a broader move toward equality.

CHAPTER 3

Bentham's Liberal Triumphalism

In the 1780s, Jeremy Bentham was already a utilitarian. In particular he already subscribed to the egalitarian criterion: the greatest happiness for the greatest number. He was also under the sway of Adam Smith's new political economy. Bentham for most of his life advocated a triumphalist liberal view that saw in Smith's simple system the best economic order that could be generated for the greatest number. Chapter 2 considered briefly Bentham's broad endorsement of security vis-à-vis equality. Bentham's most dramatic defense of laissez-faire capitalism can be found in his famous *Defence of Usury* (1787).[1] In that work Bentham mounted a bold argument for the triumphalist case. Whether we consider the plight of the poorest or the ambitions of the most creative, laissez-faire capitalism achieves the best possible outcome, without exception.

The immediate purpose of Bentham's exercise was to reprimand Adam Smith for failing to appreciate the general utility of laissez-faire financial markets. For both rich and poor alike, for projectors and savers, the brave new world of finance promised real opportunity. Specifically, in a series of letters, Bentham argued that the *Wealth of Nations* contained a serious error in its support of usury laws.[2] Bentham's argument asserted that unregulated markets providing finance to creative projectors will hasten capital accumulation and growth. The prosperity generated by such a system will trickle down to the population at large. The happiness of the

1. Note that the essay is written well in advance of Malthus's tract and therefore doesn't address the implications of Malthusian population principles.

2. The passages are in Smith's *Wealth of Nations*, book II, ch. 4 ([1776] 1976).

greatest number depends on free markets, innovation, and growth. The young Bentham made no suggestion that the liberal order can or should lead to a broader transition. Whatever its blemishes, the system of laissez-faire capitalism does better than any other system by the great mass of people. It is an end in itself. The only result of constraining interest rates will be a lower level of welfare for the society as a whole.

Through the first four editions of the *Wealth of Nations*, Adam Smith supported state-imposed caps on the rate of interest. Much to the chagrin of many of his followers then and since, Smith thought 5 percent was just about enough for any borrower in Great Britain to pay on a loan ([1776] 1976, 357). In 1787, writing from the estates of the Russian Count Potempkin in the backwater of Zadobrast, near Krichev in Belarus, Jeremy Bentham penned his *Defence of Usury* as a series of letters.[3] From the remote periphery of the expanding industrial revolution, Bentham claimed a place for usury in Smith's own system of economic liberties. In doing so, he explicitly sought to convince Adam Smith to give up his support for interest-rate limits. Smith, for all his faith in a system of natural liberty, was unwilling to let all interest rates float. Bentham argued anything else must reduce the welfare of the greatest number. The last edition of the *Wealth of Nations* to appear in Smith's lifetime, in 1789, left the usury passages unchanged.

From a superficial perspective, the entire affair amounted to nothing more than a modest dispute between a failing master (Smith died in 1790) and an overeager disciple. (Bentham acknowledged in the *Defence* that all he knew of political economy originated in Smith's works.) Certainly this view is sometimes taken by those embarrassed by Smith's support of usury laws. For an example of modern chagrin, see Milton Friedman (1976), who viewed Smith's stubbornness on the issue as merely a sentimental gaff. Hollander (1999, 525) discusses the similar reactions of Robbins (1968) and Stigler (1988).[4] Yet for others the argument strikes a fundamental chord. G. K. Chesterton (1933), for one, identified Bentham's essay on usury as the very beginning of the "modern world." I tend to agree with him. In his day, Chesterton surely meant the "modern

3. With one exception, the letters were addressed "to a friend," presumably Bentham's close friend George Wilson. Letter XIII was addressed directly to Adam Smith. Bentham had journeyed into White Russia to assist his brother, Samuel, in various projects on behalf of Potempkin's efforts at Russian modernization. For a fascinating treatment of the two brothers' experiences in Russia, see Christie's (1993) *The Benthams in Russia, 1780–1791*.

4. Keynes, however, often noted his own support for usury laws and his general approval of Smith's views on the subject (1936, ch. 23).

liberal world." But before entertaining such ambitious claims, let's consider the historical context of the debate.[5]

HISTORICAL CONTEXT

In modern economics, interest is defined as the rental price of money. But the word has a complex and less than fully resolved etymology. The origins of *interest* are intimately connected to the changing meaning of *usury*. Canon law in the Middle Ages forbade usury, which was generally interpreted as charging a loan repayment in excess of a loan's principal amount. Our modern word *interest* derives from the medieval Latin *interesse*. The Oxford English Dictionary explains that *interesse* originally meant a penalty for the default on or late payment of an otherwise legitimate, non-usurious loan. As more sophisticated commercial and financial practices spread through Europe, fictitious late payments became an accepted if disingenuous way of circumventing usury laws. Over time, "interest" became the generic term for all legitimate and accepted payments on loans.

Since the Middle Ages, each epoch has participated in the debate over the conditions under which lending should be prohibited as usury. As the European economy developed from a feudal system, through a mercantilist one and on toward an explicitly capitalist economy, changing attitudes toward interest reflected the underlying transformation of the mode of production.

In their open hostility to usury, the medieval churchmen of Britain, including Occam and Duns Scotus, subscribed to the traditional scholastic interpretations of Aristotle. Their writings, like those of Aquinas, defined usury in straightforward fashion as the practice of requiring payment for a loan (Noonan 1957).[6] The late scholastics in Salamanca—Catholic academics writing on economic issues between 1350 and 1650—began chipping away at this definition, excluding an ever-broader range of normal business loans. Among the Reformation thinkers, Luther largely held to the ban on usury, while Calvin saw little logic in the Church's traditional position.[7] With the enlivening of commercial markets, the "new men" of

5. The interchange between Smith and Bentham over usury has been the subject of several insightful articles, including Hollander (1999), Kelly (2000), and Paganelli (2003).

6. However, as a Franciscan, Duns Scotus occasionally took exception to the interpretations of the Dominican, Aquinas, as discussed in Noonan (1957).

7. On Luther's somewhat nuanced position, see Singleton (2011). For a quick introduction to Calvin's thoughts on usury, see Geisst (2013, 75–76).

the English Renaissance supported the trend toward openness and began to change the meanings of the business vocabulary.[8]

This shift in practice and thinking was not an unseen evolution; it was clearly observed. For traditionalists it was controversial. And not all the traditionalists were scholastic churchmen. In the late sixteenth century, Thomas Wilson, a scholar, judge and diplomat, wrote his impassioned *A Discourse on Usury* ([1572] 1925), a broad attack on the spreading acceptance of interest-bearing loans among the merchant classes in England. As suggested by R. H. Tawney, Wilson was representative of a traditionalist impulse, reflecting early Protestant efforts to rebuild community and reestablish a sense of structured equity. Tawney quotes a letter of Wilson's (1572 [1925], 15), "The state is unfortunate in which nothing is permitted to anybody, but much more unfortunate in which everything is permitted to all."

Offering any number of traditional arguments, Wilson would not countenance the proposed difference between normal loans and usury at high interest. In "The Preachers Oracion," he makes clear that taking a low rate of interest "excuseth no man, when god forbiddeth all maner of taking" (229). Lending according to the Preacher "shoulde be . . . free, simple, and for charityes sake . . . without anye thinge at all more than the principall."[9]

But this strong moral argument was increasingly undermined by the growing availability of profitable and relatively safe financial investments. In his essay, "Of Usurie" ([1601] 1985), Francis Bacon endorsed a system of state regulation fixing a lower interest rate (5 percent) for most loans and a higher rate (9 percent) for loans to merchants in large centers. Some ninety years later, John Locke ([1691] 1824) doesn't even consider seriously the possibility of an objection to interest per se. Instead, he wrests only with the pragmatic issue of where to set the legal rate. A reduction to 4 percent from 6 percent had been proposed by the mercantilist Josiah Childe and a number of British merchants. For Locke, the point was clear. The experienced and clever would work their way around the law, while only widows and orphans would be left lending their money at the lower legal rate.

8. On this point, see the brilliant discussion by R. H. Tawney in his introduction to Thomas Wilson's *A Discourse on Usury* ([1572] 1925).

9. Lest lenders think such a bargain foolish, Wilson assured them in his "Christian Prologue" of greater rewards to come: "I will teache others to be greater usurers . . . to gaine more in a daye then others are able to get in seven yeres. . . . Lend to your poore neighbors in time of their great neede for gaine on gods name . . . and you shall yerely, daylie, and howerly reape infinit gain. For as god is better able to rewarde you then man, so will he for his promise sake make you recompense with encrease infinitely" ([1572] 1925, 189).

Anticipating much of the core machinery of supply-and-demand theory, Locke argues that promised benefits from such a price ceiling would not materialize as the quantity supplied of funds contracted ([1691] 1824, 124).

SMITH ON USURY

By the late eighteenth century, virtually all economic commentators in Britain and many on the continent asserted the usefulness and accepted the legitimacy of interest payments in commerce and finance. Still, a writer as savvy as Adam Smith felt the need to defend the taking of interest. In the *Wealth of Nations*, Smith ([1776] 1976, 356) stated what he took to be straightforward when he wrote, "[A]s something can every-where be made by the use of money, something ought every-where to be paid for the use of it." Expanding on this observation, Smith went on to make a classic argument about black markets similar in spirit to Locke's. Efforts to outlaw interest only have the effect of raising the cost of borrowing: "This regulation, instead of preventing, has been found from experience to increase the evil of usury; the debtor being obliged to pay, not only for the use of the money, but for the risk which his creditor runs by accepting a compensation for that use. He is obliged, if one may say so, to insure his creditor from the penalties of usury."

The stage seemed set for Adam Smith to endorse the removal of all legal restraints on interest and to move on. But Smith balked. Rather than making the case for a free market in loans, Smith made a case for limiting interest rates at something a bit above the lowest market rate. Smith was worried about usury: "[I]n order to prevent the extortion of usury, [a country which allows interest] generally fixes the highest rate which can be taken without incurring a penalty" (356). Smith saw nothing wrong with this practice. Indeed, he went on to discuss where the legal maximum should be set: "This rate ought always to be somewhat above the lowest market price, or the price which is commonly paid for the use of money by those who can give the most undoubted security. . . . The legal rate, it is to be observed, though it ought to be somewhat above, ought not to be much above the lowest market rate" (356).

The major rationale offered for his famous and much discussed limit on financial rates was Smith's fear that at higher legal rates such as "eight or ten percent . . . the greater part of the money which was to be lent would be lent to prodigals and projectors, who alone would be willing to give this high interest" (357). It's pretty easy to guess who Smith meant to include among "prodigals," but who exactly did Smith have in mind when he wrote of "projectors"? The term was common in the eighteenth century. It included a surprisingly broad range of innovative financial and real investors. Ponzi schemes and wild speculations could be advanced by projectors, but so could real productive inventions. Elsewhere in the *Wealth of Nations*, Smith indicates that while some projectors might invest in attractive ventures, great harm was to be expected from "chimerical projectors, the drawers and re-drawers of circulating bills of exchange, who would employ ... money in extravagant undertakings, which ... would never repay the expence which they had really cost" (316). Thus Smith was concerned about both spendthrifts and inventive speculators.[10]

Without caps on interest rates, Smith was convinced that these prodigals and projectors would outbid "sober people." And as a result, "[A] great part of the capital of the country would ... be ... thrown into those [hands] which were most likely to waste and destroy it." In contrast, a judicious ceiling on interest rates guaranteed the safety of lenders' money and the productive use of the "capital of the country" (357).[11]

BENTHAM'S *DEFENCE*

It's not clear exactly why Bentham undertook his *Defence of Usury*. The standard story is that Bentham had picked up a rumor while traveling concerning plans to lower the legal interest rate in Britain. Bentham had heard from Sir Richard Worsley (Member of Parliament and occasional diplomat, author of a book of travel observations, and plaintiff in a rather notorious adultery case against his wife, Lady Seymour) that William Pitt, the prime minister, planned to lower the legal interest rate maximum from 5 to 4 percent. Worsley's information was only a rumor.[12] However, Bentham made clear in a letter to a friend, dated December 19, 1786, that he already had "arguments against it *ready cut* and *dry*: the former epithet you may have some doubt about; the latter you will not dispute. You know it is an old maxim of mine, that interest, as love and religion, and so many other pretty things, should be free" (quoted in Everett 1931, 169).

10. The classic text on projects and projectors is Daniel Defoe's *An Essay upon Projects* (1697).

11. There is a neat parallelism between Smith's famous distinction between productive and unproductive labor and his distinction between productive and unproductive uses of capital. This point is made by Steven Medema (2009).

12. While Pitt did not put forward such usury legislation, had he in fact done so he would have been a prime example of the frequent observation that legislators of usury laws were more often debtors than creditors. Pitt, the youngest Prime Minister in British history, died virtually bankrupt at age forty-seven.

In any event, Bentham's (1787a) argument started with five potential rationales for regulating "money bargains" (not quite in this order): (1) prevention of usury; (2) prevention of prodigality; (3) protection of indigence against extortion; (4) protection of simplicity against imposition; and (5) repression of the temerity of projectors. Let's follow Bentham through each of these.

Prevention of Usury

Bentham argues that there is no guide to defining usury except custom. There is no "natural fixed price." There is only custom—and customs differ. "[B]lind custom . . . has varied, from age to age, in the same country, it varies from country to country, in the same age." Custom has led to substantial variations in the legal interest rate: for example, 30 percent in Constantinople and 5 percent in England, (1787a, 4).

At this point, Bentham makes a key thrust. Why regulate this exchange of lending money at interest and regulate no other transactions? Asserting as a given that broad systems of price controls are generally not feasible, Bentham makes one of his deepest arguments: "[B]ut why a policy, which as applied to exchanges in general, would be generally deemed absurd and mischievous, should be deemed necessary in the instance of this particular kind of exchange, mankind are as yet to learn" (4). This argument is often passed over in discussions of Bentham's essay, but it must surely be the central one. For the early scholastics, the conception of just prices was a seamless whole. An extortionate price cost the customer a few coins, but it cost the seller his soul. The early scholastics believed that this was true both for goods and for money lending. Bentham in effect turned the early scholastic argument on its head. Where the scholastics looked for a justification for every price, Bentham argued that it makes little sense to look for a justification for this price of interest and this price only. We live in a material age. There is no difference between "a man who takes as much as he can get . . . for the use of a sum of money" and the man who buys "an house with it, and made a proportionable profit by the house" (4). This same argument comes up in Bentham's extended discussion in Letter IX of a comparison between fixing interest rates and fixing the prices of horses.

Prevention of Prodigality

Having accepted the existence of a customary rate of interest, Bentham made an empirical observation. Prodigals generally have property to run down, and where security exists, prodigals are likely to get the customary rate. Hence, usury laws won't stop the greater part of prodigality—even if they effectively set an interest rate near the customary level. Moreover, even if the prodigal is kept by a usury law from borrowing against his inheritance and estates, the prodigal simply will sell or pledge to sell his property. No true prodigal is likely to be constrained in such circumstances. Prodigals are not done in by interest rates that are a few percentage points higher, but by their pattern of excessive spending and much borrowing.

Again, Bentham's argument rests on the increasing prevalence of unfettered markets in the world around him. The point here is reinforced by Bentham's discussion of purchasing on credit from tradespeople, who often charged higher interest on their accounts than the money lenders. The prodigal in the marketplace has just too much opportunity to achieve his ruin. According to Bentham (and J. S. Mill after him), the only effective means of preventing prodigals from dissipating their wealth would be an "interdict" that disallows the sale or pledging of property.

Protection of Indigence

In the modern period, protection of the indigent has perhaps been the most common argument for usury laws. For example, arguments for restrictions on the business practices of pawnshops and payday loans often emphasize how such practices can be especially attractive and injurious to those with low incomes. Bentham emphasized the difference between poverty and simplicity. The poor man with "no particular defect in . . . judgment, or his temper" knows as well as the rich what his interests are. In a market, the poor would be glad to take a lower rate if they could obtain it. But their willingness to pay a higher rate is evidence enough of the value of the loan to them. How is the legislator "who knows nothing, nor can know any thing, of any one of all these circumstances, who knows nothing at all about the matter" to justify interfering? In Bentham's view, such interference was pure folly (1787a, 7).

Protection of Simplicity

Lest anyone be unsure, by simplicity Bentham had in mind "absolute idiocy." For nothing "short of absolute idiotism, can cause the individual to make a more groundless judgment than the legislator." But in Bentham's view, the problem of simpletons in the market involves the simpleton's everyday buying of goods, both the prices paid and the quantities bought, not just the problem of borrowing and interest. Again, markets surround us all. If anything, as Bentham noted, the simpleton may have a better chance at appreciating the one dimension of interest rates than the multiple dimensions of quality of goods, which may be easier to misrepresent.

Repression of the Temerity of Projectors

Although Smith had identified the usefulness of usury caps with harnessing both prodigals and overeager projectors, Bentham connected Smith especially with this latter aim. Bentham directly addressed Letter XIII, by far the longest of the volume, to Smith. In what has long been judged a sincere tribute to Smith,[13] Bentham acknowledged Smith as his intellectual teacher, claiming any persuasive argument he could make on usury must necessarily be fashioned out of the tools that Smith had constructed. Then Bentham plunged into such an argument. Far from being the scourges of the modern economy, he argued, projectors are the very fount of "invention" and "improvement." To Bentham, invention and improvement are the core of the growth of productivity. The simple accumulation of capital in the "routine" can do only little for the standard of living. The projects of projectors, however, have allowed the "species" to advance "from that state in which acorns were their food, and raw hides their clothing, to the state in which it stands at present" (1787a, 22).

Precisely because projectors deal with the "new" they should rightly face high interest rates. In modern terms, projectors act through risky projects with little security, and so they must pay a risk premium. The process favors success because seeking finance generates substantial discussion of the projects. Similarly, as knowledge has grown, projectors are better at weeding out unpromising projects before seeking financing. Whatever the gains to the immediate parties, the gains to the public are far greater. Rather than fear the nation's savings would be wasted in the hands of mountebanks, Bentham celebrated the role of entrepreneurship and finance in driving the creative powers of the new industrial order. It makes little sense to accept all the rest—consumer sovereignty, market prices, and free trade—and reject this fundamental process of financing innovation. From Bentham's perspective, lending to projectors may well be the best of market transactions, rather than the one that should be

13. For an example, see Everett (1931).

limited or prohibited. Lending to projectors brings an improved standard of living for all.

THE SMITH ENIGMA

Bentham made it very clear that he was eager to gain Smith's endorsement of his *Defence*. He explicitly addressed Smith in Letter XIII and asked for Smith to abandon support of usury legislation. The degree to which Smith concurred has been debated ever since. In his early biography of Smith, John Rae quoted a letter from Bentham's good friend George Wilson, in which Wilson related that Smith in late 1789 told a mutual friend, William Adam, the "'Defence of Usury' was the work of a very superior man, and that tho' he had given him some hard knocks it was done in so handsome a way that he could not complain,' and seemed to admit that you (Bentham) were right." Rae went on to suggest that Smith might have changed his mind (Rae 1895, 422–424).

In 1790, Bentham was apparently still optimistic that he might win Smith over. He addressed a second letter to Smith as the preface of a second edition of the *Defence*. Here he referred to a bill likely to be introduced in the Irish House of Commons that would lower interest rate maximums there (Bentham 1981). There is no known written response of Smith to Bentham's continued urgings. Smith died in 1790. It is known, however, that Smith sent Bentham a copy of the new 1789 edition of the *Wealth of Nations*, which contained no recantation of his support for usury limits and a copy of the 1790 edition of the *Theory of Moral Sentiments*. Paganelli (2003) has suggested Smith was not so subtly hinting that Bentham would do well to read the latter volume to appreciate the argument in the former.

Throughout, Bentham identified the difference between his position and Smith's as one centered on the role of projectors in the economy. As several observers have pointed out,[14] Bentham was himself very much a projector in the sense of advocating both private-sector innovations and public-sector reforms. Even as Bentham wrote the *Defence* in the Belarusian outback, he and his brother, Samuel, were putting together their ambitious scheme for prison reform and industrial organization, the Panopticon. Jeremy Bentham published the resulting short volume, presented in the form of a series of letters and entitled with impressive completeness: *Panopticon; or the Inspection-House: Containing the Idea of New Principle of Construction Applicable to Any Sort of Establishment, in which*

14. For example, see Crimmins (1998).

Persons of Any Description Are to be Kept Under Inspection; And in Particular to Penitentiary-Houses, Prisons, Houses of Industry, Work-Houses, Poor-Houses, Lazarettos, Manufactories, Hospitals, Mad-Houses and Schools: With a Plan of Management Adapted to the Principle (Bentham 1787b). The Panopticon has taken an iconic position in various critiques of modern institutions. While Jeremy Bentham did suggest in his introduction that his discussion of schools was something of a humorous fancy, he and his brother meant this exercise in the design of control and monitoring as a very real project. The Benthams invested heavily and expected substantial profits from various applications of the Panopticon. Their largest project sought to sell their Panopticon system to prison authorities in Britain.

Under the circumstances, it was little wonder that Bentham identified with projectors and argued that this odd breed was responsible for great improvements in human happiness. If those attempting to be social benefactors like the Benthams could find loans at something above the legal rate, how could Smith object?

Most likely for Smith the term "projectors," applied to agents very different from social reformers and benefactors of humanity. As suggested by Hollander (1999), Smith identified as projectors the various financial promoters of highly dubious projects aimed at fleecing the public of their savings. Their projects were not accidental failures, but virtually planned failures. Only by accident might they succeed. By promising high returns, they appealed to the greedy and fleeced the gullible.

While Smith had a deep commitment to his obvious and simple system of natural liberty, he was not a slavish or didactic follower of the invisible hand.[15] Smith's views on usury seem not to be oversights but, rather, strongly held positions.

CHESTERTON'S CLAIM

In 1790, Adam Smith saw nothing awkward in the state's capping interest rates. Jeremy Bentham's defense of usury held otherwise. In 1790 Smith still advocated a role for the social regulation of finance. Bentham saw nothing to be gained by such interference in private contracts. What in this policy debate convinced G. K. Chesterton, writing almost 150 years later, that Bentham's tract marked the beginning of the modern world?

15. For an interesting treatment of Smith's attitude toward the invisible hand, see Rothschild (2001). Rothschild makes a novel case that Smith "did not especially esteem the invisible hand," and that he meant it "as a mildly ironic joke" (116).

The claim is put forth in Chesterton's short biography of Thomas Aquinas (Chesterton 1933). Chesterton did not offer an extended explanation of his position. But it is not difficult to reconstruct his case.

Chesterton yearned for a reestablishment of the traditional communitarian Christian ethics of Aquinas. In that system, production was primarily for use and loans were a manifestation of charity. Usury was a sin precisely because it took advantage of the needs of others. More broadly, Chesterton, like Aquinas, saw markets not as the center of the community's life but as a modest appendage, useful only when strongly controlled by a religious morality. Little wonder that Chesterton bemoaned a modern world built on the principles of triumphalist British liberalism. From Chesterton's vantage point, Bentham's *Defence* can be viewed as offering the clearest and least adorned early statement of those principles. Without excuses, Bentham insisted on the individual as the locus of responsibility. The spread of market relations empowered individuals to chart their own course. The market offered opportunity to individual creativity and a harsh respect for even the poor. And no market did so more explicitly than that for borrowing and lending money.

Bentham's *Defense* anticipates his assertion in "Radicalism Not Dangerous" (Bentham 1819) that private property and the investment process characterizing the new capitalism generate the best possible outcomes for the working classes. This is the unadorned liberal triumphalist argument. From this perspective, even the poorest workers under a fully laissez-faire capitalist regime are far better off than the rich of antiquity. Free markets in and of themselves meet the utilitarian criteria of the greatest happiness for the greatest number.

Over the years the arguments in favor of leaving interest unregulated have become emblematic of the broader case for a triumphal, libertarian capitalism. Even today, the debate resonates. For example, most states in the United States have legally defined usury rates that limit interest on loans between persons and corporations (Glaeser and Scheinkman 1998). A number of state legislatures have implemented prohibitions on the most egregious aspects of "payday lending," in which a borrower gives a payday lender a postdated personal check and receives cash, minus the lender's fees.[16] For a triumphal liberal, interference in such simple private exchanges promises not a welfare gain but a welfare loss. According to one

16. For example, with a $300 payday loan, a consumer might pay $40 in fees and receive $260 in cash. Such high fees on short-term loans repayable in a few weeks imply per annum interest rates reaching reach 1000 percent and more (Stegman and Faris 2003).

academic defender of the payday loan industry, the evidence shows "on balance that many borrowers are helped by access to short-term credit even at prices that some observers might consider 'high'" (Stango 2012, 33). And that is all there is to it.

To establish triumphal liberalism, the core economic sin of traditional ethics—usury—had been transmogrified into a manifestation of the core social engine of the new age: self-interested exchange. Quite simply, the new mode delivered the goods. The sin of usurious commercial exploitation of the needs of others had been recast into the liberal equality of the marketplace. Where Smith sensed a new world abuilding, Bentham embraced it and declared its manifesto. The seamless web of community advocated by Aquinas and Chesterton was pronounced unuseful and unworkable, replaced by a web of impersonal but empowering contracts. Smith, never the extremist, looked to hedge the point. The young Bentham refused to let Smith have it both ways.

CHAPTER 4

Utilitarian Perspectives on Private Property

Bentham's *Defence* was a dramatic and clever piece. But it was not a full-scale apology. The obvious foundational step in building a utilitarian justification of the triumphalist position would have been a thick and convincing defense of private property generally, and more specifically of the private ownership of industrial capital. Yet, one looks in vain for the deep utilitarian work on private property rights in the means of production. The early utilitarians, Bentham and Paley, provide no detailed analytical/historical rationale for this institution in its various forms: household tools and possessions, land and other natural resources, merchant capital, financial capital, slave capital, and most importantly in the nineteenth century, the large machinery and plant of the new factories and other industrial enterprises. Instead, we find what can at best be described as a thin defense—a short, highly abstract discussion here, a chapter or two there.[1] The early utilitarian defense of private property is largely rhetorical in character.[2] Given the utilitarian commitment to exploring the

1. The major example from the early utilitarian writings is the treatment by Bentham ([1838] 1962) in ch. 8 of the *Civil Code*.

2. Rhetorical arguments, at least for our purposes, are those which are not meant to convince but, rather, to act as signs or symbols. Rhetorical arguments, lacking serious bolstering, show where a writer or school is "coming from." They provide a shorthand statement easily identified by the reader. *Rhetorical* in this context has a mildly negative connotation and corresponds closely to the everyday use of the word. This common use of *rhetorical* can be distinguished from the broader meaning that refers less judgmentally to methods of persuasion as discussed by Deirdre McCloskey in *The Rhetoric of Economics* (1998). The common definition adopted here can also

underlying logic of institutions, the lack of a serious defense appears a major lacuna in the triumphalist liberal position.

Rhetorical arguments are almost by definition thin. However, it is difficult to specify what type of defense would qualify as appropriately substantial. It is beyond the scope of this book to lay out definitive guidelines for utilitarian argumentation. But the general consequentialist position of utilitarians[3] would seem to demand that a defense of property rights starts from a well-reasoned theoretical argument deducing the likely outcomes of alternative institutional structures. Where possible, it would be bolstered with careful historical/anthropological/empirical exhibits demonstrating the soundness of the theoretical exercise. Both theory and empirics would aim at providing a measure of the aggregate welfare generated by the institutional forms considered.

Against this background, we can proceed to ask why the early utilitarian defense of the institution of private property typically took such a rhetorical form.[4] At least four hypotheses suggest themselves: irrelevance (the interests of utilitarians did not particularly depend on a defense), triviality (the defense at the time was considered a closed book), impossibility (the subject at least in utilitarian terms was simply too complex for any serious analysis), and ambivalence (utilitarians were painfully uncertain about the relation of the institution to their own stated goals).

IRRELEVANCE

It is particularly difficult to argue that the utilitarian position did not require a defense of private property. From its origins the utilitarian school committed itself to a deep and unflinching reanalysis of major social institutions. Jeremy Bentham had brought a new energy to a social-materialist view of rights. Bentham in particular took exception to the liberalism of John Locke, with its metaphysical talk of natural rights.

be distinguished from a much more pejorative meaning of "rhetorical" suggested by Albert Hirschman in his *The Rhetoric of Reaction*, where "rhetorical" arguments are those "that are in effect contraptions specifically designed to make dialogue and deliberation impossible" (1991, 170).

3. For example, as subsequently laid out in Mill's *Logic*, ch. 12, "Of the Logic of Practice, or Art; Including Morality and Policy" ([1843] 1974).

4. I leave it as an open matter whether others offered more robust defenses. Perhaps most relevant and most consistent among the classical economists was Malthus's defense of private property, based on his theory and empirics of population growth (Malthus [1798] 1970, 139–145).

Rights made sense for the utilitarian only to the extent they served to advance the greatest good of the greatest number. This key precept put virtually all the civil institutions of society in question. John Stuart Mill called Bentham "the great *subversive* . . . the great *critical* thinker of his age and country" (Mill [1867] 1987, 134). In principle, the philosophical radicals held up all rights and social institutions to serious questioning. Given such a starting point, it would be difficult to imagine that the utilitarians would avoid subjecting the institution and character of property rights to careful scrutiny.

Apart from their general commitment to a full reappraisal of society, utilitarians had more particular reasons to explore carefully the consequences of different systems of property. Virtually all utilitarians make a commitment to equality. Jeremy Bentham had explicitly asserted the universality of diminishing marginal utility. For a pie of any given size, equal slices would generate the highest total utility. Similar commitments had prompted any number of agrarians, including the Diggers of the Cromwellian revolution and Thomas Spence in the 1790s, to advocate substantial redistribution of property. Given the utilitarians' strong endorsement of equality, it would seem that they must either accept the agrarian conclusions or develop an explicit and serious defense of private property.

The utilitarian commitment to equality was built on a conviction that the greatest proportion of people were fairly similar in their ability to produce and in their capacity to enjoy.[5] Such notions were characteristic of the Enlightenment philosophers on whom the utilitarians relied, most specifically Claude Adrien Helvetius, David Hume, and Adam Smith.[6]

A number of scholars have previously noted the deep tension in utilitarian thought between the endorsement of equality and the announced commitment to the institution of private property.[7] Both Paley and Bentham end with sweeping endorsements of private property. Because

5. I think this is what Sandra Peart and David Levy (2005) mean by "analytical egalitarian." One might reasonably ask why the utilitarians didn't provide a thicker defense of their egalitarianism. But perhaps that is another book.

6. As argued in chapter 1, the three mentioned were of a similar mind: Hume spoke of "how nearly equal all men are in their bodily force, and even in their mental powers and faculties, till cultivated by education" (Hume [1748] 1826, 511), while Smith famously observed, "The difference between the most dissimilar characters, between a philosopher and a common street porter, for example, seems to arise not so much from nature, as from habit, custom, and education" (Smith, [1776] 1976, 25). Helvetius had simply asserted "education makes us what we are" (Helvetius, [1772] 1969, 2:405).

7. In particular, Alan Ryan (1984).

of the tensions in their thought, these utilitarians could hardly deny the need for a serious foundation for such endorsements.

TRIVIALITY

To the extent that early utilitarians viewed the defense of private property as trivial they presumably based their conclusion on the scholarly understanding of the day. Where, in that scholarly mix, had a serious defense already been made? Three related strains of thought are potentially relevant to such a claim: seventeenth-century political philosophy, eighteenth-century history, and eighteenth-century moral philosophy. A reconsideration of these literatures suggests that both philosophers and historians offered little empirical support for their largely speculative endorsements. Perhaps over the years their positions took on the authority of age and an appearance of self-evidence. But utilitarians with their commitment to the reconsideration of root arguments should have approached these earlier defenses with a degree of skepticism. To drive this point home, here is a short review of the less than sturdy materials the utilitarians had available at the time.

Seventeenth-Century Political Philosophy

Bentham's argument about security would hardly have been novel for his readers. He had simply restated (not even repackaged) the Hobbesian description of the state of nature.[8] Hobbes's position was well known to Bentham's contemporaries. As read today, Hobbes is far from a utilitarian (Tuck 1996). Yet in the most famous passage from the *Leviathan*, Hobbes comes quite close:

> Whatsoever therefore is consequent to a time of Warre, where every man is Enemy to every man; the same is consequent to the time, wherein men live without other security, than what their own strength, and their own invention shall furnish them withall. In such condition, there is no place for Industry; because the fruit thereof is uncertain: and consequently no Culture of Earth; no Navigation, nor use of the commodities that may be imported by Sea; no

8. As several observers have noted, Bentham rarely refers directly to Hobbes's work, in part because of his hostility to Hobbes's penchant for natural law. Nevertheless, there is a strong consensus that Bentham read and was very much influenced by Hobbes. See Crimmins (2002).

> commodious Building; no Instruments of moving, an removing such things as require much force; no Knowledge of the face of the Earth; no account of Time; no Arts; no Letters; no Society; and which is worst of all, continuall feare, and danger of violent death; And the life of man, solitary, poore, nasty, brutish, and short." (Hobbes [1660] 1996, 89)

Hobbes never would endorse the utilitarian greatest good, but he is not above suggesting that his "state of nature" lacks virtually all the useful material and cultural achievements that contribute to the attractiveness of civilized life. Given Hobbes's central place in British political philosophy, it is understandable that Bentham and other utilitarians, where convenient, drew on the Hobbesian description of the state of nature. But in doing so, did the utilitarians draw on a richness of argument that rendered unnecessary their further defense of property? Put somewhat differently, was the Hobbesian case so well developed that no further elaboration was really required of utilitarians like Bentham? I think the answer is no.

Hobbes's argument in the *Leviathan* is itself quite thin; it's little more than a speculation. In a short paragraph, Hobbes acknowledged that his "warre of every one against every one" never generally existed "over all the world." But he goes on to suggest two empirical examples: (1) "(For) the savage people in many places of America, except the government of small Families, the concord whereof dependeth on naturall lust, have no government at all; and live at this day in that brutish manner" (89); and (2) "Howsoever, it may be perceived what manner of life there would be, where there were no common Power to feare; but the manner of life which men that have formerly lived under a peacefull government, use to degenerate into, in a civill Warre" (89–90). A bit later Hobbes refers to the "miseries, and horrible calamities, that accompany a Civill Warre; or that dissolute condition of masterlesse men, without subjection to Lawes, and a coercive Power to tye their hands from rapine, and revenge" (128).

From this base Hobbes goes on to justify the state, and in particular the institution of private property. In a very utilitarian fashion, Hobbes justifies the property rights established by the power of the state in terms of their consequential value: "For before constitution of Soveraign Power (as hath already been shewn) all men had right to all things; which necessarily causeth Warre: and therefore this Proprietie, being necessary to Peace, and depending on Soveraign Power, is the Act of that Power, in order to the publicque peace." These are the "Rules of Propriety (or *Meum* and *Tuum*)" (125). The establishment of property rights is the critical action of the sovereign. Before, all is state of nature and insecurity, after all is industry.

That is it for Hobbesian anthropology, empirics, and historicism. The entire evidentiary structure of Hobbes's argument rests on a brief allusion to American Indians and a reminder of the miseries of the English Civil War. For Hobbes, the Leviathan is justified as virtually self-evident. Property rights come with the state. While obviously Hobbes could not have anticipated the new industrial forms of property, he makes no effort to distinguish among the other several classes of property. The sovereign makes the rules, but it is far from clear the degree to which the same rules are to cover all forms of property.

Bentham and other utilitarians certainly echoed Hobbesian notions about the state of nature. But neither Bentham nor Paley emphasized a debt to Hobbes. Hobbes, of course, was under no responsibility to demonstrate that property rights as they existed historically, or as they might be reconstructed in the future, fully met the utilitarian standard—that is, the greatest happiness of the greatest number. And Hobbes never elaborates such an argument. The utilitarians, however, faced just such a responsibility. By simply echoing Hobbes, Paley and Bentham hardly settled the matter.

Of course, between Hobbes and the utilitarians, the traditional argument in favor of private property had undergone its own history. Most important, John Locke had attempted to anchor private property as a natural human right, not a civil right. Locke, like Hobbes, is not a committed utilitarian so he, too, is under less pressure than Bentham's followers.

But the utilitarians could hardly endorse Locke's natural right. Thus Bentham had explicitly and famously argued, "there is no natural property" (Bentham [1838] 1962, 308). For Bentham, property was created by the law and to be judged on utilitarian principles. Indeed, Bentham repeatedly makes fun of efforts to establish natural rights. The man who posits "an eternal and immutable Rule of Right" that "dictates so and so: and then begins giving you his sentiments upon any thing that comes uppermost" (Bentham [1780] 1987, 79). Bentham can't fall back on Locke.

Eighteenth-Century Historians

Utilitarians, as Leslie Stephen observed long ago, claimed to base their reforms on empirical evidence, but had only the crudest appreciation of history (Stephen [1900] 1950, 298).[9] Bentham especially was fond of

9. Stephen, something of a professed utilitarian, was the grandson of James Stephen of the Clapham sect, evangelical allies in the antislavery crusade with the utilitarians. He was also the father of Virginia Woolf and Vanessa Bell.

shortcuts. For him, "a rough sketch of a science is the same thing as its definite constitution." Even John Stuart Mill was to criticize Bentham for his attitude toward history. As Stephen suggested, history for the utilitarians was only a "record of crimes and follies and of little else" (297). Hence, when the utilitarians offered historical examples in defense of private property, it would be surprising if they brought forth more than a few sketches.

But the eighteenth century had witnessed a flowering of historical researches. Edward Gibbon had produced his striking history of the Roman Empire. In Scotland, David Hume had undertaken a massive history of England. And his friend William Robertson had written a number of histories, the most relevant to the current discussion being one of America. To what extent had the eighteenth-century outpouring of historical scholarship established a defense of private property?

The works of none of these prominent historians are directly cited by early utilitarians in their (admittedly short) defenses.[10] The history they do draw on amounts to little more than commonplaces. Paley restricts his history of property largely to some thoughts on Bible stories. Bentham makes an off-hand reference to the lack of economic development in lands ruled despotically by the Ottomans (Bentham [1838] 1962, 310–311).

The finding that the early utilitarians made little use of the new historical scholarship of the late eighteenth century is perhaps not surprising. Quite simply, the historians offered the utilitarians relatively little "data" on property rights. The following (admittedly cursory) overview of what the major historians had to say about property rights points toward this negative conclusion.

Gibbon: Gibbon's famous work had little to offer about the importance of private property to Roman successes and failures. Early in the *Decline and Fall*, Gibbon shows respect for the genius of the Antonine emperors in providing an inclusive and stable religious, political, and legal system to the empire. He contrasts their inclusive approach with the dualism of the Middle Eastern empires, characterized by central despotism and loose control in the rebellious periphery. But he gives no specifics here.

Later in his discussion of Roman law and its reforms under Justinian, Gibbon offers a brief consideration of Roman property rights. Gibbon starts philosophically with a Lockean argument, but quickly acknowledges

10. However, in his autobiography, Mill mentions reading the histories of Hume, Gibbon, and Robertson at an early age (Mill [1873] 1981, 10).

"the common rights, the equal inheritance of mankind are engrossed by the bold and crafty; each field and forest is circumscribed by the landmarks of a jealous master." His position becomes explicitly utilitarian:

> In the progress from primitive equity to final injustice, the steps are silent, the shades are almost imperceptible, and the absolute monopoly is guarded by positive laws and artificial reason. The active, insatiate principle of self-love can alone supply the arts of life and the wages of industry; and as soon as civil government and exclusive property have been introduced, they become necessary to the existence of the human race. (Gibbon [1776] 1932, 357)

But there is little of history here. Gibbon goes on to defend the institution of property in land as consistent with "the wisest legislators" who with the "singular" exception of the Spartans had "disapproved an agrarian law as a false and dangerous innovation." In this vein he sees the wisdom of the Roman rejection of egalitarian folk traditions:

> Among the Romans, the enormous disproportion of wealth surmounted the ideal restraints of a doubtful tradition, and an obsolete statute; a tradition that the poorest follower of Romulus had been endowed with the perpetual inheritance of two jugera; a statute which confined the richest citizen to the measure of five hundred jugera, or three hundred and twelve acres of land. (357)

Overall, it is hard to see much historical justification for the broad opinions Gibbon offered. Indeed, his material is largely a restatement of the views of philosophers. One suspects that in Gibbon's discussion of private property, history followed moral philosophy and not vice versa.[11]

Hume: Hume, of course, was a historian as well as a philosopher. And his history of England clearly stated the theme that commerce and industry were dependent on the security of private property. For example, in discussing the lack of commerce in England after the Norman invasion, Hume wrote "[T]he improvements of agriculture were also much checked, by the immense possessions of the nobility, by the disorders of the times, and by the precarious state of feudal property; it appears, that industry of no kind could then have place in the kingdom" (1778, 1:484). Hume also commented on the bad "police" of the country that

11. The connection may be quite direct. Gibbon's discussion of Roman agrarian law closely parallels Smith's treatment in the *Wealth of Nations* (Smith [1776] 1976, 4:ch. 7). Similarly, his exception of the Spartan lawgivers appears in Hume's *Enquiry Concerning the Principles of Morals* (Hume [1740] 1978).

left private property insecure (2: 69). The history of the country was one of an improvement of security such that by the time of the Tudors, Hume suggested "that the instances of a high exerted prerogative were not so frequent as to render property sensibly insecure, or reduce the people to a total servitude" (4:200). Hume is by and large concerned with the threat of tyranny and/or chaos to property. The lesson of English history is that commerce and industry require safety from arbitrary tyrants and marauding robbers.

But the historical subject matter Hume has to work with offers little else in the way of lessons. In particular, he has virtually no material that allows a comparison among alternative property arrangements. The only real challenge to traditional views of private property in the period he covers was raised by the Diggers. Hume dismisses their radicalism in a cursory fashion. In doing so, he offers opinion, not history.

Robertson: William Robertson's history of America, written in very much a Humean spirit, opened a serious investigation of the favorite example of a state of nature: the Native American tribes. Presumably, when Paley and Bentham made the claim that no one in a society with common property lived as well as the lowest in developed commercial societies, they had the tribes in mind.

Robertson sets the stage in a conventional enough manner:

> In America, man appears under the rudest form in which we can conceive him to subsist. . . . The greater part of its inhabitants were strangers to industry and labour, ignorant of arts, imperfectly acquainted with the nature of property, and enjoying almost without restriction or controul the blessings which flowed spontaneously from the bounty of nature. (Robertson [1777] 1847, 90)

But he is admirably careful not to overgeneralize his conclusions with respect to property, or for that matter utility. He is acutely aware of the range of exceptions to the standard characterizations. While critical of Rousseau's glorification of the savage state, Robertson is far from dismissive of Native American virtues. He also is appreciative of the effectiveness of tribal loyalty in stimulating contributions to common production.[12]

Rather than a greedy war of all against all, Robertson sees the savage state as supportive of equality and hostile to privilege at least within the tribe. Robertson simply observes "nations which depend upon hunting

12. Interestingly, Robertson seems strongly critical of the treatment of women in Native American cultures.

are, in a great measure, strangers to the idea of property" (108). This was especially the case in the temperate zones of North America.

Robertson's general view suggested that where agriculture and settled life dominated, simple property rights were likely to be established and following those rights was an elaboration of government and control. Robertson in particular discusses the Natchez and the people of Bogotá in this light:

> Among people in this state, avarice and ambition have acquired objects, and have begun to exert their power; views of interest allure the selfish; the desire of preeminence excites the enterprising; dominion is courted by both; and passions unknown to man in his savage state, prompt the interested and ambitious to encroach on the rights of their fellow-citizens. (111)

Reinforcing the influence of agriculture, Robertson also invokes a climatic determinism in his discussion of Native American governments. "[I]f we proceed from north to south along the continent of America, we shall find the power of those vested with authority gradually increasing, and the spirit of the people becoming more tame and passive. In Florida, the authority of the sachems, caziques, or chiefs, was not only permanent, but hereditary" (110).

And everywhere the suppression of independence is intricately linked to the manipulation of superstition. "Even among nations of this state, the spirit of subjects could not have been rendered so obsequious, or the power of rulers so unbounded, without the intervention of superstition. By its fatal influence, the human mind, in every state of its progress, is depressed, and its native vigour and independence subdued" (111).

Robertson's nuanced discussion of the historical varieties of American cultures did little to *justify* the traditional Hobbesian uses of the state of nature in the defense of property rights and the Leviathan. He offers a positive theory, not the normative evaluation required by the utilitarians.

This sketch of eighteenth-century historiography is obviously superficial. However, it hardly suggests that the historians had offered strong proofs on the central question raised by the utilitarians. The opinions of the ancients on the role of private property hardly could weigh in a utilitarian calculation. Nor was any defense of equality likely to advocate a return to medieval despotism. Just the opposite; a defense of equality would most probably be linked to the democratic political reforms strongly endorsed by most utilitarians. As such, the history of tyrants was of little relevance. American history, while interesting for pointing out the oversimplifications of common wisdom, hardly could establish the critical claim that an empowered egalitarianism would lead back to the state of nature. Rather, it just suggested that the American "state of nature" was more complicated than most Europeans thought.

Eighteenth-Century Moral Philosophy

David Hume made the question of private property central to his theory of morals. His was surely the most sophisticated theory of property rights to emerge from eighteenth-century philosophy.

In his *Enquiry Concerning the Principles of Morals* (1751), Hume begins with a quick historical review. He point out the "fanatical" quality of the Levelers and somewhat more ambivalently the ancient examples of egalitarian legislation in Sparta's constitution and Rome's agrarian laws. But he leaves no doubt as to how obvious in the light of history he views the utility of private property:

> But historians, and even common sense, may inform us that, however specious these ideas of perfect equality may seem, they are really, at bottom, impracticable; and were they not so, would be extremely pernicious to human society. Render possessions ever so equal, men's different degrees of art, care, and industry will immediately break that equality. Or if you check these virtues, you reduce society to the most extreme indigence; and instead of preventing want and beggary in a few, render it unavoidable to the whole community. (Hume 1751, ch. 3, pt. 2)

Hume had long been interested in the role of "selfishness" in human society. In his *Treatise of Human Nature*, he had expounded at some length on how property rights cleverly set selfishness against itself. Our avidity for acquiring goods and possessions "is insatiable, perpetual, universal, and directly destructive of society." Moreover, "no affection of the human mind has both a sufficient force, and a proper direction to counter-balance the love of gain, and render men fit members of society, by making them abstain from the possessions of others. . . . There is no passion therefore, capable of controlling the interested affection, but the very affection itself, by an alteration of its direction" ([1740] 1978, 492). By providing protection for the bounty of selfish energy, property rights used a commitment to long run selfish ambition to thwart the urge to steal in the short run. And these rights could not be compromised or partial in any respect, but according to Hume must be "perfect or none at all" (529).

Hume went on to build his entire theory of justice around the social psychological forces that he saw as stabilizing the notion of private property.

Justice is not natural to the "mind of man." Rather, it derives its origin "from the selfishness and confin'd generosity of men, along with the scanty provision nature has made for his wants" (495). Justice like property, but unlike natural virtues, must be "full and perfect or none at all." Society then more or less spontaneously establishes rights in private property based on "Occupation, Prescription, Accession and Succession" (505).

The philosophical argument is profound and utilitarian in spirit. But can it serve the purposes of a utilitarian defense? Does it reasonably trace the consequences of the institution in its various forms? Throughout Hume's discussion, as stated in the *Treatise* and the *Enquiry*, the social usefulness of private property rights is asserted as a trivial observation, without need of any substantial support. From a utilitarian perspective, Hume regarded the defense of private property as trivial. The "peace and order" of society make "every individual person . . . a gainer, on balancing the account; since, without justice, society must immediately dissolve and every one must fall into that savage and solitary condition, which is infinitely worse than the worst situation that can possibly be suppos'd in society" (497).

David Hume's thought had a profound effect on the utilitarians. William Paley, a devout churchman, restricted himself to criticizing the agnostic Mr. Hume, but is generally credited with legitimizing Hume's utilitarianism. Bentham enthusiastically recognized Hume as a major source of his own utilitarianism. Still, Paley, Bentham, and Mill did not explicitly invoke Hume's philosophical arguments on property.[13] While elegant, Hume's theory could add little in the way of consequential support to the utilitarian defense of property rights. Many of the utilitarians undoubtedly noted Hume's simple historical examples, but his deeper philosophical speculations provided little in the way of concrete evidence for their position.

IMPOSSIBILITY

Hume regarded the "historical proofs" against absolute equality as trivial. But did those "proofs" really justify claims for property rights? Early

13. Mill came very close, however. As pointed out by Margaret Shabas, Mill in his essay "On Nature" paraphrases Hume's discussion of justice (which as noted following is intimately linked to Hume's philosophical defense of property rights) when he asserts "Justice is entirely of artificial origin" (quoted in Shabas 2006, 132–133). Mill suggests in that essay that early concepts of justice were linked to the acceptance of the law of property. But both here and in his essay *Utilitarianism* ([1861] 1987), where he discusses justice at length, Mill does not bring the Humean argument to the fore.

utilitarians could hardly ignore in good conscience the wide range of alternative arrangements of property, taxation, and redistribution that clamored for evaluation. It may just be beyond us (and the early utilitarians) to imagine the full range of social organizations that might be substituted for "perfect" private property rights and then evaluate them from a utilitarian perspective? The utilitarian standard is just too difficult to meet. And indeed, the multiple categories of property must further complicate any such analysis. Yet, none of the early utilitarians seemed to suggest the impossibility of what was required.

Put somewhat differently, the history of the utilitarian defense of property in the works of Paley and Bentham seems to be a history of the excluded middle. By largely focusing on the extremes, the early utilitarians seem to avoid the most difficult work. Paley and Bentham were convinced that efforts to achieve absolute equality were chimerical and destructive. The vast majority of their audience undoubtedly agreed. But what they certainly hadn't proved was the case for a "perfect" property right, whatever that might be. They typically made security into an absolute. The result was embarrassingly Panglossian. Not satisfied with suggesting that the institution of private property served a range of useful functions, the utilitarians at their most aggressive pushed on to claiming a need for virtually unfettered property rights. All of this is somewhat odd, given the clear recognition by utilitarians that variations on the institution of private property in all its manifestations were considerable across the countries of Europe and elsewhere.

We might reasonably ask what type of social science the utilitarians actually imagined capable of deciding among and then evaluating these various alternative sets of rules. Paley gave us few hints in this regard and never formalized a social science that could be used to make fundamental decisions about institutions such as property rights. While he spoke of a "science of politics," he did so in an off-hand and highly informal manner. Thus in discussing hereditary monarchies and elective monarchies, he cited "the confession of every writer on the subject of civil government, the experience of ages, the example of Poland, and of the papal dominions" as establishing the superiority of the former to the latter. But Paley didn't seem to expect much from such researches, since he placed this conclusion "amongst the few indubitable maxims which the science of politics admits of" (Paley [1785] 2002, 319).

Bentham clearly had a more elaborate vision of social sciences in general and political economy in particular. He saw the "science" of political economy as informing the "art" of governing. And he felt that Smith had made major gains in advancing that science (Bentham [1843] 1962, chs. 1–2). Bentham attempted then to reconcile his own greatest-happiness principle with Smith's political economy. This promising project led to a number of acute observations, including the endorsement of a proto-benefit-cost analysis. However, so much was assumed from the start that the resulting analysis could hardly have provided a serious foundation for a defense of private property. The "general rule" for government was simply "Be quiet." Bentham concluded, "The art, therefore, is reduced within a small compass: *security* and *freedom* are all that industry requires." In effect, Bentham's rhetorical commitment to laissez-faire and private property preceded his social science. It would have been virtually impossible to use that social science to broadly and seriously test the normative merits of alternative approaches to private property.

AMBIVALENCE

It is not hard to appreciate the sources of ambivalence in the utilitarian defense of private property. At root is that same tension between egalitarianism and property that makes the defense necessary in the first place. Istvan Hont speaks of the "paradox of commercial society": "The economic efficacy of inequality was a paradox because it drove a wedge between the traditional egalitarian intuitions of Western moral thought and the guiding assumptions of modern political economy" (Hont 2005, 92). The result for most all moral philosophers is an element of ambivalence. For triumphalists, this tension leads to an almost compulsive need to rush to a conclusion that all was in fact for the better. Hont suggests that Hume and Smith had constructed "an argument that resembled in structure and purpose the Christian defense of 'evil' in the world by a theodicy, that is a reconciliation of the existence of evil with the benevolence of God" (91).

But even in the case of triumphalists, the underlying ambivalence can show through. For example, Paley's famous discourse on the egalitarian behavior of a flock of pigeons suggests considerable ambivalence toward the institution of private property. As D. L. LeMahieu has commented, "Wrenched from context, the analogy was perhaps the most radical declaration against property in the Enlightenment" (Paley [1785] 2002, xviii). Paley's passionate statement belies his thin resolution and suggests considerable ambivalence. And even more than Paley, Jeremy Bentham over his long career evinced conflicting judgments of the institution of private property. In his most extensive, but still relatively short defense of private property in *Principles of the Civil Code*, Bentham reiterated the

Humean arguments. Recognizing the pull of equality, he argued that security and the ability to plan into the future are fundamental to the advance of the economy. But as Bentham grew older and politically more radical, his prescriptions for the economy verged on redistributional. He advocated for public education, inheritance laws, and welfare. And for all this Bentham has been attacked by more than one libertarian, including von Mises and Rothbard. But what the libertarians see as apostasy is more reasonably viewed as an ambivalence in the face of the demands of equality. Better to fall back on a superficial consensus and not to explore too deeply the quagmire.

J. S. MILL AND THE ORIGINS OF THE UTILITARIAN ANALYSIS OF PRIVATE PROPERTY

John Stuart Mill inherited the utilitarian mantle. He brought it together with the greatly expanded set of tools generated by political economy. The moment was ripe for a new survey of the usefulness of private property in all its various forms. Like Bentham, John Stuart Mill made clear the utilitarian challenge to the social sciences. Like his father James Mill, he understood that the goal of achieving the greatest happiness of the greatest number opened "a wide and difficult field, and that the whole science of human nature must be explored to lay a foundation for the science of government" (James Mill 1825, 3). Admittedly a charge of such breadth might prove a daunting task. But a scholar of the caliber of John Stuart Mill, when well motivated, could demonstrate an impressive ability to put together such consequential arguments. While he did not always show the same resolve or focus, it is fair to say that J. S. Mill began the serious analysis of the varieties of private property.

In the *Principles*, Mill included two relatively short chapters on property. While provocative in a number of ways, the chapters are not Mill at his best. In place of a strong historical argument Mill offers a rather rarified thought experiment: a colony considering a system of private property or collective ownership. Here he sets out in a highly abstract fashion to consider the usefulness of the institution not in the midst of the horrendous inequalities of the industrial revolution but, rather, in an egalitarian colonial Eden, "a community unhampered by any previous possession; a body of colonists, occupying for the first time an uninhabited country; bringing nothing with them but what belonged to them in common" (Mill [1848] 1965, 201). And in this Eden, Mill works mightily to reconcile property and equality. He analyzes a private property "accompanied by none of the initial inequalities and injustices which obstruct the beneficial operation of the principle in old societies." In this ideal experiment:

> Every full grown man or woman, we must suppose, would be secured in the unfettered use and disposal of his or her bodily and mental faculties; and the instruments of production, the land and tools, would be divided fairly among them, so that all might start, in respect to outward appliances, on equal terms, accompanied by none of the initial inequalities and injustices which obstruct the beneficial operation of the principle in old societies. (205)

He even goes so far as to provide an original "compensation . . . for the injuries of nature."

The question is, What consequences flow from such a system in comparison to one of collective ownership? Both alternatives are to be fully purged of any imperfections. Private property is initially distributed in the fairest possible manner. Collective ownership is governed by democratically elected magistrates. He intends to compare "communism at its best, with the regime of individual property, not as it is, but as it might be made" (208).

The exercise does not produce a defense of private property as it is in the real world. That real world he roundly condemns, virtually endorsing "communism" with all its potential faults over the then real-world system of private property that, according to Mill, rewarded people in almost inverse proportion to their work effort. Rather, Mill's highly conditional defense is for a "principle of private property [which] has never yet had a fair trial in any country" (208). Mill goes on:

> The laws of property have never yet conformed to the principles on which the justification of private property rests. They have made property of things which never ought to be property, and absolute property where only a qualified property ought to exist. They have not held the balance fairly between human beings, but have heaped impediments upon some, to give advantage to others; they have purposely fostered inequalities, and prevented all from starting fair in the race. That all should indeed start on perfectly equal terms is inconsistent with any law of private property: but if as much pains as has been taken to aggravate the inequality of chances arising from the natural working of the principle, had been taken to temper that inequality by every means not subversive of the principle itself; if the tendency of legislation had been to favour the diffusion, instead of the concentration of wealth—to encourage the subdivision of the large masses, instead of striving to keep them together; the principle of individual property would have been found to have no necessary connexion with the physical and social evils which almost all Socialist writers assume to be inseparable from it. (209)

The thought experiment evinces an almost sentimental attachment to the possibilities of a purified system of private property. The result is more of a daydream than a serious program.

Had Mill left it at that, his approach to property rights would have been even more ambivalent and hardly more serious than that of his utilitarian predecessors. But he doesn't leave the matter there. Indeed, he explicitly considers the various categories of property throughout the *Principles*. From his utilitarian perspective he takes up slavery, land systems, handicrafts, and elements of financial capital. For example, his discussion of peasant proprietors and alternative systems of tenancy ([1848] 1965, 2: chs. 6–10) displays a mastery of theory linked to a rich empirical effort. On that canvas, Mill combines positive economics with a strong normative argument in favor of independent proprietorships. This is institutional analysis of the highest order. In this case Mill approached the standard he himself set for utilitarian discourse.[14]

Most central to the present argument is Mill's treatment of industrial capital. As discussed in chapter 9, Mill anticipated the emergence of worker-owned cooperatives that rent and eventually own the industrial capital with which they work. This prediction is founded in his understanding of the social psychology of the wage relation. The analysis is serious and the insights are still relevant. Mill's work on the capitalist employee-employer relationship amounts to a full-scale critique of private property in the form of industrial capital. Not surprisingly, cooperatives became the focus of Mill's radical reform agenda and his central hope for meaningful progress.

But here, I am running ahead of the argument. Mill did not expect the industrial transformation to take place quickly. Despite his own critique, he did not think the system of laissez-faire capitalism had yet run its course. Even as he began to anticipate and endorse substantial cooperative reforms for the future, Mill made a radical case for accepting laissez-faire capitalism in the near term. He was convinced that private property in the form of industrial capital still had a historic role to play. The success of broader reforms hinged on a period of extensive accumulation by the capitalists coupled with the assertion of control over their own growth by the working classes.[15] These developments, then, were to make up the very core of the political economy of progress.

14. Mill's broader consideration of land questions are taken up in chapter 6.
15. It is hard not to see strong parallels here to Marx's materialist view of early nineteenth-century history. For more on this comparison, see chapter 10.

CHAPTER 5

Mill's Radical Case for Laissez-Faire Capitalism

Even in the absence of a full-scale defense of private property, the utilitarian position of Bentham and James Mill held to a triumphal liberalism. Whatever nagging egalitarian concerns they may have had, these early utilitarians read history as culminating in laissez-faire capitalism. In this view, capitalism emerged as the economic parallel to the slow development of civil and political rights. The spread of markets had steadily expanded the range of economic freedoms open to the population. The serfdom and bondage of the largest portion of the population had been replaced with a web of market relations that left almost all individuals free to pursue their own interests as best they could. From the triumphalist perspective, the emerging capitalist system raised all boats. What more could the working classes reasonably expect? Such arguments pointed toward a general endorsement of the new economy and the industrial revolution it had spawned. On this point the utilitarians, Bentham and James Mill, largely agreed with the position adopted by the mainstream classical economists, Robert Malthus, David Ricardo, and Nassau Senior.[1]

Imbued with an Enlightenment commitment to progress, and sensitized by the harshness of the industrial revolution, John Stuart Mill balked at

1. In defense of Bentham, James Mill, Malthus, and Ricardo, it can be noted that inequality in Britain grew steadily and sharply through the first half of the nineteenth century. Had they been alive at mid-century, they might well have altered their position. No such defense can be offered for Nassau Senior, who died in 1864.

an unconditional endorsement of laissez-faire capitalism. To demonstrate the inadequacy of the liberal triumphalist position and the possibilities open to a more radical set of policies, Mill turned to the new social science of political economy. For the first time a radical economics was built on a rigorous theoretical analysis. Mill's effort to weave together radical theory and programmatics, if not his specific claims, became the model for all serious left analysis.

The early classical economists claimed to read the future from their emerging analytical model. For Malthus and Ricardo, the new political economy pointed toward an unkind and sluggish stationary state. Using the same set of tools, Mill dissected the classical claim and instead found considerable cause for radical optimism. The course of development was not as dark and the possibilities for radical reform were much greater than Ricardo had concluded. Indeed, Mill saw in the political economy of accumulation a base for a range of radical reforms.

The notion of applying a rigorous analysis to the economy had been growing since the late mercantilists. The idea of basing policy on such analytics had developed in step with the sophistication of political economy. The mercantilists, the physiocrats, and the early classical economists—Smith, Malthus, and Ricardo—all claimed their sciences capable of improving policy. Ricardo had entered politics precisely to bring this view to the political arena. Only with John Stuart Mill, however, does analytical political economy become the foundation for a radical program that envisions a fundamental change in the organization of production.

Mill anchors his hopes for the greatest number in the possibilities to be opened by further capital accumulation. That promise, Mill argues on the basis of his social science, can be abetted by radical reform, but only lost through revolution. Reading this radical vision into Mill's political economy of progress forces a sharp distinction from sympathetic, but less radical, left liberal understandings of Mill's position. For example, David Brink, in his *Mill's Progressive Principles* (2013), makes a cogent argument for the consistency of Mill's liberalism. But such an analysis stops short of appreciating the full radical content of Mill's utilitarianism. Self-consciously stumbling over the claims of equality, while evincing support for liberal reforms, this approach to Mill fails to express the depth and fire of his rejection of the economy of his day.

If radicals have inherited their worldview from Mill, they also have inherited his deep ambivalences. Mill drew out the uncertainties that surrounded the predictions of classical political economy. In his analytical researches, the uncertainties intertwined with the radical utilitarian's unresolved ambivalences toward more classical liberalism. The result was a rigorous, but at some points inconclusive analysis of capitalist progress. An overarching tentativeness has characterized radicalism ever since. If for no other reason, it is worth exploring Mill's political economy with the purpose of identifying the analytical sources of this radical tentativeness.

At the core of his theorizing, Mill constructed a radical case for laissez-faire capitalism that casts that system, not as the final achievement of progress, but as a transitional stage in social evolution.[2] Capital accumulation in this stage promises progress toward a very different economy, an economy capable of significantly raising the material conditions of the working classes and significantly reducing the extent of inequality. Achieving the transition requires a broad education of the masses. Education acts as a foundation for enlightened political action and, even more important, a new moral responsibility among the people at large. At his most optimistic, Mill envisioned a progressive transition in which the political and economic power of the working classes proved sufficient to build an economy far less grasping than the capitalism of his day, an economy characterized not by capitalists' private ownership of the means of production, but rather by the workers' cooperative ownership of their workplaces.

Utilitarians in the nineteenth century struggled with two stories. For lack of better terms we continue to label these as "triumphal liberal" and "radical." Exploring the struggle reveals a multilayered intellectual effort replete with a range of still relevant theoretical complexities and uncertainties. But the struggle also stands as a warning, as a morality tale, cautioning against too easy rationalization and wishful thinking. The exploration is undertaken, not with the intent to judge those long gone, but with sympathy for their efforts. In particular, John Stuart Mill's radical dilemmas gain poignancy to the extent that radicals today also wrestle with the seductive promises of progress.

Modern radicals are drawn to Mill because of his egalitarian commitment, a commitment much stronger than that of the neoclassicists of the first half of the twentieth century or the neoliberals of the second half. Troubled by Mill's deep involvement in British colonialism,[3] modern radicals still respect him for his efforts in support of meaningful reform.

2. Mill's vision of laissez-faire as a progressive, but transitional stage has been noted by John Gray (1989). Gray, however, dismisses much of Mill's radical political economy as "proto-socialist Utopianism" (217). The present work might be viewed as an attempt to provide a more constructive view of the radical themes in Mill.

3. Mill worked most of his adult life for the East India Company. See Zastoupil (1994). For an interesting discussion of Mill and imperialism, see Harris (1964), who sees Mill as not a racist, but still a defender of "benevolent despotism" (201).

Admittedly, his membership in the high middle class may have multiplied his biases, distorted his understanding of the economic system, and limited his dissent. But that said, his promotion of the utilitarian goal, the greatest happiness of the greatest number, summarizes an appealing materialist understanding of the purposes of a society with moral content. His effort to find in liberal institutions a foundation for a radical transformation of the economy can resonate with radicals even today.

PROGRESS AND LAISSEZ-FAIRE CAPITALISM

Where triumphalist liberals saw laissez-faire capitalism as a final stage of progress, the radical Mill's political economy is an analysis of continuing movement. The forces that encourage investment and capital accumulation will inevitably wind down. Profit rates will fall and the economy will eventually enter a stationary state. For the radical Mill, such developments were not symptoms of a dreaded decline but, rather, of a hopeful transition. The stationary state promised not misery but a greatly expanded set of opportunities for the greatest number.

Mill is very cautious in advancing this view of progress. He repeatedly warns that the future is difficult to read. Given the major theoretical tendency—that is, for the profit rate to fall—he identifies a number of important counter-tendencies. These counter-tendencies leave the timing of the anticipated stationary state shrouded in uncertainty.

Admittedly, there is something convenient, perhaps even disingenuous, about a radical theoretical position that accepts the status quo as the means to transitions placed in the distant future. Theories of progress often run the risk of such criticisms. Mill is as vulnerable as most prophets of progress. Over the course of his life, Mill embraced romanticism, classical liberalism, and radicalism. Toward the end of his life he moved toward a cautious socialism. A story of progress must have had great appeal for a Mill influenced by all these tendencies. It provided an optimistic future, even as it allowed the acceptance of much of the status quo. But we do the radical Mill's ideas a disservice if we dismiss them only because they may have provided him psychological relief from conflicting or even contradictory affinities.

Mill's radical utilitarian acceptance of laissez-faire capitalism is premised on the current economic organization's being one not of permanence but of transition. Throughout the *Principles* and many of his other writings, Mill was clear in his criticisms of the British economy of his day. For Mill, widespread greed and poverty weighed heavily in his assessments of the system.

But recognizing such major social problems, he was still deeply impressed that British capitalism had generated a machine capable of rapid accumulation. Mill was convinced that laissez-faire policies constituted the lynchpin of this system. If capital accumulation provides the path to a new economy, laissez-faire guarantees the most rapid pace of that accumulation.

Laissez-faire capitalism provides the instrumental means for accumulation. The radical Mill recommended laissez-faire, but not because of any commitment to triumphal libertarianism. Indeed, he was clear that once the stationary state has been achieved, a broad range of public interventions financed by taxation would be useful and welfare enhancing. Laissez-faire becomes a means to an end, not an end in itself.

Book 4 of the *Principles* is entitled "Influence of Progress of Society on Production and Distribution." Yet Mill seemed reticent to publish loudly the radical scope of the changes he envisioned and desired. Almost every conclusion is carefully hedged with academic conditionality. It is difficult to avoid the conclusion that Mill was tentative with respect to the most radical aspects of his analysis. And yet the radical pieces are there. They fit into a coherent whole, a promise of meaningful progress.

Ultimately the argument or the hope is that laissez-faire will generate rapid capital accumulation and thus provide a base for a fairer economy and better society. Accumulation generates the dynamics of utilitarian political economy. But the arc of progress is not just the quantitative expansion of the economy. Progress promises qualitative change.

MILL'S THEORY OF PROFIT

To appreciate Mill's progressive argument, the logical starting point is his general understanding of the classical theory of profit. In his central discussion of profit (*Principles*, book 2: ch. 15), John Stuart Mill radically declares, "The cause of profit is, that labour produces more than is required for its support" (Mill [1848] 1965, 411). Mill advances the proposition against the notion (on occasion, but not consistently, put forth by Adam Smith) that profit is the product of exchange or "purchase and sale." Mill insists we redirect our gaze from the "outside surface of the mechanical machinery of society" toward "the operations of the producer." Here, below the surface of exchange, one fact dominates attention: workers can produce more than they need to live.[4] Understanding the analysis of profits requires directing attention to production itself.

4. The similarity here to Marx is obvious. Marx's rather ungenerous observations on this key passage from Mill will be discussed in chapter 10.

Mill warns against extrapolating from individual markets to the general rate of profit. In individual commodity markets, supply can easily outpace current demand. It is a common phenomenon and greatly influences businesses in any given market. All enterprises must fear the real possibility that demand in their field will be insufficient to purchase supply at historically expected prices. Equally true, merchants with a good eye for market trends can prosper by avoiding sluggish commodities in favor of those most in demand. But Mill categorically rejects the extension of such micro-observations to the macro-determination of the general profit rate.

The lynchpin of the argument is the proposition now known as Say's Law and usually rendered as "supply creates its own demand." While Mill acknowledges Say's "judicious" championing of this proposition on the continent, he credits his father, James Mill, with effectively advancing it in England. J. S. Mill is gentle but firm in his criticisms of three prominent writers: Thomas Malthus, Thomas Chalmers, and J. C. L. Sismondi. These "distinguished economists" have made two errors. At times they have confounded commercial crises with general gluts. But the source of commercial crises, Mill maintains, is not overproduction but an "excess of speculative purchases" and the resulting "contraction of credit." Their second error is to mistakenly confound the long-run tendency of the profit rate to fall with a broad insufficiency of demand (66–67).

For Mill the underlying source of profits in a capitalist economy is the productivity of labor. The vagaries of profits in individual lines of enterprise simply reflect an ongoing struggle as to how the overall surplus of production will be divided among capitalists in various sectors. With Say's Law in the background and abstracting from any crises of realization,[5] Mill asserts that the mass of profits depends only on the portion of output that doesn't go for wages. Workers can produce more than they need to reproduce themselves. In the context of the wage bargain, the capitalists as a group have laid claim to the surplus.

What is at issue is the distribution of the product. The distribution reflects the class character of the capitalist system. Mill is clear that he

5. It should be noted that Mill's classical argument here divided his position fundamentally from the revolution brought on in economics by John Maynard Keynes and Michal Kalecki. While Mill acknowledged that in a financial crisis speculation may lead to an exorbitant increase in the demand for money, he insisted this is a short-run situation. Given time capitalists will always invest their savings. Keynes held that such investment was far from automatic. Unlike the classical school, Keynesian theories of profit emphasize the willingness (or reluctance) of capitalists to consume and invest. For an insightful discussion of Say's Law in relation to classical economists of the nineteenth century and to Keynes's criticisms, see Cottrill (1997).

is describing an economy in which "labourers and capitalists are separate classes" (411).[6] The capitalists take the profit because their contracts with labor give them residual rights to any surplus. Earlier in his discussion of distribution, Mill had dealt with the system of slavery in which the slaveowners forcibly wrest the surplus from the labor force. But Mill was convinced that such a system was necessarily less efficient than capitalism.[7] And a similar conclusion applied to systems of serfdom. The driving forces undermining all such systems of compulsory labor originated in Malthusian population pressures. (See Mill [1848] 1965, 249.) These raised labor's cost and lowered its productivity. But in a slave system or capitalist system, the point remained that workers eat less than they produce.

Mill's logic couldn't be clearer.[8] The mass of profits is determined by the productivity of workers and their wages. At any given time the rate of profit is simply this mass of profit divided by the existing pool of capital. At this point in the argument, however, there is an analytical wrinkle. The issues are well discussed by Hollander (1985). In an early essay, *Of Profits, and Interest* ([1830] 1844), Mill had raised the question as to the impact of intermediate inputs and capital goods (what Marx was to call constant capital) on the determination of the profit rate. Mill suggested that some portion of current surplus must be devoted to covering the return on inputs supplied by other capitalists. He argued that all that is required is to distinguish between a broader concept "cost of wages," which includes these profit payments on wages previously advanced to generate intermediate inputs and capital goods, and the "value of wages," which should be limited to the actual wage payments direct and indirect.

As pointed out by Hollander, the problem with Mill's solution is that it breaks the clean metaphor of the working day divided into two portions: wages going to the worker and profits going to the capitalist. Perhaps sensing the difficulties, in the *Principles*, Mill seems to waffle. He again

6. While in this discussion of profits Mill plays with the idea that such a division would not be necessary if workers had "funds on hand" to cover their own support, he drops the thought and doesn't return to it until later in the *Principles*, when he takes up cooperatives.

7. By the sixth edition of the *Principles*, Mill gives as his major authority on this point Frederick Law Olmsted, the widely traveled reporter of conditions in the American South. Modern treatments of slavery, such as Fogel and Engerman (1974), throw serious doubt on Olmsted's conclusions.

8. Yet at least one authoritative commentator has insisted that Mill's theory is "no Marxian exploitation theory different from the abstinence theory" (Blaug 1985, 193).

observes that intermediate goods, "materials," and capital goods, "implements," are themselves produced by labor. If those other goods are created by the capitalist himself, there is no issue. But if not, the only change is: "certain of the capitalists concerned have, for the sake of general convenience, had their share of profit paid to them before the operation was completed. Whatever, of the ultimate product, is not profit, is repayment of wages" ([1848] 1965, 412). The logic here seems a bit strained. The division between wages and profits is tautological. The entire problem is precisely the timing of profits, and Mill avoids this conundrum.

If Mill didn't solve the timing question, his intuition still remains credible. Indeed, considerable energy has gone into understanding such questions in the context of Marxist economics. Characterizing the equalization of profit rates when industries differ in their capital-labor ratios forms the core of the so-called transformation problem between labor values and prices. Avoiding a rigorous treatment of Marxist value theory, we can just note that at least one way to summarize the current Marxist understanding of the problem is as follows: "A necessary condition for the existence of a positive profit rate is that the workers wages be less than the labor value they produce."[9] The proposition comes very close to Mill's basic claim.

ABSTINENCE AND SAVINGS

Though Mill was convinced that profits ultimately derive from labor, he argued that as distributed under the capitalist system the pool resolved into payments for abstinence.[10] At any given time the profit rate is simply the ratio of the surplus to the accumulated stock of capital.

The motive for capitalist abstinence is simple. Since he makes an advance to productive labor "to support them during their work, he can, and naturally will, claim remuneration from the produce. He will not be content with simple repayment; if he receives merely that, he is only in the same situation as at first, and has derived no advantage from delaying to apply his savings to his own benefit or pleasure," (34). As Mill said late in his life, "No merit is claimed for this *abstinence*; those to whose persevering frugality the labouring classes owe this enormous benefit,

9. This is called the fundamental theorem of Marxism by Morishima (1973).

10. The importance of abstinence in regulating the supply of savings was most closely associated with Nassau Senior (1854). Mill also mentions risk and superintendence, but in his view, the latter is effectively a payment for labor rendered and the former is a compensating differential between undertakings.

for the most part thought only of benefiting themselves and their descendants" ([1869] 1967, 656). The rate of profit and the interest rate serve as an incentive to saving.[11]

While incentives are necessary to motivate savings, the willingness to abstain and save is subject to substantial changes over time. In particular, Mill was convinced that the willingness to abstain from immediate gratification in pursuit of future benefits and wealth had been rising in the modern period. As life becomes more secure, and as "great prizes are less and less to be hoped for by any other means than long perseverance, mankind become more willing to sacrifice present indulgence for future objects" ([1848] 1965, 738).

Of course, the alternative to savings is consumption, either of market goods or directly through the hiring of servants and others. The desire for luxury stands as a major obstacle to the accumulation of wealth, one of three Mill lists. The other two are a desire for leisure and Malthusian population pressures. The search for pleasure inhibits capital accumulation. For many countries, luxuries and pleasures loom large in peoples' consciousness. England and Holland, however, are exceptions. Mill, anticipating R. H. Tawney, connects the rapid accumulation of capital in England to "that extreme incapacity of the people for personal enjoyment, which is a characteristic of countries over which puritanism has passed" (171).

Mill also acknowledges that for a few, presumably very rich persons, savings can become a matter of "mere habit." They accumulate "not because they have any object in growing richer, or desire to add in any respect to their consumption, but from *vis inertiæ*. They continue producing because the machine is ready mounted, and save and re-invest their *savings* because they have nothing on which they care to expend them" (573).[12]

In general, though, abstinence determines the carrying capacity of the capitalist economy. The pool of accumulated savings provides the support for workers and their families. "There will be no greater number of productive labourers in any country, or in the world, than can be supported from that portion of the produce of past labour, which is spared from the enjoyments of its possessor for purposes of reproduction, and is termed Capital" (160).

11. Actually, Mill saw the interest rate as the return for saving. The somewhat larger profit rate also reimbursed superintendence and other administrative functions. Still, he always considers the two as closely linked.

12. Again Mill ignores the Keynesian possibility that the rich might just hold wealth in the form of money, thus generating an insufficiency of demand.

THE FALLING RATE OF PROFIT

For all classical economists, the accumulated savings of the past built the so-called wage fund and limited the number of productive workers who generate further profits. And for just about all classical economists, accumulation was bounded by a tendency for the profit rate to fall. Ricardo in particular had emphasized that population growth forced the expansion of agricultural activities to less and less fertile lands. In what Samuelson (1978) called the "short-circuited" case of the "classical canonical model," land rents rose sharply in response to the expansion, squeezing down profits to the capitalist.

Land rents rose because as less fertile lands came into production, agricultural prices necessarily rose and access to more fertile lands became more and more valuable. The ample surplus on more productive lands increasingly fell into the hands not of capitalists but of landowners. On less fertile lands, the surplus was small from the start. In principle the process could continue until the margin of cultivation extended to lands so low in fertility that they could just support a labor force, leaving no surplus for the owners of such parcels. At this point, the entire surplus on more fertile lands accrued to their landowners, leaving no profits for capitalist farmers anywhere in the economy.

Of course, the system would not be likely to actually reach a zero profit rate for the capitalist farmers. Before such an absolute zero was reached, the declining profit rate would undermine the incentive for savings and accumulation. At this minimum point, growth would stop and the system would enter a stationary state. It was a situation that Ricardo considered a disaster. Hence, Ricardo's strong support for free trade, which he hoped would keep down food prices and greatly reduce the pressure on British agriculture. With cheap imported foods, capital could keep its pace of expansion and national wealth would continue to grow.

It is an old story, retold many times. And there is no doubt that it held sway over much of classical political economy. With his strong Ricardian background, Mill could never quite turn his back on the approach and always put it forth as a distinct possibility. The realization of the outcome hinged on the growth rate of population. If that growth rate remained high, always matching the growth in capital, and never allowing an increase in real wages, the pressure on land was close to inevitable. Under such circumstances, capital accumulation served little purpose other than to raise rents. And ultimately, it must come to an end when the rents absorbed virtually all of the surplus. The radical Mill could hardly be excited by the prospects held out to the great mass of population even if imports were effectively opened, for the bottom line remained the same even then. Imports allowed population growth to continue, but in themselves could not address the welfare of the working population.

Mill always acknowledged this depressing story; never did he fully repudiate it. But he did offer a clear alternative, an alternative that promised progress, not impoverished stagnation. I will refer to the older story as the "Ricardian theory" of the falling rate of profit and to this second story as the "radical theory" of the falling rate of profit. Here, too, profit rates would fall, but now that fall resulted not from rising rents but, rather, from rising wages. The driving force in capital accumulation was abstinence by capitalists. The key to turning such accumulation to the betterment of the general population was abstinence in reproduction among the laboring classes. This second Millean invocation of abstinence echoed themes suggested by, but never fully developed in, the later writings of Malthus.

Mill was assuming that population won't expand at anything like geometric proportions. In part, he attributed the reprieve to the rising level of general education among the working classes and in part to continued emigration to America and colonies of the British Empire. In any case, without extensive population growth the pressure on land is much reduced and rents remain relatively flat. Slow population growth undermines the traditional Ricardian threat to the profit rate. But rapid capital accumulation builds up the demand for labor. With a given labor force, rising demand for labor necessarily puts upward pressure on wages. In the radical theory, it is this rise in wages that provides the alternative mechanism for bringing down the profit rate.

The new mechanism, like the first, had its roots deep in Ricardian economics. Mill strongly endorsed the classical Ricardian proposition that, other things equal, a rise in the wage rate will necessarily reduce the profit rate.[13] In the presence of strong population growth, the wage–profit trade-off has no influence on fundamentals. But working-class abstinence implies that the accumulation of capital will far outstrip the growth of labor. In these circumstances, so much more favorable to workers, the continuing expansion of savings must result in competition for labor and increases in wages.[14] As wages rise, profit rates fall. But the

13. The Ricardian wage–profit trade-off is sometimes interpreted as applying only in the short run, while Ricardian rent theory is left to establish the long-run profit rate (Cottrill 1997). The wage–profit trade-off is the centerpiece of Sraffa's (1960) attempt to reconstruct classical economics. The trade-off is generally acknowledged from a neoclassical perspective as well (Burmeister 1984).

14. The basic framework here is consistent with the wage-fund theory that Mill supported most of his life—i.e., an increase in accumulation and the demand for

surplus now accrues not to indolent landowners but, rather, to the mass of laborers ([1848] 1965, 740). Here is the radical Mill's much-hoped-for arc of progress.

In a somewhat surprising manner, Mill conflated his discussion of his two alternative theories of falling profits. He made the central point the assertion that profit rates will eventually fall while avoiding a decisive statement as to which of the two alternative mechanisms would hold sway. At places in the narrative it seems only a matter of secondary importance whether that decline resulted from rising rents or rising wages. In either case, Mill predicted the emergence of a stationary state. The position may be the product of Mill's commitment to objectivity in face of a quandary. But it rings quite odd, given the radical Mill's strongly expressed optimism concerning the character of the stationary state. Indeed, it is hard to fathom, let alone accept, that optimism if the fall in profit rates is brought about by rising land rents that leave workers with subsistence wages.

Whatever the mechanism bringing down the profit rate, Mill was sure that such a tendency would eventually bring to an end the traditional growth of capital through capitalist investment. As long as the profit rate is above some minimum, savings will continue to expand. But according to Mill, the critical point was not so far away. He repeatedly asserted that the interest rates then current in Britain were approaching the minimum. The rapid accumulation of capital was in the process of greatly expanding the denominator of the profit rate. With a declining or only slowly growing surplus available to capital, the pace of accumulation must push the rate of profit down toward its minimum. At that point, accumulation would slow to a halt.

Two possible counter-tendencies to the falling rate of profit should be considered. The first counter-tendency is the free importation of relatively cheap wage-goods. Notice the implications of such trade differ dramatically depending on which path the economy is following to lower profit rates. If population growth is not checked by working-class abstinence, then real wages must remain at the Malthusian subsistence level. Under such a scenario, cheap imports of foodstuffs put a cap on agricultural rents, lower nominal wages, and expand the surplus available to capitalists

labor will raise wages if supply is static or only slowly growing. However, Mill (like Smith before him) understood that the bargaining power of employers was likely to be much stronger than that of workers. Hence, wages might actually be below the "equilibrium" level. This observation played a central role in his support of trade unions and later in his so-called recantation of the wage-fund theory. For a discussion of the wage-fund theory and the recantation, see Kurer (1998).

and savers. Capital accumulation brings forth ample labor at low wages, and the whole of the increase in surplus accrues to capitalists and their backers. Rather than fall, profit rates then rise to a new plateau. And that higher level of profit rates can be maintained on an expanding basis as long as cheap agricultural imports are available.

Alternatively, if the working classes through abstinence succeed in controlling their fertility, they effectively disrupt the connection between population growth and capital accumulation. With a stable population and relatively cheap foodstuffs, the real wage achieves a higher level than previously attainable. The fall in the rate of profit may be somewhat delayed, but is inevitable. The rising demand for labor and high wages puts ever greater pressure on the profit rate. A stationary state, now at a real-wage level higher than that achievable without imports, emerges.

Finally, Mill also considered the counter-tendency of technological change. Like Marx, he associated this with the increasing share of fixed capital in the capital stock. Over time investors find new ways of doing things that raise the productivity of the labor force. While Mill considered the short-run (Ricardian) possibility that new machinery may reduce the circulating capital pool available for labor, he was convinced that once a large capital stock has been accumulated, such effects will be relatively modest. More important, he differed from Marx in his view of the effects of fixed capital on the rate of profit. Mill was clear that such investments are productivity enhancing. For Mill, the expansion of fixed capital raises the productivity of all workers in the economy.[15] As fixed investment raises output per head, it also slows the decline in the profit rate.

Mill argued that just as in the case of imports of cheap foodstuffs, new technologies raise the available surplus. Thus, the consequences for the profit rate again depend on the population dynamics of the working classes. Without abstinence, new technology forestalls the decline in profit rates. If, however, population remains constant, then the surplus created by new technologies eventually contributes to higher real wages.

What is the net result of the tendency of profit rates to fall and the various counter-tendencies? This is clearly an empirical matter. Weighing the various effects, Mill suggested that the profit rate will fall and the economy will approach a stationary state. But he left irritatingly vague exactly which of the two regimes of falling profit will prevail.

15. Mill's argument is broadly consistent with that of Okishio (1961) and other commentators on Marx who hold that new investment would not be introduced unless they raise productivity levels.

THE STATIONARY STATE

As the rate of accumulation falls toward zero, the economy approaches a stationary state. Without the incentive of the profit rate, potential savers and investors greatly curtail their activities. In his assessment of these expected developments Mill broke sharply with earlier classical economists. He asserted that the onset of a stationary state may well prove highly beneficial to the society as a whole. Taking exception to Smith and McCulloch, the radical Mill claimed that not continuing growth but, rather, the stationary state promises prosperity for the greatest number.

Mill leaves unclear which of the two paths to falling profits the economy is likely to follow. Taking up the character of the stationary state, Mill alluded only sketchily to the profound differences in welfare that follow upon one course or the other. If the stationary state has been launched by the expansion of population and rents, then society enters that state with the largest sustainable population living at the minimum habitual standard of wages. Alternatively, if the stationary state has been achieved through the abstinence of the working classes, then society enters that state with high wages and prosperity for the great bulk of the population.

It is hard to believe Mill's endorsement of the stationary state can assume anything but the second, radical course of development, the one premised on working-class abstinence. Mill does hint at just this outcome, connecting his argument to that of the mature Malthus. He recounts Malthus's repudiation of "the acknowledged errors of his first edition" and that author's subsequent efforts "to promote these juster and more hopeful anticipations" (753). The notion that the "progress of society must 'end in shallows and in miseries' . . . can only be successfully combated on his [Malthus's] principles" (753).

But that said, Mill fails to make explicit how or why this attractive course and not the traditional Ricardian one is the most likely outcome. Mill's paean to the stationary state only seems credible under the assumptions of the radical theory. Only under the assumption that workers have wrested a major share of the surplus does this famous chapter take on the character of utilitarian political economy and not poetic romanticism. Mill's attack on the economy of getting and spending must lose relevance if the great majority of people are left at the habitual minimum. While elements of the chapter border on the romanticism of Carlyle and Ruskin,[16]

16. For example, in early editions of the *Principles*, Mill engaged in a bit of bourgeois baiting, pointing to the United States as a materialist society without deeper values. After the Civil War, he recast these paragraphs into a rather confusing testimonial to the "heroic virtues" of the American North (754). In either case, Mill here seems at his most romantic.

Mill touches ground again when he asserts: "[T]he best state for human nature is that in which, while no one is poor, no one desires to be richer, nor has any reason to fear being thrust back, by the efforts of others to push themselves forward" (754). This "best state" can only be achieved through Mill's second, radical story in which falling profits are the reflection of rising wages. Entwined in the rhetoric is the simple statement that the wealth of the nation is of little value if "the increase of population or anything else prevents the mass of the people from reaping any part of the benefit of them" (755).

While Mill is everywhere clear on the benefits achievable through slower population growth, he seems reluctant to make explicit the need for aggressive educational and organizational efforts to achieve these goals. Perhaps his early association with Francis Place, the advocate of working-class birth control, had encouraged caution on this score.[17] In any case population control, however achieved, must be seen as the fundamental precursor to the radical stationary state. Only on this reading, and admittedly Mill makes this reading a bit difficult, the stationary state offers the chance to stabilize the economy at a relatively high level of productivity and wages.

RADICAL LIMITS

In Mill's radical story, laissez-faire capitalism is the quickest and most effective way to move from an undeveloped economy to a high-productivity economy capable of supporting a sizable population of increasingly sophisticated workers. The incentives characterizing laissez-faire capitalism strongly favor the capital owner over the laborer. The profits generated from the productivity of workers encourage high rates of saving and accumulation. And with fixed investments, the savings enhance productivity further.

In a radical reading of Mill, laissez-faire capitalism becomes a means and not a goal. The capitalist economy is a period of transition between

17. On the history of Mill, Place, and the birth control movement, see Miles (1988, ch. 9). As a young man J. S. Mill had spent two days in jail for distributing Place's pamphlets on the subject of birth control. This incident was parodied by a poet in the *Times*:

> There are two Mr M—'s, too, who those that like reading
> Through all that's unreadable, call very clever;—
> And, whereas M—Senior makes war on *good* breeding,
> M—Junior makes war on all *breeding* whatever?
>
> (Reproduced in Miles 1988, 149)

the pre-capitalist economy and one of much greater utility per capita. The new economy is not to be guided by the narrow logic of the private ownership of the means of production. It will be an economy of abundant capital and wealth. In such an environment, taxation for public purposes will not only be allowed but also encouraged. Inheritance will be greatly curtailed. Most important, cooperative production and worker ownership will be widespread. We will return to the specifics of the Millean reform agenda for a stationary state in Part II.

Even at his most radical, Mill seemed convinced that meaningful reform could only be achieved if it were based on the rapid pace of capital accumulation made possible by laissez-faire capitalism. Mill offers no formal, or even informal, "proof" that this capitalist transition is optimal. His argument is often no more than implicit in his writings. He defended neither the pace of improvement nor the ultimate endpoint as welfare maximizing. But he held that attempting a sharp break with laissez-faire capitalism too early will result in failure, or worse. In particular, he is hostile to any efforts at immediate direct redistribution.

From a radical perspective, it must have been difficult at the time, and remains difficult even today, to judge how compelling Mill's argument really was. That argument was firmly rooted in Malthusian population theory. But the Malthusian insistence on population control might have just as easily been combined with direct and significant taxation of the capitalists.[18] The radical Mill's endorsement of laissez-faire capitalism on utilitarian grounds, while conditional, still seems more than required by the theoretical argument. Within his radical theory of falling profits, it is difficult to understand why he could not see as constructive a significant redirection of portions of the surplus to pressing working-class needs. He looks forward to just such a redirection after the stationary state is achieved, so it can't merely be Mill's concerns over the power of the Leviathan. Mill seems compelled to delay such efforts to a point where capitalists' historic role has been fully played out. Radicals in the late nineteenth and twentieth centuries would not prove so reluctant.

Key to Mill's position is his absolute conviction in Say's Law. Market mechanisms for Mill represent the fastest and surest way to achieve capital accumulation. As long as profits are acceptable and investments are forthcoming, policy should eschew any interference in the accumulation

18. In a modern context, such taxation forms the very heart of the radical reform program advocated by Piketty (2014). But also note that Piketty rejects out of hand the long-run tendency of profits to fall and hence the radical hope of a transition through the stationary state.

process. Surely Mill's faith in Say's Law was overly optimistic. The last two centuries are replete with evidence that for extended periods capital's animal spirits can be significantly repressed or depressed. But that said, Mill's focus on long-run growth through private accumulation does not require the strong version of Say's Law that he invoked.

At the same time, Mill can be faulted for not fully appreciating the potential welfare-improving effects of technological change. He clearly recognized that technological change was capable of supporting profit rates. And he acknowledged that technological progress had been historically realized through the processes of capital accumulation.[19] Yet in his discussion of the stationary state he completely fails to consider the extent to which such an economy might forgo further technological progress through its curtailing of private capital accumulation. We can only speculate on the extent to which Mill thought profit-driven technological change might be replaced with worker-developed innovations in a more cooperative economy.[20]

In Mill's view, the scientific analysis of progress pointed toward a radical program most capable of achieving the greatest good for the greatest number.[21] Even recognizing its historical shortcomings, we do well to give serious consideration to Mill's political economy of progress, since it identifies for the first time the key components of modern radicalism: an analytical approach based on political economy, the progressive power of market-driven accumulation, the ultimate emergence of an abundant economy, and the need for radical institutional change.

19. On this point he was well ahead of Malthus, but of course, he had more experience on which to draw.

20. An argument might be made that in the stationary state a more open society might encourage the development of creativity including advances in technology. On Mill's hopes for such an open society, see Donner (1991).

21. Mill seems to have thought his view was shared by the working classes who, if they chose to blatantly exercise their latent power, could achieve an immediate revolution:

> The existing social arrangements, and law itself, exist in virtue not only of the forbearance, but of the active support of the labouring classes. They could effect the most fundamental changes in the whole order of society by simply withholding their concurrence. (Mill [1869] 1967, 655)

In effect, Mill interpreted working-class forbearance as rooted in a commonsense, pragmatic utilitarianism. While this Millean observation contains insight, it surely oversimplifies the complexities of working-class politics as they have played out in modern times.

PART II

Progress and Radical Reform

CHAPTER 6

Inheritance and Land

The radical Mill looked forward to progress generating a more equal and a more gentle economic system over time. Most dramatically he advocated and expected capitalist owned production to eventually be replaced by worker cooperatives. That process, discussed in Chapter 9, would take time. In the here-and-now, Mill argued that Britain would benefit from legislating radical reforms to the institution of private property. Such reforms would enhance economic efficiency in the short run and facilitate the transitional role of the competitive economy in the long run. Mill identified two major areas for restructuring: the overhaul of inheritance laws and land reform. In both cases, he advanced the radical content of utilitarian principles while eschewing almost all efforts at direct redistribution. He was convinced that progress required time for further capital accumulation and the maturation of the working classes. Direct redistribution would serve little purpose other than to erode incentives. Mill advanced a radical program of institutional reform, but he did so in a fashion that gave considerable deference to the status quo. Presumably he based this caution on utilitarian calculation.

BENTHAM'S "SUPPLY WITHOUT BURDEN"

Mill's position on inheritance was a radical extension of Bentham's more tentative suggestions. Bentham had laid down the basic framework. Surprisingly, the otherwise triumphalist Bentham had asserted the usefulness of seeking a progressive reform of inheritance laws. Discussing the tensions between security (by which Bentham essentially meant the civil rights associated with private property) and equality, Bentham observed, "Time is the only mediator between these contrary interests. Would you follow the counsels of equality without contravening those of security, wait for the natural period which puts an end to hopes and fears—the period of death" ([1838] 1962, 312). While "up to a certain point" security and equity are "incompatible . . . with a little patience and skill they may be brought by degrees to coincide."

Bentham was generally optimistic that in a prosperous country "large properties will be seen, without effort, without revolutions, without shock to subdivide themselves by little and little, and a much greater number of individuals will participate in the advantage of moderate fortunes" (313). To speed this process he argued for an extension of the state's power of escheat—that is, the lapsing of property to the crown. Bentham described his basic proposal as "Supply without Burden" ([1795] 1962). Bentham pushed for "the appropriating to the use of the public all vacant successions . . . on the failure of near relations, will or no will" (586).

Unlike Mill, Bentham felt strongly that close relations had a right—indeed, a natural right[1]—to full succession. In particular, children developed legitimate expectations that they would live in the same conditions as their parents, supported by the same accumulation of wealth. Bentham argued, in this case as in many others, that the frustration of expectations generated serious pain. Governments should avoid exacerbating such pains. Under the greatest-happiness principle he included the "disappointment-prevention principle." According to Bentham, inheritance by a near relative fell under this principle.[2]

In his usual manner Bentham was quite detailed as to the specifics of his scheme. Relations "within the pale" who are childless and "without prospect of children"[3] might be allowed only the interest on the principal. Moreover, he proposed that even for those within the pale who can reasonably be expected to have never anticipated the inheritance—for example, an uncle or aunt—the state might be awarded half the capital sum. Similarly, Bentham would allot a general power of bequest with respect to half the property that might "be at present subject to that power" (586).

1. This invocation of "natural rights" is highly unusual for Bentham.

2. Bentham defines near relatives as those standing "within the degrees termed prohibited with reference to marriage" ([1795] 1962, 586).

3. Bentham suggests an age qualification here: females childless at forty-eight and males childless at sixty.

Bentham identified the role of inheritance in generating inequality. His reform proposal was cautious, but it marked inheritance as a question for the utilitarians. While Bentham hesitated, one might expect that his more radical disciples would push more aggressively. In general, that doesn't seem to have been the case. For example, William Thompson, the socialist utilitarian, hardly went further on this score than Bentham himself.

Thompson was known for his effort to merge the teachings of Bentham and Robert Owen. Thompson, a well-off Protestant landowner from Cork in Ireland, had spent "several years" as a student and guest in Bentham's home (Lowenthal [1911] 1972, 16). Thompson clearly asserted his allegiance to the Benthamite principle of the greatest happiness of the greatest number. He built his own version of cooperative socialism in this context. Mill was familiar with Thompson and held him in high regard. Most notably, the two had faced off in a famous debate over Owenite cooperatives at the Cooperative Society in 1825. And Mill very much came to share Thompson's opinions on the liberation of women.[4] On most counts, Thompson was by far the more radical of the two. Yet in the matter of inheritance, Thompson was decidedly more cautious.

In his *Inquiry into the Principles of the Distribution of Wealth* ([1824] 1963), Thompson devoted considerable attention to the need to reform a range of institutions along utilitarian lines. Of the first importance are "constitutional institutions." But after these, the institutions governing inheritance are a priority. Echoing Bentham's conviction that disappointment generates particularly sharp pains, Thompson emphasized that children reasonably build expectations of enjoying the living standards of their parents. These expectations should not be disappointed. Children should inherit equal shares of their parents' wealth. That wealth should not be allowed to concentrate from generation to generation through primogeniture or similar means but, rather, should be shared equally among all siblings.

Thompson argued that wills that try to maintain fortunes intact work not only to encourage inequality but also to undermine the political sphere. He asserted, "The hereditary possession of wealth is one of the most tremendous and efficient expedients ever devised for depriving mankind of the benefits of self-government" (310). Thompson was particularly concerned that while fortunes are concentrated on first-borns,

4. While Mill mentioned Thompson's *Appeal of One-half the Human Race, Women* ([1825] 1970) in passing in his *Autobiography*, Lowenthal suggests that he failed to note the similarities of Thompson's volume with Mill's own *Subjection of Women* (Lowenthal [1911] 1972, 16).

younger members of wealthy families monopolize a range of public offices, offices that by rights should be open to all.

In sum, Thompson concluded, "The evils then arising from the power of uneven distribution of wealth by will among children, being obvious, the pretended advantages of the practice mere fallacies, it is to be reckoned . . . as one of the most pernicious [institutions] as affecting the distribution of wealth, production and knowledge" (312). The policy prescription is to require equal shares for all children in a family. This is as far as Thompson goes. His position is not much different from Bentham's own and certainly is less radical than Mill's.

THE SAINT-SIMONIANS

Taking an overview of British radical thought in 1830, Mill would have been aware of Bentham's and Thompson's views on inheritance. He would have found little else on the subject.[5] But if British radicals had only limited interest in the inheritance question, Mill was certainly aware that the question commanded considerable attention on the other side of the channel. In particular, Mill's thinking on inheritance was undoubtedly influenced by the Saint-Simonians.

Mill was a Francophile. At the early age of fourteen, he spent about a year in France and was very much taken with the intellectual atmosphere of that country. He was hosted by J. B. Say, the outstanding French political economist and friend of James Mill. At Say's home he met Henri de Saint-Simon, the early proponent of a system of industrial meritocracy within a progressive view of history. While the young Mill didn't take up the Saint-Simonian cause, he did continue to follow closely the Saint-Simonians as they evolved after the founder's death in 1825. In particular, he maintained a lifelong friendship with Gustave d'Eichthal, a Saint-Simonian he met in 1828 at the London Debating society (Mueller 1956; Cairns 1985).[6]

Saint-Simon himself never explicitly addressed the question of inheritance.[7] It was his followers, the Saint-Simonians, who developed a critique

5. This statement puts aside, for the moment, the perennial radical question of land reform, which is considered separately below.

6. Mill also had a close but ultimately acrimonious connection to Auguste Comte. Comte had been an early follower of Saint-Simone, and while breaking with the Saint-Simonians he had preserved much of the seer's view of progress. Mill wrote extensively on Comte's philosophy of positivism (Mill 1866).

7. "Saint-Simon did not question the right of inheritance, except possibly in one place and there only by implication" (Iggers 1958, 86).

of the institution of inheritance in their volume, *The Doctrine of Saint-Simon* (Iggers 1958). The first volume of *The Doctrine* was produced in the years 1828–29. In the "Sixth Session," the Saint-Simonians put forward a theory of the "Successive Transformation of Man's Exploitation by Man and of the Rights of Property." Asserting that "property is a social institution, subject, as are all other social institutions to the law of progress," the Saint-Simonians argued, "the exploitation of man by man must disappear. The constitution of property which is hereby perpetuated must, therefore also disappear." Progress is moving toward a new order in which "the state, and no longer the family, will inherit the accumulated riches insofar as these form what the economists call production resources" (89).

Now the Saint-Simonians were far from levelers. Indeed, quite the opposite. They explicitly distinguished themselves from those who supported a "community of goods." Rather, the Saint-Simonians envisioned a strongly meritocratic society in which education would be universal and each would be "classified according to his ability and remunerated according to his work" (89).

Mill was very much aware of the Saint-Simonian position on inheritance. This was the period of his closest connection with that tribe. It seems reasonable to conclude that Mill found encouragement in the Saint-Simonians' attack on inheritance. It is not too much to claim that he adapted that attack to his own views, and thus strengthened the Benthamite utilitarian hostility to inheritance.

Mill was also sympathetic to the meritocratic message offered by the Saint-Simonians in opposition to privilege. But Mill would never couch his hostility to inheritance in terms of any grandiose plans for state control of production. Mill's grounding in traditional political economy and distrust of the state left him extremely wary of Saint-Simonian projections of a new industrial order.[8]

MILL ON INHERITANCE

J. S. Mill was adamant in his attacks on inheritance. Still, his proposed reforms of the institution are best viewed as a compromise. Rooted in

8. Even Mill at his most radical—for example, as the champion of worker cooperatives (see chapter9)—remains leery of central-government control. In his famous defense of laisser-faire, he gives numerous reasons for his distrust of government expansion, not the least of which are (1) that government inevitably holds "an inferior interest in the result" than those most immediately involved and (2) that government generally fails to build the "habit of collective action in the people" (Mill [1848] 1965, 942).

Benthamite principles, Mill was at pains to suggest that his approach to limiting inheritance would work not only to reduce inequality but also to benefit prospective heirs. Where the Saint-Simonians looked to the state actively to determine which citizens merited the control of productive assets, Mill assigned the state a more limited role: to guarantee against the unattractive concentration of wealth.

While Mill was generally hostile to using the state to directly redistribute income and wealth, he strongly endorsed the use of the state in limiting the size of inheritances. Mill's position reflected his commitment both to equality of opportunity and to the utilitarian acceptance of incentives. While Mill argued that those who had acquired capital or other wealth should have the right to leave it, he held that society and even the recipients had an interest that such bequests not be concentrated. The result was a radical inheritance policy designed to check the intergenerational concentration of wealth.

In the *Principles*, Mill argued that it was a mistake to leave children "rich, without the necessity of any exertion." The society, and most often even the heirs themselves, suffered from overly generous inheritances. He went on, "Without supposing extreme cases, it may be affirmed that in a majority of instances the good not only of society but of the individuals would be better consulted by bequeathing to them a moderate, than a large provision." This conclusion he claimed was not only his, but also "a commonplace of moralists ancient and modern" ([1848] 1965, 221).

In advancing this position Mill held it to be consistent with the institution of private property. He acknowledged that inequalities arising from "unequal industry, frugality, perseverance, talents, and to a certain extent even opportunities, are inseparable from the principle of private property." And if we endorse the principle, "we must bear with these consequences of it." That said, however, Mill saw "nothing objectionable in fixing a limit to what any one may acquire by the mere favour of others, without any exercise of his faculties, and in requiring that if he desires any further accession of fortune, he shall work for it" (225). Subject to such constraints, any individual should have the right to determine his or her bequests. The key point was that large fortunes must be divided among a number of inheritors.

The utilitarian calculus behind this position is clear. Mill endorses the institution of private property largely for the incentives it creates. These incentives, especially during the transitional period of the progressive state, generate considerable benefit for the society as a whole. Be that as it may, Mill is certain that the concentration of wealth over generations is unlikely to strengthen these positive effects. Rather, concentration will reduce effort and energy among the inheritors. To the extent successful accumulators are motivated by narrow bequest motives, there may be a loss in the effort they expend. But Mill is confident that such losses are minor compared to the increased energy shown by their less than richly endowed children.

THE NEW CLASS

His proposal for the reform of inheritance was not just a minor issue for Mill. While achieving voluntary population controls always maintained first place in Mill's hopes for the future, reform of inheritance laws would seem to have occupied a near second place in his speculations. In an 1847 letter to John Austin, Mill wrote, "What does seem to me essential is that society at large should not be overworked, nor over-anxious about the means of subsistence, for which we must look to the grand source of improvement, repression of population, combined with laws or customs of inheritance which shall favour the diffusion of property instead of its accumulation in masses" (Letter to John Austin, 13 April 1847, in Mill 1963, 713).

In his *Principles*, when Mill glowingly describes the possibilities of the stationary state, he again emphasizes the positive effects of limitations on inheritance. In the stationary state, Mill looks forward to "a better distribution of property attained, by the joint effect of the prudence [voluntary population controls] and frugality of individuals, and of a system of legislation favouring equality of fortunes." The latter he identifies as "a limitation of the sum which any one person may acquire by gift or *inheritance*, to the amount sufficient to constitute a moderate independence." Mill argues, "under this two-fold influence" society would now be characterized by "a well-paid and affluent body of labourers; no enormous fortunes, except what were earned and accumulated during a single lifetime; but a much larger body of persons than at present . . . with sufficient leisure, both physical and mental, from mechanical details, to cultivate freely the graces of life" ([1848] 1965, 755).

The new class was to act as a model for "the classes less favourably circumstanced." In addition to participating in the development of "all kinds of mental culture," it would serve to speed "social and moral progress." Mill goes on to suggest this class would become the source of many improvements of industrial culture. Unlike most earlier technological changes, these new efforts would focus not on increasing the rate of profit but, rather, on lightening the burdens of common workers.[9]

Mill's connection with the Saint-Simonians permeated his admittedly less than detailed description of the new class. Mill echoed the Saint-Simonian emphasis on meritocracy. The new class will develop a more moral and social view of its work. Mill explicitly praised August Comte for anticipating this sea change. According to Mill, Comte created an idea of "great beauty and grandeur." Comte encouraged us to "regard working for the benefit of others as a good in itself. . . . [W]e should desire it for its own sake, and not for the sake of remuneration, which cannot justly be claimed for doing what we like: that the proper return for a service to society is the gratitude of society." Mill went on to assert: "To this opinion we entirely subscribe" (Mill 1866, 147–149).

LAND AND LANDLORDS

A radical utilitarian analysis seriously questioned the role of concentrated inheritances. In Mill's political economy, control of private property was not justified on the basis of natural rights, but drew its utilitarian legitimacy from its role as an inducement to labor and enterprise. Large inheritances served to lessen incentives rather than to strengthen them. In much the same manner, the concentration of landed property raised serious questions for Mill. Historically, landed property had been the most important medium of large inheritances. For this reason alone, land ownership was suspect. But even more than other types of property, the concentration of land ownership undermined enterprise and incentives. Large land holders were likely to be careless and inefficient in managing their affairs, while their labor force sank into apathy and squalor. This inefficient and dehumanizing system, rather than the original wrongdoing associated with their ancestors' appropriation of nature's bounty, was the true sin of the landed classes. Mill's radical land reforms were not aimed at settling scores for past wrongs, but at building a foundation for prosperity through a higher

9. Mill was vague as to the institutional context in which these improvements in technology will be generated and dispersed. He simply looked forward to the time when "the conquests made from the powers of nature by the intellect and energy of scientific discoverers become the common property of the species, and the means of improving and elevating the universal lot" ([1848] 1965, 757). He is clear, however, that control of population is a necessary prerequisite of these general advances.

level of efficiency. Thus Mill eschewed broad calls for the expropriation and direct redistribution of land. He undoubtedly regarded such schemes as dangerous. In any case, they were politically impractical. Rather, his proposals paralleled the approach Britain had taken with respect to slave holders under the Slavery Abolition Act of 1833. They call for compensation to be paid to existing owners. Like the Abolition Act, the immediate purpose of such reforms was to put an end to the wastage of human resources.

BRITISH AGRARIANISM

Of course, Mill was hardly the first to wrestle with the inconsistencies surrounding efforts to justify private ownership of land. In England the case against private property in land went back at least to the "True Levellers" or "Diggers" of the mid-seventeenth century. A hundred years later, agrarian ideas had infused radical thought throughout the country. In particular, the agrarian Thomas Spence called for the direct appropriation of land and the institution of common ownership. In the early nineteenth century, the Ricardian socialists advocated a range of proposals with respect to land reform. All of these threads influenced Mill's position.

Gerrard Winstanley and the Diggers

The English Civil War (1642–1651), with its questioning of monarchal and religious authority, led naturally to a number of radical themes. Taking a cue from the Parliamentary party, the Levellers empowered by their experiences in Cromwell's New Model Army looked to a broader democracy. They called for universal male suffrage rooted in a conception of natural rights (Hill 1972). Purging the government of corruption would create a new, fairer society.

Further to the left were the "True Levellers" or Diggers. The Diggers held that reforming the government could not in itself achieve the broader goal of a just society. In particular, the Diggers maintained on the basis of scripture and reason that the "Creator Reason" had fashioned the world as a "Common Treasury." "Not one word was spoken in the beginning, That one branch of mankind should rule over another." But the earth had been "hedged in to In-closures by the teachers and rulers, and the others were made Servants and Slaves." And now the Earth "is bought and sold, and kept in the hands of a few, whereby the great Creator is mightily dishonored." Landlords had amassed their estates "by oppression or murder or theft" (Winstanley [1649a] 1951, 379).

Oppression stemmed from "subtle, imaginary, and covetous wit," which enabled landlords to trick "the plain-hearted poor . . . to work for them for small wages." This made possible steady accumulation. The same landlords were clever dealers and manipulators of public trust. But even earlier, starting with military power, the landlords had established a bloody rule, breaching the Seventh Commandment against murder and the Eighth Commandment against stealing. At root, the landlords had "stolen the earth from their fellow creatures, that have an equal share with them by the law of reason and creation" (382–383).

While the Diggers clearly questioned all private property in land, their major direct action was aimed at collectively farming commons and waste lands. Most famously, under the leadership of Gerard Winstanley, a group of Diggers set up a commune on St. George's Hill in Surrey in 1649. Eschewing violence, they attempted to establish an egalitarian community. In defending their actions to Thomas Fairfax, commander-in-chief of the Parliamentary forces, the Diggers asserted:

> Wee desire noe more of yow then freedome to worke, and to enioy the benefitt of our labours—for here is wast land enough and to spare to supply all our wants. . . . [I]f this freedome were granted to improve the common lands then there would bee a supply to answer every ones inquire, and the murmurings of the people against yow and the Parliament would cease, and within a few yeares wee should have noe beggers nor idle persons in the land." (Winstanley [1649b] 1894, 220)

Not surprisingly, local landowners took considerable offense at the Diggers' plan and eventually succeeded in driving them off. Several other Digger communes were also established and were similarly disbanded.

Winstanley's arguments echoed earlier themes of the Peasants' Revolt (1381). John Ball had famously puzzled, "When Adam delved and Eve span, who was then a gentleman." And popular agrarian unrest over enclosures had continued throughout late medieval and early modern English history. These earlier protests blended easily into the Diggers' broad claims based on natural rights. In addition, we should note, the Diggers presented the beginning of an efficiency argument. They held that the reclaiming of common lands would greatly reduce if not eliminate rural poverty. The mechanics of this efficiency argument remained vague.

Thomas Spence

A similar emphasis on natural rights characterized the agrarian writings of Thomas Spence (1750–1814). "That property in land and liberty among men in a state of nature ought to be equal, few . . . would be foolish enough to deny" (Spence [1775] 1920, 5). Spence held that these natural rights, like the right to liberty and air, should be protected by society and the state. Those privileges should be infringed on no further than "necessity absolutely required" (7). This claim might be the end of the matter, but Spence felt obliged to demonstrate the feasibility of a plan based on man's natural right in land. He put forward his proposal in direct contrast to present arrangements, "lest it should be said that a system whereby they may reap more advantages consistent with the nature of society cannot be proposed" (10).

Spence's plan envisioned each parish taking control of all local land. The takeover would be accomplished peacefully if possible, but by force if necessary. Spence had no misgivings about seizing land without compensation. He specifically argued that buying land was equivalent to purchasing goods known to be stolen. Land purchasers greedily eager to make a profit at the expense of the people deserved no compensation. Once common ownership was achieved, the parish would simply rent out all of its lands. Spence didn't suggest that the rentals be to the highest bidder. In fact, he didn't make clear how rents would be set at all. However, he did expect that parish voters would insist "the land is let in very small farms, which makes employment for a greater number of hands, and makes more victualling of all kinds be raised" (14–15). Spence was sure that this system would be more productive than private property in land.

Spence devoted the parish rents to financing all national and local public expenditures. Although he estimated no figures, he was quite optimistic as to revenues available. After paying necessary sums to Parliament, he thought the parish would be able to put its revenues to work,

> in maintaining and relieving its own poor, and people out of work; in paying the necessary officers their salaries; in building, repairing, and adorning its houses, bridges, and other structures; in making and maintaining convenient and delightful streets, highways, and passages both for foot and carriages; in making and maintaining canals and other conveniences for trade and navigation; in planting and taking in waste grounds; in providing and keeping up a magazine of ammunition, and all sorts of arms sufficient for all its inhabitants in case of danger from enemies; in premiums for the encouragement

> of agriculture, or anything else thought worthy of encouragement; and, in a word, in doing whatever the people think proper; and not, as formerly, to support and spread luxury, pride, and all manner of vice. (11–12)

Although not included in his original plan, the direct redistribution of any public surplus over and above expenses was envisioned in later versions.

Throughout his life Spence maintained his position as a popular radical publicist and pamphleteer. He influenced a number of the most militant British radicals, who took on the name of Spencean Philanthropists. In the Cato Street Conspiracy (1820), these men plotted the overthrow of the British government, for which several were hanged. More relevant to the present history, Spence was well known to Mill's friend Francis Place in his early days in the London Corresponding Society. Place was strongly supportive of Spence's land plan and had anticipated writing a memoir of Spence (Miles 1988, 42). Place looked forward to the time "when men will be sufficiently wise to agree that all the land shall belong to all the people . . . and upon . . . some such plan as Mr Spence has promulgated . . . the people shall be the sole landlord and receive all the rent" (quoted in Miles 1988, 42). Through Place, Mill undoubtedly was familiar with Spence's scheme. Although Mill mentioned that plan once or twice in his own writings, he never discussed it in any detail.

The Ricardian Socialists

In the first half of the nineteenth century, the Ricardian socialists held to Ricardo's labor theory of value. Indeed, they held to it far more literally than Ricardo himself. Not surprisingly, they generally accepted Ricardo's theory of land rent as well. Coupling Ricardian land-rent theory with Spence's basic morality pushed some Ricardian socialists such as John Gray toward the conclusion that land should be nationalized.

Early on, Gray had been one of Robert Owen's managers at Orbitson, which he thought very poorly run (Gray 1831, appendix). He was also well versed in classical political economy and "[h]is writings are filled with quotations from the economists," including Adam Smith, James Mill, and J. M. McCulloch (Lowenthal [1911] 1972, 48). Gray fully understood Ricardian rent theory. In his view, Ricardian rent was essentially a tax created by the private ownership of land. As he put it, "The variations in the quality of land are the instrument of power—the act of Circumstantial Parliament—by which the people are now taxed to a most enormous amount" (Gray, 1831, 297). Nationalization could effectively remove this tax. Once nationalized, Gray argued for food prices being set to average (not marginal) costs. In this way,

> all the land worth cultivating would be cultivated; the whole produce would be divided by the whole cost of production; the extra cost of cultivating inferior land, in proportion to the result obtained therefrom, would be equally divided amongst every eater of bread in the kingdom, and the price of corn would be lower than it is now by the whole amount of rent that is annually paid for permission to cultivate the land on which it is grown. (297)

Now a well-versed Ricardian might object that Gray's plan sends no signal as to the intensity with which each piece of land should be farmed. Gray seemed vaguely aware of such an objection. He left the question to skilled paid managers: "[T]he precise number of farmers should be the number that may be sufficient to cultivate the land in the best manner, and with the least sufficient expense of superintendence and management" (298). The laborers would constitute a paid workforce.

Unlike Spence, Gray advocated the purchase, not the expropriation, of land. The voluntary National Chamber of Commerce would prove so successful in its business dealings that it would easily be able to purchase the land of the country. Nor did Gray see any reason to derive tax revenue from land rent. Instead, he argued for a proportional tax system achieved through a value-added tax on finished goods.

Gray's emphasis on nationalization can be contrasted with the position of William Thompson, who looked, not to land nationalization, but to cooperative agricultural arrangements (Thompson [1827] 1969). Thompson, of course, was an enthusiast of the cooperative movement. He envisioned voluntary cooperatives of 300 to 2,000 or more individuals renting if necessary and purchasing if possible about one-half to one and one half acres per head. In this plan, current landowners were to receive compensation for selling their land. The purpose is not the reclaiming of a common birthright, but the achieving of social advantages and economic efficiencies inherent in cooperative production.

MILL ON LAND

Mill was exquisitely aware of the basic radical arguments against private property in land. To the extent that land is a productive gift of nature and not itself produced by labor, it is something different from capital. In effect, Mill echoed the Diggers and Spence in his opening propositions.

"The essential principle of property being to assure to all persons what they have produced by their labour and accumulated by their abstinence, this principle cannot apply to what is not the produce of labour, the raw material of the earth" (Mill [1848] 1965, 227). But in classical utilitarian form, he eschewed arguments based on natural rights in favor of those based on efficiency.

On the grounds of efficiency Mill thought that land must be privately managed. He put the point as follows: "The use of the land in agriculture must indeed, for the time being, be of necessity exclusive; the same person who has ploughed and sown must be permitted to reap" (227). Notice the almost off-hand qualification here that the need for private control holds "for the time being." Possibly this suggests that at some future date an alternative to private control and use might be possible. Perhaps there's a faint hint here of the Diggers collective communal approach, but with the proviso that it can only be considered at some future time when progress has achieved new technological or moral conditions.

For the time being, Mill avoided considering such experiments. But he offered as possibilities just about every other plan from the radical agrarian canon: "the land might be occupied for a season only . . . or might be periodically redivided as population increased: or the State might be the universal landlord, and the cultivators tenants under it, either on lease or at will" (229–230).

Having made the broad radical point, Mill in characteristic fashion offered a major counter-argument: "But though land is not the produce of industry, most of its valuable qualities are so." Labor is required to clear and drain the land. Labor is required to fence and improve the land. Mill pointed to the Bedford Level, the bogs of Ireland, and Pays de Waes in Flanders as prime examples of land requiring extensive investment of labor. And Mill drew the conclusion: a potential maker of agricultural investments must be able to look forward to "a sufficient period before him in which to profit by them: and he is in no way so sure of having always a sufficient period as when his tenure is perpetual."[10] This is the heart of the "justification, in an economical point of view, of property in land" (230–231).

Mill's discourse became almost a scholastic dialectic moving from one position to its obverse. He allowed "In Great Britain, the landed proprietor is not unfrequently an improver." But that is not the general rule, for primogeniture is hardly compatible with a serious approach to agriculture.

10. At this point in the argument Mill offered in a footnote a long supporting quote from J. C. L. Sismondi.

Landlords generally lack the resources to improve their land. And "[w]ere they ever so much inclined, those alone can prudently do it, who have seriously studied the principles of scientific agriculture: and great landlords have seldom seriously studied anything." Burdened by debt and struggling to provide for their children who will except for one not inherit their estate, landlords fail miserably at maintaining those lands. To add insult to injury leases generally are limited to short terms and absolutely discourage any improvements by tenant farmers (231–232).

Somewhat surprisingly, Mill made no specific argument for the reform of land ownership in England. But Ireland was a different matter. If landed property was difficult to justify in England, in Ireland it was impossible to justify. There, the landlords "[r]eturning nothing to the soil . . . consume its whole produce, minus the potatoes strictly necessary to keep the inhabitants from dying of famine; and when they have any purpose of improvement, the preparatory step usually consists in not leaving even this pittance, but turning out the people to beggary if not to starvation" (229–230). Such a situation requires institutional reform. And Mill was clear that it is the responsibility of the state "to deal with landed property as the general interests of the community may require."

Even in Ireland, however, Mill insisted on full compensation. Landowners, even Irish landowners, do have a civil right to full compensation. Whereas Spence thought landholders had compromised all such claims by their very efforts to extract gain from the common wealth, Mill saw the claim to compensation as "indefeasible." Landowners shared it with the "owners of any property whatever, recognized as such by the state." They were owed either a capital sum or "an annual income equal to what they derived from it." In defense of this position, Mill offered two arguments. The first was that virtually all privately owned land was at some time purchased with the "produce of the labour and abstinence" of the buyer and hence purchased in good faith. The second argument privileged the status quo very much like the welfare economist's notion of a Pareto improvement—that is, an insistence that all parties be made better off by a change. Mill observed it can never "be necessary for accomplishing an object by which the community altogether will gain, that a particular portion of the community should be immolated" (231).[11]

11. A possible exception to Mill's insistence on Pareto improvement can be found in his assertion that while Britain's emancipation of slaves through compensation of slaveowners increased total output, the compensation paid was probably less than the loss imposed on the owners. Mill voiced no objection to this outcome ([1848] 1965, 249).

In the case of Ireland, Mill felt something must be done.[12] He endorsed a general act of Parliament that would turn Irish tenants into owners subject to a sort of quit rent. However, he was much more enthusiastic about voluntary societies that attempt to develop waste lands or purchase land outright (324–336). He was particularly concerned that whatever reforms are instituted they be developed with an eye to encouraging the efficiency obtained by indefinite or long-term tenure.

Whatever the mechanism, Mill envisioned the establishment of an energetic and prosperous class of new farmers. The point was not to redistribute, but to reorganize in a fashion that increased efficiency and overcame rural lethargy.[13] Mill was constantly on the lookout for structural changes that build up the self-sufficiency and competency of classes that have heretofore been trapped in an enforced indolence.

As in the case of broadening inheritances, Mill's radical thought was more focused on the inherent capabilities of people to produce than on their immediate consumption needs. At root, Mill was convinced of the fundamental equality of people. Institutional reform, then, must aim at unlocking this productive potential in an orderly and useful manner. Without threatening chaos, reform must open paths to progress, encouraging the active and conscious participation of a wider and wider share of the population.

LAND TAXES

Mill was a classical economist, fully committed to the classical analysis of land rent as laid out by Ricardo and dating back to Smith. As such, Mill recognized a fundamental difference between taxing land rents and taxing other income. In particular, he held that a tax on pure location rents in no way reduced incentives to produce. Since the landowner, qua landowner, played no part in production but simply rented the land to the highest bidder, reducing the net rent left supply unaffected.

The question then became to what extent land rents should be taxed. As in his general discussion of private property in land, Mill was concerned with what he considered the legitimate expectations of landowners. To the extent that the state has levied a longstanding land tax, there was no problem. Unfortunately, when estates in England were freed from feudal

12. This is true at least for the editions of the *Principles* up to 1857.

13. And such a goal was, of course, fully consistent with offsetting Malthusian pressures.

obligations, the state created only a very modest land tax. At that point a much higher tax might have been legitimately instituted, in effect making the state a co-owner. But now owners who have purchased lands at market values have the expectation that land taxes will not be increased (821–822).

The state missed an opportunity in the distant past. But it still had major opportunities in the future. Mill held that the progress of society inevitably raises land values. Landlords increase their wealth and income "independently of any trouble or outlay incurred by themselves. They grow richer, as it were in their sleep, without working, risking, or economizing" (819). It is impractical to try to determine the past growth in land values owing to this social process. However, in going forward, a general valuation of land could be made. With such data on hand, "It would be easy to keep the tax within the amount which would reduce the market value of land below the original valuation: and up to that point, whatever the amount of tax might be, no injustice would be done to the proprietors" (821).[14]

Mill's position can be contrasted with that of Spence, who essentially held landowners culpable for having purchased property stolen from the common wealth. Spence's position also characterized the radical Henry George, famous for advocating a single tax on land. Writing in 1879, George insisted that the single tax appropriate virtually the entire land rent, without concern for compensation. Although he greatly respected Mill, in this case George specifically targeted Mill's position. He argued that the principles of common law make no allowance for compensation when stolen property is at issue. George stated:

> The law does not say, as John Stuart Mill says: "The land belongs to A, therefore B who has thought himself the owner has no right to anything but the rent, or compensation for its salable value." . . . The law . . . gives the innocent purchaser of a wrongful title no claim, it allows him no compensation. And not only this, it takes from him all the improvements that he has in good faith made upon the land. . . . And not merely that. According to the common law,

14. Mill is clear that current land values include expectations of rising rents. To this extent, one of his proposals—i.e., to measure increase in location rents through an index of commodity prices—would seem flawed. But his proposal to use the increase in land values directly fails to address his concern to not mix the effects of improvements with general increases in site rents. In his 1871 pamphlet on land tenure reform, *Programme of the Land Tenure Reform Association, with an Explanatory Statement by John Stuart Mill*, he adds to the scheme the ongoing "registration . . . of subsequent improvements made by the landlord" ([1871] 1967, 692).

> when you have surrendered the land and given up your improvements, you may be called upon to account for the profits you derived from the land during the time you had it. (George [1879] 1886, 329)

Mill was never likely to argue for the outright expropriation of land as had Spence before him or George after him. His reform proposals were defined within his understanding of utilitarian principles. Yet, his position was still radical and he advanced that position as a major supporter of the Land Tenure Reform Association.

In the case of land, as in the case of inheritance, Mill was committed to rebuilding institutions, but he saw little purpose and no hope of unraveling the wrongs of the past. In both cases, the focus must be on the future. The point was to put inefficient and inequitable past practices to rest while building new productive classes. It was useless to attempt to rewrite history, but most useful to correct the course going forward, to strengthen the nation's institutions, and to hasten the pace of progress.

CHAPTER 7

Poverty, the Poor Laws, and the Family

The English Poor Laws, which provided indigent families various kinds of public assistance, commanded a considerable share of the energy of the new discipline of political economy in the first third of the nineteenth century. Among classical economists, there was probably greater agreement on the Poor Laws than on any other policy, including free trade. Malthus and Ricardo disagreed on whether to protect Britain's market from imported grains, but they were in complete agreement on the need to overhaul the Poor Laws.

Despite the general policy consensus among classical economists, John Stuart Mill's writings on the Poor Laws reflect his conflicting instincts with respect to poverty. These almost contrary perspectives tap into core ambivalences in Mill's radical thought. On the one hand, Mill saw that Poor Laws recognize a genuine concern and public responsibility for the impoverished. The greatest happiness of the greatest number demanded an effective safety net. Yet, the insurance of a basic livelihood raised the specter of Malthusian population growth unchecked by scarcity. Presumably, such growth financed out of taxation could end only with the complete absorption of the surplus and the halt of accumulation.

Caught between these concerns, Mill endorsed the classical formula that asserted those receiving aid must be relegated to a state of "less eligibility," a state less attractive than that of the lowest paid worker. While the classical liberal diatribe against indolence and laziness infects Mill's writings on the Poor Laws, the central problem for him was population growth—population growth that threatened the welfare of the greatest number. Mill's advocacy of workhouses as opposed to "outdoor" relief was based precisely on the control such institutions promised for preventing sexual relations among the impoverished. As in the case of his radical endorsement of laissez-faire, Mill looked forward to the day when progress would make possible a right to work without the destruction of basic liberties.

A QUICK HISTORY OF THE EARLY POOR LAWS

Until the sixteenth-century Protestant Reformation in England, virtually all of what we would now call welfare—subsidized employment, food distributions, charity health care, and elder care—had been carried out by the Catholic Church. Spurred by the waning power of Catholicism in England and the breakdown of feudal relations more generally, the Tudor monarchs experimented for half a century with a series of Poor Laws. Finally, during the reign of Queen Elizabeth I in 1601, a firm fiscal base for poor relief was established (Smith [1776] 1976, 152–153; E. Leonard [1900] 1965). Compulsory taxation to support the poor was mandated by the central government, but the Poor Laws were administered locally.

In each parish, an annual vestry meeting elected an overseer who carried out the law under the supervision of the justice of the peace. The Poor Laws left considerable discretion to the local administrator to pick whatever mix of relief policies seemed most appropriate to local conditions. These included "outdoor relief," which might take the form of subsidized food, direct transfers, wage subsidies, and/or public employment; and "indoor relief," which required recipients to enter a parish poorhouse. Whatever their charitable purposes, from the beginning the Poor Laws were wrapped up with legislation to control the movements and behavior of vagrants. While enforcement of these laws was clearly lax, one can glean from the legislated penalties a notion of the intensity of concern with vagrancy. In the late sixteenth century, various laws sanctioned prison sentences, whipping, and even death for "sturdy vagabonds" (Senior [1841] 1973).

England's civil wars of the seventeenth century greatly diminished the national effort to bring relief to the poor, but after the Restoration in 1660 put Charles II on the throne, his administration both expanded relief and attempted to strengthen control of the mobility of the poor. The problem was that "poor people endeavour to settle themselves in those parishes where there is the best stock, the largest commons or wastes to build cottages, and the most woods for them to burn" (Senior [1841] 1973, 10). Local overseers had long refused to provide assistance to those paupers residing in their parishes but born elsewhere. And if these refusals weren't enough, the overseers would attempt to remove such paupers to their original locale. In 1662, the Law of Settlement standardized these local constraints on mobility. Justices of the peace were empowered to remove any new resident of a parish who could not give a substantial bond, regardless of whether the newcomer had actually applied for aid (Oxley 1974, 39–42).

Over the next half-century, expenditures under the Poor Laws grew substantially. This expansion attracted much criticism from various proponents of natural law, including Daniel Defoe and Bernard Mandeville.[1] Providing generous support to the poor, these commentators argued, simply undermined work incentives. The Poor Law of 1722 checked the rise of expenditures. This harsh legislation encouraged parishes to build workhouses and to separate pauper families. One historian has called this the "nadir" of social responsibility, as many parishes farmed out their poor to contractors (Cowherd 1977, 1). The rest of the century witnessed a movement toward more humanitarian reform, but it was reform still rooted in the notion that England's village communities should look after their own, despite the increasingly national character of the economy.

Humanitarian efforts were again matched by increases in expenditures. To a large degree, though, this expansion reflected the ongoing changes in the British economy. The continuing modernization of agriculture, the decline of domestic manufactures, and the beginnings of industrial activity all put pressure on the poor. Modern economic history documents a broad and steady expansion of relief in response to changing conditions (Boyer 1990). The 1795 Speenhamland allowance system, a wage supplement based on the difference between a worker's income and an established minimum, was a revolutionary innovation. By 1803, about 1 million people, or 11 percent of the population of England and Wales, received some sort of relief from the Poor Laws. About 16 percent of these recipients were aged or infirmed. Of the million recipients, only

1. Thus Daniel Defoe, the creator of Robinson Crusoe and part-time writer of mercantilist tracts, traced the sources of impoverishment to the indolence of able-bodied men, an indolence encouraged by the Poor Laws. In his influential pamphlet "Giving Alms, No Charity," Defoe asserted, in fine mercantilist form, that England had "more labour than hands to perform it" (Defoe [1704] 1970, 9). Similarly, Bernard Mandeville, the author of *The Fable of the Bees*, concluded, "The poor have nothing to stir them to labour but their wants, which it is wisdom to relieve but folly to cure" (Mandeville 1924 [1732], 2:351. See also Mandeville 1924 [1729], 1:194 and 1:248). See further discussion of Defoe and Mandeville in Webb and Webb (1927 [1963], 114–116).

83,000 were year-round residents of workhouses (K. Williams 1981, 230). As estimated by Williams, "[T] he weekly dole per pauper works out as just under one and a quarter shillings a week in an era when even an underpaid agricultural labourer could expect to earn the better part of ten shillings a week" (38–39). For most recipients, these were modest supplements to wages perilously close to subsistence.

Despite some improvement in the wages paid to agricultural laborers during the first three decades of the nineteenth century, expenditures on the Poor Laws continued to rise. Total nominal expenditures by 1830 had reached 6.8 million pounds, or about 2 percent of national product (K. Williams 1981, 148; Blaug 1963). Especially in rural areas, public relief had become a virtually permanent fixture in the incomes of the poor. For the new Whig government and its prophets of political economy, this state of affairs was untenable.

THE CLASSICAL ECONOMISTS' ATTACK ON THE OLD POOR LAWS

Classical economists from Adam Smith on had found fault with the Poor Laws. In the *Wealth of Nations*, for example, Smith ([1776] 1976, 157) had attacked the settlement requirements of the Poor Laws as violations of "natural liberty and justice." The culmination of the classical attack came in 1834, after nine Royal Commissioners had been named to investigate and recommend changes to England's Poor Laws. The commission's report was largely authored by Nassau Senior, one of the first professors to hold a chair of political economy,[2] and by Edwin Chadwick, a disciple of Jeremy Bentham who was quite sympathetic to the theories of classical political economy.

The commissioners made a considerable show of basing their report on empirical findings. They appointed twenty-six assistant commissioners to gather information by visiting parishes around England and Wales. In addition, the commissioners sent out two extensive questionnaires directly to the parishes, one for urban and one for rural areas. While the questionnaires and the instructions to the assistant commissioners would

2. Senior, a member along with the Mills of the Political Economy Club, broadly subscribed to the pragmatic outlook and purposes of utilitarianism. However, among classical economists, he stood out for his criticisms of Malthus, Ricardo, and J. S. Mill. He is sometimes classified as a "proto-marginalist." For a brief introduction to Senior, see De Marchi (1987).

undoubtedly be considered biased by modern standards, the commission amassed a huge amount of data that today still provides a broad field for economic historians. But as virtually all students of the Poor Laws agree, Senior and Chadwick paid little attention to this mass of data. Instead, they put together their final report by drawing a few supporting instances from the subcommissioners' reports as best fitted their argument (Boyer 1990, 60–61; Oxley 1974, 24–28).

The Poor Laws, according to the classical critique, had combined the worst aspects of slavery and freedom—that is, the worker's freedom and mobility were sharply constrained while his initiative and diligence had been destroyed. In 1830, before he joined the Royal Commission, Senior ([1830] 1966) wrote: "The poor-laws, as administered in the southern districts of England, are an attempt to unite the irreconcilable advantages of freedom and servitude. The labourer is to be a free agent, but without the hazards of free agency; to be free from the coercion, but to enjoy the assured subsistence of a slave. He is expected to be diligent, though he has no fear of want" (ix). This combination of coercion and missing incentives could only lead to pauperism and dependency. In fact, the chief constraints placed on laborers' liberty by the Law of Settlement had already been removed by the first two decades of the nineteenth century. But Senior and others remained concerned that the custom of granting outdoor relief on relatively attractive terms would exacerbate the incentives for indolence.

The heart of the commissioners' (Poor Law Commissioners [1834] 1905) report built on the classical awareness of the importance of incentives in economic behavior. Their report stated this worldview as a dictum: "Every penny bestowed, that tends to render the condition of the pauper more eligible than that of the independent laborer, is a bounty on indolence and vice" (228). The central purpose of reform must be to force the pauper into a state of "less eligibility," a state less attractive than that of the lowest worker. To achieve this goal, the commissioners proposed a return to the principles of 1722—that is, to a system of harsh workhouses.[3] The threat of the workhouse, as opposed to the relative generosity of outdoor relief, would lead to a conversion of the great bulk of "able-bodied paupers" into "independent laborers," a concomitant reduction in

3. Interestingly, this proposal actually implied a substantial increase in the powers of the central government, rather than implying any sort of reduction, since administration of the workhouses was to be standardized across regions. Driver (1993, ch. 2) suggests the reformers, in a Benthamite mood, were less worried about free markets than about effectively encouraging labor-market participation.

taxes, an improvement in wages (since employers enjoying lower taxes would demand more labor), an increase in productivity, a lower birthrate, reduced crime rates, and an increase in morality and frugality.[4]

Senior held the Poor Laws responsible for the very existence of pauperism: "The able-bodied pauper is the result of art. He is not the natural offspring of the Saxon race. Unless his pauperism is carefully fostered by those who think it their interest to preserve it, he rapidly reverts to the normal type-the independent labourer" ([1841] 1973, 33).[5] Yet he also acknowledged that the price of independence and productivity might at times be a high one. And here, Senior ([1830] 1966, xiv–xv) fell back on a rougher version of Adam Smith's invisible hand: "Nature has decreed that the road to good shall be through evil—that no improvement shall take place in which the general advantage shall not be accompanied by partial suffering."

In the extreme, the argument suggested not the reform of the Poor Laws but the complete eradication of such interventions. Early on, Malthus had toyed with such a conclusion. For Malthus, any improvement in the standard of living inevitably led to earlier family formation and higher population growth. In his view, this consequence was bad enough if the spur came from high wages, since it would eventually result in misery and famine, but even worse if it originated in Poor Laws, which perversely rewarded fecundity.

In support of his policy position, Malthus developed a surprisingly rich theory of family dynamics. He argued that the family lay at the heart of a natural system of economic incentives. The most potent counterforce to a man's potential indolence and inconsistency came from the knowledge that his wife and children were totally dependent on his efforts. "By the laws of nature a child is confided directly and exclusively to the protection of its parents," Malthus ([1798] 1970, 265) wrote. "By the laws of nature, the mother of a child is confided almost as strongly and exclusively to the man who is the father of it." Thus, the dependency of women and children, "by the laws of nature," encouraged the productive behavior of males.[6]

4. From the vantage point of economic history, Blaug (1963, 1964) provides a famous refutation of the classical analysis of Poor Law reform. But see also Boyer (1990, ch. 5) for evidence on the stimulus of the Poor Laws to birthrates.

5. Senior here touches on the most ancient claim that poor relief, far from solving the problems of poverty, plays a major role in creating and exacerbating those problems. Hirschman (1991) calls this mode of conservative arguing the "perversity thesis."

6. Thus Malthus would not be surprised at modern evidence of a "marriage premium" rooted in greater effort among married men. See Korenman and Neumark

In the context of this patriarchal theory of the family, Malthus worried that any cash transfers intended for the welfare of dependents would, in effect, be heavily shared with the patriarch. Malthus assumed that the altruism of a large number of men extended only to the bare necessities of their dependents, and that their desire for leisure was quite high. For such men, the presence of dependents and the absence of family support became major incentives to their work effort. Malthus was so sure of the effectiveness and rightness of this natural set of incentives that he worried as to the usefulness of any poor law, even a reformed one.

A number of critics pointed out that a full abolition of public support would leave large numbers of women and children in dire straits, suffering because of the inadequacy of their husbands and fathers, whether because men were unable to provide or because they simply lacked the altruism to be motivated by the predicament of their dependents. Malthus responded by claiming the vital necessity of maintaining the dependency of women and children:

> It may appear to be hard that a mother and her children, who had been guilty of no particular crime themselves, should suffer for the ill-conduct of the father; but this is one of the invariable laws of nature. If a man could neglect or desert his wife and children without their suffering any injury, how many individuals there are who, not being very fond of their wives, or being tired of the shackles of matrimony, would withdraw from household cares and difficulties, and resume their liberty and independence as single men! . . . In the moral government of the world, it seems evidently necessary that the sins of the fathers should be visited upon the children; and if in our overweening vanity we imagine that we can govern a private society better by endeavoring systematically to counteract this law, I am inclined to believe that we shall find ourselves very greatly mistaken. (Malthus [1798] 1970, 266–267)

Malthus held up the "naturalness" of the unregulated system of motivation. Like Smith's invisible hand, this arrangement encouraged the maximization of total labor effort and production.

For Malthus, the family unit when functioning properly played a key role in social organization. It provided motivation and purpose to males,

(1991) for a discussion of the empirical evidence on this point. More generally, Malthus's analysis of the internal economics of the family anticipated more modern treatments. The Malthusian view of fathers can be interpreted as an anticipation of Gary Becker's (1991) parental-altruist's utility function, which explicitly makes the utility of the altruist a function of the utility of spouse and child. Becker cites Malthus's theories of fertility, but seems unaware of Malthus's discussion of the family as an incentive to male effort.

and protection for females and children. It was capable of generating contentment for all ranks of society. Through example, it engendered virtue and prudence. The Poor Laws, according to Malthus, threatened and disrupted this central institution.

Malthus's patriarchal views on the family were widely shared by both liberals and conservatives of his time. Tory Radicals were particularly fond of recalling the "comforts of the cottage" that had characterized a recent golden age of patriarchy.[7] Not surprisingly, Malthus's themes were developed at length by the Poor Law Commissioners. Their report identified the breakdown of the traditional bonds of family dependency as one of the most destructive consequences of the Poor Laws:

> The worst results are still to be mentioned: in all ranks of society the great sources of happiness and virtue are the domestic affections, and this is particularly the case among those who have so few resources as the labouring classes. Now, pauperism seems to be an engine for the purpose of disconnecting each member of a family from all the others; of reducing all to the state of domesticated animals, fed, lodged and provided for by the parish, without mutual dependence or mutual interest. (Poor Law Commissioners [1834] 1905, 95–96)

The commissioners went on to cite examples to show how the breakdown in the family undermined the role of the father, who as a pauper now might "threaten to abandon his wife and family unless more money is allowed him." (97).

Conversely, as the Poor Laws worked to break down the natural dependency of children, the commissioners realized that the young would have less interest in their parents' welfare. When children of fourteen were eligible for their own parish relief, they were likely to defy and even mistreat their parents. Young women would not nurse their aged parents without payment from the authorities.

Anticipating the charge that even in a world free of poor laws some men would lack the will (or altruism) to take care of their dependents, the commissioners argued that society had no serious intention of intervening within the family structure and hence could achieve little benefit for such women and children: "The ground on which relief is ordered to the idle and dissolute is, that the wife and family must not suffer for the vices of the head of the family; but as that relief is almost always given

7. For a discussion of mid-nineteenth-century Tory Radical perspectives on the family, see Persky (1998).

into the hands of the vicious husband or parent, this excuse is obviously absurd." (87).

Senior and his fellows could hardly avoid the fact that many poor women with children had either never been married or had been deserted by their husbands. One might anticipate that these early welfare reformers, with their strong concerns for the natural family, would have approved forced marriages with the father or at least the imposition of child support. Curiously this was not the case. Indeed, just the opposite. In a flurry of concern over the inefficiency of state intervention, the Poor Law Commissioners asserted that little was gained by haranguing an accused father. Perhaps the man was innocent. Even if not, forcing the payment of child support could only send a signal that children born out of wedlock would bring economic bounties to their mothers. Unscrupulous women would take advantage of both their lovers and the parish. At places, the excruciating logic became almost comical, as when one of the subcommissioners asked,

> Whether marriages [taking place among the labouring classes in rural districts] are not in most instances, brought about by the threat which the woman holds out to the man of swearing the child to him if he does not marry her; and whether the power afforded to the man of suggesting to the woman that she may place him in this predicament is not the infallible topic of seduction and persuasion which he employs in the rare instances which require persuasion? (Poor Law Commissioners 1833, 392)

When the commissioners opposed policies such as forced marriages and/or child support, they argued that such policies encouraged illegitimacy and population growth. Of course, they might have taken just the opposite view. Wouldn't the enforcement of child support have made men more careful, and thus reduced the number of births out of wedlock? Such a proposition would arguably have been more logically consistent with the Malthusian emphasis on family and children as economic motivator.

At a deeper level, Senior and Chadwick seemed to balk at the independence women might achieve from child-support payments from an absent father, or from public grants made directly to the mother. The Poor Law Commissioners suggested that women with children to support must rely on their own parents. Their plight could only be answered by a renewed dependency. In the end, Senior and the classical economists assumed that the dependency of women and children was natural, and that the Poor Laws should seek to preserve it rather than to disturb it. In short, they were hostile to subsidies directed at men because it destroyed their initiative and freedom, but hostile to subsidies for women and children because it would destroy their dependency and injure the patriarchal family, the fundamental unit of the society.

MILL'S RADICAL UNDERSTANDING OF THE POOR LAWS

John Stuart Mill, like almost all classical economists, supported the reform of the Poor Laws and the harsh incentives it was meant to enforce. But at the same time he strongly opposed proposals such as Malthus's to do away with the Poor Laws in their entirety. His reading of the Poor Law Commissioners is that, in the short run, competent and efficient management of the Poor Laws would be able to resolve the tension between the social need for a safety net and the negative incentives created by too generous support. Indeed, he saw the commissioners' report as a major contribution of serious inquiry to public policy.

Mill argued that the researches of the commissioners demonstrated the feasibility of "an absolute right to be supported at the cost of other people ... without fatally relaxing the springs of industry and the restraints of prudence." The commissioners, although often seen as "hostile to the principle of legal relief," had in fact "proved the compatibility of [a] Poor Law, in which a right to relief was recognised, with the permanent interests of the labouring class and of posterity." They had done this with "a collection of facts, experimentally ascertained in parishes scattered throughout England." Their careful investigation demonstrated, "[T]he guarantee of support could be freed from its injurious effects upon the minds and habits of the people, if the relief, though ample in respect to necessaries, was accompanied with conditions which they disliked, consisting of some restraints on their freedom, and the privation of some indulgences" (Mill [1848] 1965, 360).

Mill's claim is basically a restatement of the classical proposition of "less eligibility." But Mill couches it in a broader context, stressing his concern with the welfare of the greatest number. Throughout his life, Mill emphasized that chance played a major role in people's lives. Through no fault of their own, many in poverty were simply the victims of chance. But now, with the reformed Poor Laws, "the fate of no member of the community needs be abandoned to chance." He goes on:

> [S]ociety can and therefore ought to insure every individual belonging to it against the extreme of want; that the condition even of those who are unable

> to find their own support, needs not be one of physical suffering, or the dread of it, but only of restricted indulgence, and enforced rigidity of discipline. (360)

Rather than resignation, Mill saw the new Poor Laws as "something gained for humanity, important in itself." This argument very much distinguishes Mill from the most extreme statements of Malthus and Senior, who at times seem to prefer no poor laws at all.

But that is not all. For Mill, the new Poor Law is most important as "a step to something beyond." Here, Mill returned to his central theoretical theme of the promise of progress and the dependence of that promise on the working class's willingness to assert control over population growth. Admitting that many regard a meaningful change in working-class views on population as "chimerical," Mill asserted that such a change is quite possible. The logic of population control is simply the extension of workers' visceral understanding that limiting competition is the key to raising wages. Mill observed, "The dependence of wages on the number of the competitors for employment, is so far from hard of comprehension, or unintelligible to the labouring classes, that by great bodies of them it is already recognised and habitually acted on." He gives as examples the trade union movement, in which "every successful combination to keep up wages owes its success to contrivances for restricting the number of the competitors." And skilled trades have long understood the need to restrict their own numbers (374).

Uneducated and without hope, the poorest workers had been slow to absorb these basic lessons. But the spread of literacy and rising expectations laid the groundwork for major changes in outlook. Perhaps most important, women, even poor women, when educated to a modest standard and endowed with basic civil rights, would assert a major check on population growth. Women had a longstanding aversion to families of excessive size. To be relieved from the drudgery that characterizes such families, "would be hailed as a blessing by multitudes of women who now never venture to urge such a claim, but who would urge it, if supported by the moral feelings of the community" (372).[8] In the long run, Mill anticipated that many women would increasingly find employment outside the home, and properly so. Mill looked forward to a far more open and less patriarchal family structure than that pictured in Malthus's economics of

8. Anticipating modern feminism, Mill noted in this context, "Among the barbarisms which law and morals have not yet ceased to sanction, the most disgusting surely is that any human being should be permitted to consider himself as having a right to the person of another" (Mill [1848] 1965, 372).

the family. He saw this openness as a central component in the long-run solution of the Malthusian population dilemma.

Mill's reading of the promise of progress fundamentally rejected Malthus's romantic patriarchal view of the family. Mill's description of Victorian families was the very opposite of that presented in the Tory Radicals' comforts of the cottage. Late in his life, Mill published his essay on *The Subjection of Women* ([1869] 1984). While acknowledging that "in the classes most exposed to temptation, a man's wife and children tend to keep him honest and respectable, both by the wife's direct influence, and by the concern he feels for their future welfare," Mill saw no reason why maintaining a patriarchal structure is a prerequisite of such beneficial results. Instead, Mill asserted, "[T]his beneficial influence would be preserved and strengthened under equal laws; it does not depend on the woman's servitude, but is, on the contrary, diminished by the disrespect which the inferior class of men always at heart feel towards those who are subject to their power" (331). Equality in the family, not patriarchy, would better work to enhance men's sense of responsibility, to limit family size, and to guarantee parental care for children.

Even while Mill endorsed in the short run the repressive nature of Poor Law reforms, he looked forward to progress—progress that would make much of the stinginess of such programs unnecessary. The reform of the family and the checking of population growth together with ongoing capital accumulation would put upward pressure on workers' wages. As a result, even generous relief would not compete with private employment. In such circumstances, relief could be fully focused on its true social purpose: the offsetting of the vagaries of chance. Mill's radical position on the Poor Laws accepts much of the classical reform program, but holds out the promise that the future will allow for a more compassionate safety net. The greatest good of the greatest number demands critical and even harsh reforms in the short run, but progress will prepare the ground for a more just and humane approach to social insurance in the long run.

Mill had a deep faith in progress. But at times he feared that the goal might require a more aggressive set of changes. In his discussion of the fundamental need for "a prudent regulation of population," Mill asserted that if such an outcome won't be forthcoming under the "system of hired labour," then the "system is a nuisance." In such a situation, "economical statesmanship should consider whatever arrangements of property, and alterations in the modes of applying industry" are necessary to alter existing incentives for large families (Mill [1848] 1965, 373).

In this vein, Mill put forward an almost revolutionary position in discussing the efforts of the French government to deal with the emergence of mass unemployment during the Revolution of 1848. Mill supported *le droit au travail*, or right to work, introduced by the provisional government under considerable duress. In effect, this legislation endorsed the broad project of the early socialist Louis Blanc for making the government the employer of last resort. The ambitious plan was poorly executed, perhaps sabotaged, and ended with the failure of the Revolution.

The basic classical argument of "less eligibility" clearly marks the approach of *le droit au travail* as counterproductive and virtually designed to reduce incentives and encourage laziness. A number of years later, Nassau Senior referred to *le droit au travail* as a "gross economical enormity."[9]

In contrast to Senior, Mill began his discussion of *le droit au travail* with considerable sympathy. He compared the French law aimed at the "general labour market" favorably to English Poor Laws aimed at providing "alms to the individual." More broadly, Mill asserted, "[I]t must appear to every unselfish and open-minded person, that the earth belongs, first, to all, to the inhabitants of it; that every person alive ought to have a subsistence, before any one has more; that whosoever works at any useful thing, ought to be properly fed and clothed before any one able to work is allowed to receive the bread of idleness" ([1849] 1985, 348–349).

Mill's observations in the midst of the events in France take on an almost revolutionary quality. Talk of this type is exceptional for Mill and at odds with his dominant themes of progress and patience. But the incident does serve to demonstrate that Mill saw little that was sacred in the present order if that order could not hold out the promise of a more just society, capable of greatly reducing the ravages of poverty.

9. The expression appears in Senior's journal covering August 1861 (Senior 1872, 277). He groups *le droit au travail* with two other "gross economical enormities," "the *impôt progressif sur la fortune présumée*" and "a paper currency made a legal tender without limitation of its amount."

CHAPTER 8

The Education of the Working Classes

Classical economists in Great Britain had a longstanding interest in the expansion of education. Their goal was not so much to spur national growth or upward mobility as to encourage the development of a well-disciplined working class and a responsible electorate. More than one classical economist stretched his commitment to laissez-faire to endorse government expenditures on education. That said, they all regarded state schooling as an element of charity to be focused almost exclusively on the poor. Moreover, their distrust of state functionaries suggested the need for market tests even for the education of the poor. Even as a radical, John Stuart Mill was very definitely in this classical tradition. Given the importance that he assigned to education, Mill was surprisingly reluctant to advocate for public support of schooling. While he relied on the spread of education to work the most fundamental changes, Mill balked at public provision of mass education. Mill following Smith saw a need for only a modest amount of formal education—reading, writing, and basic arithmetic. Mill's radicalism focused not on the financing of that formal education but on the encouragement of a broader political education of the mass of workers. Rightly or wrongly, Mill looked to active debate in the press, around elections, and in their own organizations to play the largest part in developing the capacity of the working class to govern.

SMITH'S CLASSICAL POSITION

Classical economists' interest in education stretches back to Adam Smith and the *Wealth of Nations*.[1] Smith's ideas on education have long been considered prescient by economists. In particular, his discussion of wages anticipates the very core of human capital theory.[2] But neither Smith nor his classical heirs developed this theme in any detail.[3] Rather, Smith emphasized the role of education in shaping character and capacity (Peart and Levy, 2005). In a famous passage late in the *Wealth of Nations*, Smith worried that the division of labor he so celebrated earlier in that volume had a darker side. A worker once confined to the continuous repetition of a few simple tasks was hardly fit for citizenship:

> The torpor of his mind renders him, not only incapable of relishing or bearing a part in any rational conversation, but of conceiving any generous, noble, or tender sentiment, and consequently of forming any just judgment concerning many even of the ordinary duties of private life. Of the great and extensive interests of his country, he is altogether incapable of judging; and unless very particular pains have been taken to render him otherwise, he is equally incapable of defending his country in war. ([1776] 1976, 782)

The upper and middling classes could afford their own educations and in general were not subjected to such mind-numbing work. But "in every improved and civilized society this is the state into which the labouring poor, that is, the great body of the people, must necessarily fall, unless government takes some pains to prevent it" (782).

Smith's solution drew on his familiarity with the local schools of his native Scotland. England at the time had a very partial and unstandardized system of charity and "ragged" schools for the poor. Smith argued for the establishment of "parish or district little schools, where children may be taught for a reward so moderate, that even a common labourer may afford it. . . ." Smith, always practical and never a laissez-faire ideologue, argued that these schools with their mission to soften the mind-deadening

1. This section and the next two draw on the introductory paragraphs of Persky (2015).

2. Smith observed that occupations requiring considerable education or training can be expected to yield a return over and above the average wage. For such a skilled worker, his higher wages must cover "the whole expence of his education, with at least the ordinary profits of an equally valuable capital" ([1776] 1976, 134).

3. Nassau Senior was something of an exception to this generalization. See Senior (1854, 134).

character of the extreme division of labor would merit public subsidies. Still he insisted that the subsidies must be partial. The master must not be "wholly paid by the publick; because if he was wholly, or even principally paid by it, he would soon learn to neglect his business." To guarantee attendance in these schools, Smith argued for imposing a system of examinations. Passing such examinations would be required of all men before they could "obtain the freedom of any corporation or be allowed to set up any trade either in a village or town corporate" (785–786).[4]

Smith's conception of mixed financing for open elementary schools became the general recommendation of almost all the British classical economists. Robert Malthus explicitly endorsed Smith's plan, adding only that the poor should be fully instructed in "the real state of the lower classes of society, as affected by the principle of population, and their consequent dependence on themselves for the chief part of their happiness or misery." In supporting Smith's argument, Malthus offered evidence that where the working classes were more educated, crime rates were lower. He also emphasized that educated workers were less likely to be attracted to radical doctrines like those of Thomas Paine[5] (1826, 2:353).

THE UTILITARIANS

In the first quarter of the nineteenth century, classical economic thought on education was dominated by the two major utilitarians, James Mill and Jeremy Bentham.[6] Like Adam Smith, they staunchly held to the role of nurture in building character and intelligence.[7] They were both committed to the political reform program of philosophic radicalism, which emphasized the expansion of the franchise and civil rights. For the most part they continued the classical tradition with respect to state subsidies

4. Interestingly, Smith also advocated for a more extensive system of exams for the middle and upper classes, who would presumably pay fully for their own educational needs.

5. Somewhat surprisingly, Paine himself had proposed a rather modest system of subsidizing the education of the English poor quite similar to that supported by Smith and Malthus (Paine 1791; E. West 1975).

6. We skip over Ricardo here, who wrote little on education; see Miller (1966) for a discussion of this lacuna.

7. James Mill developed extensively a theory of associational psychology and education broadly conceived. His basic conclusion was that humans are made by their experience far more than by any intrinsic differences. In this conclusion he strongly supported the position of the French philosopher Helvetius. For his psychology, Mill drew heavily on the work of David Hartley (James Mill 1815).

of education for the poor. Supporters of laissez-faire, these political economists made a careful but narrow exception with respect to education. While consumers were generally the best judges of their own welfare, the working classes were unlikely to fully appreciate the value of education to their children and the community at large. Hence, the state must take some action on behalf of the poor.

Still, the early utilitarians worried about trusting students to the influence of the state. James Mill, an active supporter of experiments in state education, argued that "the danger of training the people generally to habits of servility and toleration of arbitrary power, if their education be entrusted to Government" were neither "small or chimerical." Nevertheless, "it is still so very great and good to have the whole facility of reading and writing diffused through the whole body of the people, that we should be willing to run considerable risks for its acquirement" (James Mill 1813, 211–212; quoted in Burston 1969, 32). Moreover, a free press used the very skill of reading to oppose any overreach by the state.

James Mill's final argument in this debate was "The impressions, indeed, which it is possible to make at the early age at which reading and writing are taught, and during the very short time that teaching lasts, are so very slight and transitory, that they must be easily effaced whenever there is anything to counteract them." (James Mill 1813, 211–212).[8] Mill's point was that state schools would not likely have the time to seriously indoctrinate their students, who would quickly move into the labor force.

James Mill's writings on education were matched by his considerable practical efforts. These efforts were centered on the Lancaster schools, which proposed a form of assembly-line education for their students.[9] In rooms holding several hundred pupils, education was to be parceled out by a single instructor aided by a cadre of monitors drawn from older students. This was, after all, the age of Bentham with his Panopticon, promoted for factories prisons and schools. Not surprisingly, like James Mill, Bentham was a strong supporter of the Lancaster model.[10] It seems classical political

8. This observation by James Mill is commented on by Burston (1969).

9. The Lancaster schools were named after Joseph Lancaster, a Quaker who with Mill's help obtained considerable political support, but later fell from grace over his lack of financial acumen. Lancaster then carried his school plans to the United States and Latin America (J. Taylor 1996).

10. In fairness to Bentham it should be noted that he also contributed to Robert Owen's more progressive experiments in education at the factory in New Lanark. Given the considerable distance between Bentham's triumphalist laissez-faire position and Owen's support of cooperatives, Bentham deserves credit for his willingness to explore Owen's more visionary approach to education.

economists, like a number of their modern descendants, fondly hoped to improve the efficiency of the schoolhouse. And the efficiency argument formed a key element in the endorsement of state supervision and support for the education of the poor. Presumably, the state with its considerable resources and expertise could measure the quality and effectiveness of educational activities more accurately than could parents.

The classical argument was perhaps most fully realized in the work of Dr. James Kay, later James Kay-Shuttleworth after his marriage to Lady Janet Shuttleworth. As a young man Dr. Kay had written on the conditions of workers in Manchester and this research became a major source for Friedrich Engels's *The Condition of the Working Class in England*. But Kay was no socialist. Recommended by Nassau Senior for a position implementing the Poor Laws, Kay moved up to be the first secretary of the Ministry of Education, established in 1839.

As a major bureaucrat in the emerging educational establishment, Kay-Shuttleworth very much hewed the utilitarian line. Like all the utilitarians, Kay-Shuttleworth put an especially heavy emphasis on the claim that education would help to encourage discipline and morality while reducing disorder and crime. For him, the concern to maintain order in crowded industrial areas overshadowed any thought of improving skills.

Kay-Shuttleworth was fond of quoting Adam Smith, whom he called "our great economist" (Kay-Shuttleworth [1862] 1973, 201). And he endorsed Smith's view of an appropriate educational establishment. What he built up in England was a combination of national subsidies and voluntary fees. In an oft-quoted passage he made an iconic statement of the utilitarian argument:

> a weekly payment from the parents of scholars is that form of taxation, the justice of which is most apparent to the humbler classes. . . . To shift the burthen of the School pence to a tax on spirits, tobacco, barley or malt, would be an evasion unworthy of a statesman, embarrassing to the revenue, productive of ultimate discontent, and otherwise demoralizing. . . . The moral advantage of a Tax on the poor in the form of School pence is, that it appeals to the sense of paternal duty. It enforces a lesson of domestic piety. . . . Nor can the paternal charities of a wise commonwealth be substituted, for the personal ties of parental love and esteem, without undermining society at its base. . . . The parent should not be led to regard the School as the privilege of the citizen, so much as another scene of household duty, (Kay-Shuttleworth 1853, 294–295)

Kay-Shuttleworth's position with its emphasis on domestic piety reflects the deep underlying utilitarian thematic of social stability.

JOHN STUART MILL, EDUCATION, AND PARENTAL RESPONSIBILITY

A concern to guarantee an education for the poor played a central role in John Stuart Mill's early thoughts on state-supported education. After explicitly endorsing laissez-faire in most situations, Mill asserted, "Any well-intentioned and tolerably civilized government may think, without presumption, that it does or ought to possess a degree of cultivation above the average of the community which it rules, and that it should therefore be capable of offering better education and better instruction to the people than the greater number of them would spontaneously demand" ([1848] 1965, 947–948).

Of course, Mill would not tolerate the state constructing a monopoly on education. While he expected that "government teachers will probably be superior to the average of private instructors, they will not embody all the knowledge and sagacity to be found in all instructors taken together and it is desirable to leave open as many roads as possible to the desired end." The alternative would be "despotic" (950).

This suggestion of a competitive educational system in which state schools would represent only one option is developed much more aggressively in Mill's famous essay, *On Liberty*. While the passages quoted above from the *Principles* suggest a well-developed and efficient system of state schools, Mill's discussion of education in *On Liberty* presents a far more limited role for state provision. Indeed, it is fair to say that Mill, in his writings on education, state schools, and public subsidies, exhibited a level of ambivalence that was high even for him.[11]

On Liberty sought to substitute the state's enforcement of "universal education" for its direct provision of that education. Key to this scheme would be a legal requirement for all parents to educate their children. Mill wrote, "If the government would make up its mind to require for every child a good education, it might save itself the trouble of providing one. It might leave to parents to obtain the education where and how they pleased." Mill continued, "An education established and controlled by the State should only exist, if it exist at all, as one among many competing experiments, carried on for the purpose of example and stimulus, to keep the others up to a certain standard of excellence." Mill concluded, "That the whole or any large part of the education of the people should be in State hands, I go as far as anyone in deprecating" ([1859] 1977, 302).

11. Mill's ambivalence on this matter is discussed by E. G. West (1975).

Like Smith, Mill advocated an extensive system of state-run examinations to certify the quality of education provided. "The instrument for enforcing the law could be no other than public examinations, extending to all children, and beginning at an early age. An age might be fixed at which every child must be examined, to ascertain if he (or she) is able to read." And lest there be any doubt who bore the responsibility for ensuring a child's education: "If a child proves unable [to read], the father, unless he has some sufficient ground of excuse, might be subjected to a moderate fine, to be worked out, if necessary, by his labour, and the child might be put to school at his expense" (303).

At the same time, even in *On Liberty*, Mill argued that not all parents will be able to afford reasonable education for their children. The state still had the responsibility of "helping to pay the school fees of the poorer classes of children, and defraying the entire school expenses of those who have no one else to pay for them" (302).

Given Mill's insistence that parents bear a major share of the responsibility for their children's education, it is somewhat curious that he didn't emphasize the considerable private returns to education. While all the classical economists acknowledged these returns, the only one to stress their importance was Nassau Senior. Indeed, Senior was buoyantly optimistic about the promise of such returns. In his vision, "There appears no reason to doubt that, as civilization advances, every person will receive an *education* which will materially increase his power of production." Contrasting English workers who had achieved some education to uneducated Irish immigrants, Senior argued that without their schooling the former "who are now earning 40s. a-week as mechanics, might have been breaking stones and carrying hods at 2s. a-day" (Senior 1854, 134).[12]

Rather than looking to future incomes to repay educational expenditures, Mill presented an awkward and somewhat convoluted argument that workers' wages would rise if they sent their children to school as a matter of course. In the *Principles*, Mill suggested that if common workers fully recognized and acted on their responsibility to educate their children, the "standard of necessary wages" would contain a premium for such expenditures. "But inasmuch as parents do not practise this duty, and do not include education among those necessary expenses which their

12. Senior went further. He developed the hints in Smith as to the investment/capital nature of education. What is now labeled "human capital" he called "personal capital." He considered the return on this capital to be "profit." He estimated that in Britain the returns on such personal capital amounted to about twice the returns on physical capital (Senior 1854, 134).

wages must provide for, therefore the general rate of wages is not high enough to bear those expenses, and they must be borne from some other source" ([1848] 1965, 949). If Mill had gone back to reconsider this argument in light of his suggestion of state-dictated compulsory schooling, he might reasonably have concluded that the need for state subsidies would be slight. Parents forced, with legal threats, to educate their children to state standards would certainly now consider such expenditures "necessities." Under the circumstances Mill's early argument would imply that the "standard of necessary wages" would now include appropriate adjustments, thus unburdening the state from redistribution.

A SPONTANEOUS EDUCATION

Despite Mill's modest aims in the matter of mass formal education, he had great hopes for the effectiveness of even modest levels of literacy to bring a transformation in the working classes. Indeed, he was certain that literacy had already achieved a major change in those classes. The entire "paternal system" with its degrading dependency had run aground when the working classes had been "taught to read, and allowed access to newspapers and political tracts; when dissenting preachers were suffered to go among them, and appeal to their faculties and feelings in opposition to the creeds professed and countenanced by their superiors" ([1848] 1965, 762).[13] While change took time, it was under way and could not be reversed. Mill observed: "[T]here is a spontaneous education going on in the minds of the multitude. . . . [T]he instruction obtained from newspapers and political tracts may not be the most solid kind of instruction, but it is an immense improvement upon none at all" (763). These thoughts picked up on a theme he had put forth in his early essay, *Civilization*. "With respect to knowledge and intelligence" the working classes were "treading upon the heels of their superiors" ([1836] 1977, 125). Newspapers were key to these developments and the chief means of working-class education. "The newspaper carries home the voice of the many to every individual among them; by the newspaper each learns that others are feeling as he feels, and that if he is ready, he will find them also prepared to act upon what they feel. The newspaper is the telegraph which carries the signal throughout the country, and the flag round which it rallies." It

13. Mill also cited the creation of large centralized workplaces and the improvements in transportation as sources of the new spirit in the working class ([1848] 1965).

was the newspapers that "enabled the whole country to combine in that simultaneous energetic demonstration of determined will which carried the Reform Act" (123–125).

The newspapers were abetted by the development of "trade unions" and "institutions for lectures and discussion." All these forces worked to bring the working classes into the national political discussion. In later years Mill took pride in the behavior of the Lancashire cotton workers who had shown "consistent good sense and forbearance" during the cotton shortage created by the American Civil War. These workers were well informed from their newspapers and alert to the true causes of their predicament. Like the "middle classes," the "operatives of the towns" were now situated to participate in all serious political discussions. And the process itself led to their education and maturation.

With the Second Reform Act of 1867 greatly expanding the franchise, the working classes had the power to demand that their interests be considered. The political education that workers had received meant that when they acted they would not advance "the impulse of a mere instinct of leveling." Rather, they would use "the instruments" of "the press, public meetings and associations" to advance the election of as many representatives as possible. And these representatives would now act on "definite political doctrines," doctrines "scientifically studied from the point of view of the working classes" ([1879] 1967, 707).

And the spontaneous education of the working classes was continually deepened by the expanded cooperation demanded by modern production. The scale of industry generated a new cooperative intelligence. Never before had "so many hands been employed at the same time upon the same work in all the principal departments of manufactures and commerce." The nation is "covered with associations. . . . But the greatest novelty of all is the spirit of combination which has grown up among the working classes. The present age has seen the commencement of benefit societies, and they now, as well as the more questionable Trades Unions, overspread the whole country" ([1836] 1977, 125).

Even while he celebrated the largely spontaneous education of the working classes, Mill, more pointedly than most of his contemporaries, fretted over the emergence of a mass culture. Mill advocated a high standard for individual autonomy in his famous essay *On Liberty*. Already he saw the middle classes as tending toward homogeneity and mediocrity, focused too completely on the accumulation of wealth. The working classes might be expected to follow suit. Mill was quite concerned in this respect. The newspapers, the state schools, and the unions all encouraged uniformity, where a vibrant society would depend on the flowering of individuality. Indeed, for Mill, lurking in the awakening of the working classes was the threat of a potentially deadening of the prods to achievement. As civilization progressed, the children of workers were unlikely to obtain an education capable of stimulating them to great originality. And "the energies of the middle classes are almost confined to money-getting, and those of the higher classes are nearly extinct" (130).

Only in his discussion of the stationary state did Mill suggest the possibility of some richer social milieu to follow on the emergence of high wages. Accumulation and progress bring on the stationary state. That state will be characterized by "a well-paid and affluent body of labourers," no extremely rich persons, except those who have "earned and accumulated during a single lifetime" and a "much larger body of persons than at present, not only exempt from the coarser toils, but with sufficient leisure, both physical and mental, from mechanical details, to cultivate freely the graces of life, and afford examples of them to the classes less favourably circumstanced for their growth" ([1848] 1965, 755). With less emphasis on money and wealth, the middle classes would now find themselves in a position to develop "all kinds of mental culture," improve the "Art of Living," and cultivate "the industrial arts."

Thus in the stationary state, a refocused middle class would greatly extend its scope and at the same time act as an "example" to the working classes. The picture is exciting and challenging, but Mill left it somewhat undeveloped. He gave us only this slim hint of the cultural dynamics of the stationary state. He concluded with his warning that these bounties of progress will only be achieved if "in addition to just institutions, the increase of mankind shall be under the deliberate guidance of judicious foresight." Only then "can the conquests made from the powers of nature by the intellect and energy of scientific discoverers, become the common property of the species, and the means of improving and elevating the universal lot" (757). The central and fundamental lesson to be learned by the working classes must be an understanding of its own population growth.

A NOTE ON ROBERT OWEN'S COMMUNITARIAN EDUCATION PLAN

Mill's cautious approach to educational reform can be contrasted with the radical enthusiasm of Robert Owen, who saw schooling as the fundamental ingredient in societal transformation. Owen is famously remembered for his experiments in community building. He strongly argued for cooperative forms of industrial organization. The next chapter turns to Mill's ultimate conversion to the logic of worker cooperatives. But Mill never announced a similar reconsideration of Owen's educational programmatics. This lacuna seems odd, given the cogent argument Owen makes for educational reform in the context of cooperative production.

All of Owen's philosophy was built atop his understanding of education and character formation. Drawing heavily on Enlightenment thought, Owen strongly believed in the plasticity of human nature and the basic equality of human beings. Creating a new system of education was central to his efforts at New Lanark and New Harmony.

Owen readily accepted Bentham's credo. For Owen, "That government is the best, which in practice produces the greatest happiness to the greatest number; including those who govern, and those who obey" (Owen 1817, 129). Key to achieving such an end was the refashioning of childhood education in a manner designed to inculcate rationality and community feeling. Owen's approach to education anticipated much of the progressive school movement of the twentieth century. Owen sought to involve children in their education to render "all their instruction a pleasure and delight to them." This achieved, the children would be "more anxious for the hour of school-time to arrive than to end." In such an environment they would "make a rapid progress" (56).

Where classical economists fretted over subsidizing education, Owen had no misgivings about advocating free elementary schooling for all children. In this respect he fully anticipated the logic of the common school movement later in the nineteenth century. By contrast, Mill seems to have missed a rather obvious extension of his own reform agenda.

CHAPTER 9

Cooperatives, Unions, and Economic Democracy

If Mill looked to the spread of education to destroy the dependency of the working classes on unthinking habit, religion, and base instincts, he built his hopes for the material and psychological independence of workers on the emergence of a substantive cooperative movement. As education raised workers' capacities and expectations, they would be increasingly unsuited for the mindless subservience of the employment relationship. Mill's most radical response to the excesses of laissez-faire capitalism projected the replacement of the capitalist firm with the cooperative enterprise. Mill was convinced that such a transition could not be obtained overnight. It would take time and effort. It would be built on the expanding capacities of the mass of workers. As savings accumulated, as profit rates fell, as the economy moved toward the stationary state, Mill anticipated the reconstruction of the workplace—from a locus of mind-deadening exploitation to a rational and democratic institution well fitted for free, educated workers. Such a transition was at the very heart of Mill's radical conception of progress.[1]

1. Most interpretations of Mill's program largely ignore the key role of cooperatives in his thinking about the future. A major exception is Abram Harris in his essay, "John Stuart Mill's Theory of Progress" (Harris 1956), where Harris recognized the importance of cooperatives to Mill's sense of progress. Still, Harris emphasizes the subjective elements in Mill's theory of progress, rather than the material ones rooted in Mill's understanding of classical economics. Thus, Harris argued that for Mill, "progress consists primarily in the development of man's moral and intellectual capacities" (163). Another important exception is Wendy Donner's 1991 sympathetic treatment of Mill's discussion of cooperatives as an element in economic democracy.

OWEN'S BLUEPRINT

Of course, Mill was not the first to articulate the promise of cooperatives. European history was scattered with plans for agricultural cooperatives. On the continent, the Anabaptist Hutterites had experimented with communal ownership starting in the sixteenth century. In England, the basic idea of agrarian communalism extended back at least to the Diggers at the time of its civil war.

While these historical precedents were well known to Mill, much more relevant to the present discussion were the works of Robert Owen and his associates. Mill had considerable direct experience debating various representatives of the Owenite position. Owen's plan for cooperatives was based on his own experiments at New Lanark in the first years of the nineteenth century. There Owen, a prosperous philanthropist and early follower of Jeremy Bentham, had established a progressive system of child care and education, as well as an attractive working environment. But New Lanark was not a cooperative. It was a traditionally organized factory that regularly showed a profit.

Owen's plans for cooperatives were originally put forth as an alternative to the Poor Laws, but over time he saw the cooperative form as desirable in and of itself. "There is but one mode by which man can possess in perpetuity all the happiness which his nature is capable of enjoying,—that is by the union and co-operation of *all* for the benefit of *each*" (Owen 1830, 42). Owen was convinced that worker cooperatives would greatly enhance productivity.

Owen was quite specific on the character he wished to impose on cooperative communities. The basic plan as described in Owen's draft of a constitution in 1821 involved a group of 500 to 2,000 people living in a village surrounded by agricultural lands. This size was picked so as "to avoid . . . the evils and inconveniences resulting from the congregation of mankind into large masses" and yet "preserve that limit, below which the full benefit of combination could not be attained" (Owen [1821] 1825, 161). The capital for the enterprise was to be privately subscribed. At the initiation of the community it would be governed by a committee dominated by major capital contributors, those advancing 100 pounds or more. Once the initial subscribers were repaid, the committee was to be elected at large from those forty to fifty years old (162).

At the heart of the community was to be a manufactory. Workers would generally split their work time between manufacturing and agriculture. Over time, supervisors would be drawn from the community's own population, although initially some might be hired from outside as needed. Each member of the community "shall be equally supplied with the necessaries and comforts of life" (167). Once all the debts of the community were paid, any surplus was to be applied to establishing a second community. While women were to take on a number of activities based on gender, Owen argued that the positive atmosphere and attention to education characteristic of the community would reduce greatly the miseries often found in the domestic lives of the poor.

Owen based his general plan on his own reading of human psychology as outlined in his *A New View of Society*, subtitled: *Essays on the Formation of Human Character, Preparatory to the Development of a Plan for Gradually Ameliorating the Condition of Mankind.* Owen was sure that individual psychology was well attuned with fundamental utilitarian principles. Specifically, he held: "The happiness of self clearly understood and uniformly practiced . . . can only be attained by conduct that must promote the happiness of the community" (1817, 22).

Proper education was capable of shaping the character of plastic and willing children. With care and sympathy all children could be brought to value reason. A key educational message would be an understanding of the formation of personal character, so that by adulthood individuals would come to appreciate the irrationality and "partial insanities" of others as the product of destructive and misdirected education in childhood. The point was not to wipe out individuality. Owen acknowledged that variety was characteristic of nature and would remain common among people. But in healthy individuals the ability to reason was universal. The point, then, was to build individuals capable of appreciating their common interest in reason and sympathy. [2]

Because of his emphasis on education, Owen admitted that a period of transition would be necessary to build a fully "sane" population. This period would roughly match the time necessary to allow the accumulation of the community's basic capital. Together, then, it would take about a generation for the community to achieve its basic independence.

A RANGE OF PLANS

Jeremy Bentham was attracted by Owen's psychological speculations and his educational schemes. Bentham became an investor in New Lanark. Over time the two men differed regarding Owen's broader plans

2. While supportive of the education experiments of Lancaster and others, Owen considered them too focused on methods and not directed to the process of character formation.

for worker cooperatives. The liberal Bentham found the replacement of private enterprise with collective organization too radical for his tastes. But these plans, precisely because they promised to render the whole product to the laborer who produced it, appealed strongly to the cadre of Ricardian socialists that had developed on the left wing of the new science of political economy. William Thompson of Cork, Ireland, might just as easily be called a Benthamite socialist, since he was a strong supporter of the utilitarian coda and a personal friend of Bentham. Thompson was also committed to Owen's philosophy and was known to Mill as an advocate of Owenite cooperatives. As noted above, the two had engaged in an extended debate on the topic, with Mill taking the negative position. On his death Thompson left his estates in Ireland to the establishment of agricultural cooperatives.

Shortly after his debates with Mill, Thompson developed the theme of cooperatives in a volume entitled *Labour Rewarded. The Claims of Labor and Capital Conciliated: or How to Secure to Labor the Whole Products of its Exertions* ([1827] 1969). Presumably the argument of this tract reproduces much of the content of Thompson's side of those earlier debates. It also addressed the argument in support of trade unions advanced by Thomas Hodgskin in his pamphlet *Labour Defended against the Claims of Capital or the Unproductiveness of Capital proved with Reference to the Present Combinations amongst Journeymen* (Hodgskin [1825] 1963).

Thompson viewed the organization of cooperatives as "a *radical*, a *permanent* cure of the evils that afflict society" (Thompson [1827] 1969, v). He credited Owen for first advancing a plan to use cooperatives as an alternative to poor relief and a response to the periodic crises associated with capitalism. Like Owen he saw cooperatives as the basic building block of an alternative system of economic organization. Thompson argued that cooperatives would emerge more or less organically from the trade unions. Far better than supporting unemployed members in dependency was to put them to work in collectively owned productive establishments. These cooperatives would converge over time on the model proposed by Owen—that is, combinations of manufactories with agricultural activities in relatively compact communities.

In presenting his case Thompson explicitly reviewed a list of "the means recommended by political economists and political moralists, to improve the situation of the industrious classes" (vii). The list is a long one, including extension of the franchise, expanded education, free trade, and insurance schemes. Thompson found all of these to be well-meaning palliative, but not basic solutions. All were incapable of addressing the central question of ensuring workers the whole product of their labors.

Toward the end of the list Thompson addressed the usefulness of efforts to control population, efforts so central to J. S. Mill's radical program. The argument was simple. If skilled industrial workers limit their family size, then capitalists will recruit labor from the unskilled. If the unskilled industrial workers limit their family size, the capitalists will recruit labor from the agricultural workforce. If agricultural workers limit their family size, then the capitalists will recruit labor from Ireland. If all workers in England, Scotland, and Ireland limit their family size, then capitalists will smuggle labor in from abroad. And if laws are passed to limit immigration, then capitalists will simply move their capital abroad (69–73). Thompson made this last argument in a particularly modern form. If the capitalist still saw anywhere in the world relatively cheap sources of labor, what would he do?

> Would he detain his capital at home, generously to reward the prudential laborers for raising against him the price of their labor above the surrounding level? Or, would he use the language of competitive benevolence, and compassionate the neighbouring lowly-remunerated industrious, and transfer for the employment of their skill, that capital which, he would say, would be soon swallowed up by the extravagant claims of the prudential checkers of population? While capital is possessed by one man, and labor alone, without any of the means of rendering it productive, is possessed by the industrious, it will ever be thus. (73)

Thompson wrestled with a major point here. Not only did he provide a thoughtful critique of Mill's argument for population control and high wages in one country, but he (perhaps unknowingly) provided ammunition for seriously qualifying Adam Smith's definitional invisible-hand argument. Smith had explicitly assumed in that famous passage that domestic capital would avoid moving abroad because of capitalists' lack of familiarity with foreign governments, customs, and manners. The heightened uncertainty worked to keep capital at home.[3] Thompson's argument quite reasonably in an increasingly global economy assumed just the opposite—that is, domestic capital will be powerfully attracted by low wages abroad. Given that Smith was in broad agreement with the utilitarian criterion, and more particularly with the importance of workers' wage levels, the resulting qualification must be viewed as seriously damaging.

3. Ricardo had made a very similar argument. Both are discussed in Persky (1989).

At root, Thompson traced the present "monstrous systems of force, fraud, and competition" to "the fatal disseverance of capital from labor and skill, and the consequent ignorance of the industrious." The result had been "enormous inequalities of wealth, the parents of almost all the crimes and vices that desolate society." The solution was straightforward: capital and labor must be reunited. Only when workers become "capitalist laborers" in the context of self-financing co-operatives capable of achieving economies of scale and scientific production will they achieve the goal of guaranteeing to themselves the entire product of their labor.

As the industrial revolution matured in the first half of the nineteenth century, doubts about the relationship between capital and labor were not limited to the socialist left. Where the radicals Owen and Thompson advocated full worker cooperatives, more mainstream commentators worried that manufacturing workers lacked incentives and were developing an almost open hostility to their employers. While the new forces of production unleashed by the industrial revolution were increasingly identifiable, the most appropriate production relations for governing these forces were still open to serious debate, even among those in the center. If radicals started from ideas about justice, a reform-minded technocrat like Charles Babbage started from ideas about efficiency.

Babbage came from a wealthy family and had been educated at Cambridge, where he eventually became a professor of mathematics. The inventor of the difference engine, generally credited as the precursor to mechanical computers, Babbage had a longstanding interest in the entire range of technological innovations being introduced in industry. In his influential treatise *On the Economy of Machinery and Manufacturing*, Babbage included a chapter on "A New System of Manufacturing." Babbage was convinced from his "own observation" that "the prosperity and success of the master manufacturer is essential to the welfare of the workman." Yet he feared that the worker was not rewarded "in proportion to the extent to which he contributes." Babbage's goal, then, was to find a new "mode of payment" that allowed each worker to "derive advantage from the success of the whole" ([1835] 1963, 251).

In searching for such a system Babbage considered in some detail a range of profitsharing plans, starting with contracting payment schemes in the mines of Cornwall. Babbage's own plan was a system of profitsharing in relatively small production units. Skilled workers would subscribe a modest amount of capital to the scheme along with larger sums raised from small master manufacturers. Then, in normal times workers would expect to receive half their remuneration as straight wages and half as profit shares. Moreover, any technological improvements invented by workers were to command a substantial bonus once they were proven in practice.

Babbage certainly didn't see his scheme as a solution to employment for the unskilled and marginal workers. He counted as an advantage of his system that workers would insist that their fellows be "of high character and qualifications ... respectable and skillful" (257). In slow periods, workers wouldn't be laid off, but would receive payment from a reserve fund and devote their time to the repair and improvement of tools with an eye to "facilitating future production." Babbage was confident that while the new system would begin with lower than average returns to capital, its enhanced productivity would eventually lead to higher returns. He also expected that the basic format of profitsharing would reduce any tendency among the workers to seek to combine in unions—efforts he considered wasteful.

In fact, Babbage's plan was a mixture of profitsharing and cooperative organization. He clearly thought this structure capable of prospering in competitive markets. He was unclear, however, as to the extent to which it would actually replace larger factories. Babbage devoted only ten pages to the chapter in question and left the matter with no other discussion. Although pregnant with possibilities, Babbage's scheme appears to have generated no practical developments.

THE FRENCH

Mill was aware of the cooperative ideas of Owen, Thompson, and Babbage. But he was most strongly influenced by plans being generated across the channel in France. The French Revolution of 1848 brought forth a range of real-world experiments with worker cooperatives. These efforts had been prompted by the writings of Louis Blanc, a French socialist and advocate of cooperatives. Blanc traced his central concept of *droit au travail* to Saint-Simon, but his system of industrial structure was less Simonean nationalization and much closer to that of Owen and Thompson. Although Blanc's plan gave to the state the primary role for raising capital for the "*social ateliers*," after the first year of operation these workshops were to be governed by the voting of worker-members. The government, then, would retire from direct control (Blanc [1840] 1911, 51–55).[4] Blanc expected the workers to voluntarily adopt some form of communal living. The ateliers were allowed to contract for loans from capitalists, but were not allowed to promise them any share of the association's profits. Blanc was confident that the social ateliers would prove successful in competition with private firms because of their great advantage in motivating their workforces.

4. Blanc did delegate to the government the responsibility of regulating the creation of new industrial ateliers and guaranteeing that no industry expand beyond the need for its products.

At the height of the 1848 Revolution, plans were implemented for the government's establishing national workshops. The government saw these workshops as an exercise in placating the radical workers and lent less than full-hearted support. Blanc was excluded from the administration of the cooperatives. For the most part the government-initiated workshops were failures (7). However, a number of independent cooperatives launched in this period prospered, and their success greatly impressed Mill.

MILL'S EARLY ARGUMENTS AGAINST COOPERATIVES

Mill's early ideas on cooperatives are hard to specify. His most extended comments on the subject are contained in his notes for the series of debates with Thompson at the Co-Operative Society of the Owenites. Since Mill was taking the negative side of the debate, these notes are very much focused on the shortcomings of cooperative organization. More generally this period in the mid-1820s corresponds well to that Mill described in his *Autobiography* as "the days of my most extreme Benthamism." At that time he had accepted the "old school of political economists" and their understanding that there was little room for "fundamental improvement in social arrangements." By his own report, he then "reckoned chimerical" any efforts to remove the injustice "involved in the fact that some are born to riches and the vast majority to poverty." He hoped only that education and "voluntary restraint" on population might make "the portion of the poor . . . more tolerable" ([1873] 1981, 238). Given this worldview, Mill most likely took his debating points against the Owenites quite seriously.

Mill started with an introductory comment to the effect that he had the highest respect for Robert Owen. Despite that, he asserted that Owen's theory was "founded on mistaken views of human nature and of the course of human affairs" (Mill 1988, 308–309). Although Owen and his supporters sought "the greatest happiness of the greatest number," their system would not advance that end, but frustrate it.

One of Mill's first arguments was that for all the talk of profit and rent, those income streams accounted for only a small portion of the country's total produce. He estimated their share at no more than 10 percent (315).[5] Under the circumstances then, the cooperatives claiming these incomes for their members could make only a modest improvement in their living

5. I have not been able to locate the source of this estimate, but it seems even by modern standards to be quite low.

standards. Mill then went on to list four major drawbacks of the cooperative system as laid out by Thompson in the series of debates:

1. By separating labor from subsistence, cooperatives must reduce incentives and efforts. Even when well educated, most men "love themselves better than they love the community of which they are members" (320).
2. The cooperative system makes inadequate provision for the management of production. "It is a well known proverb, "What is every body's business is nobody's business" (320).
3. The cooperative system is a "system of universal regulation." Mill asserted that he is "not one of those, who set up liberty as an idol" and he is "willing to go farther than most people in regulating and controlling when there is a special advantage to be obtained by regulation and control." But the cooperative system imposes regulation and control even where it has no advantage (321).
4. Mill objected to the capital expense of 900 million sterling, presumably a figure quoted by Thompson in the debate. Mill observed that such a figure would be sufficient to give an excellent education of every person in Great Britain (321).

Mill went on to argue that if cooperatives were begun in earnest, their expansion must in the short run reduce the capital available for workers left in the competitive sector. The first step toward raising the welfare of all workers remained the control of population growth and, if necessary, the limitation of immigration.

MILL'S RADICAL CASE FOR COOPERATIVES

Mill's early arguments in his debate against Thompson and the Owenites were cast in a classical liberal form, almost triumphalist in nature. Thompson clearly took them seriously and attempted to answer them in his own book. It is not clear what effect those responses had on Mill. Blanc and the events in France in the Revolution of 1848 very likely had a greater impact. In any case, by the time Mill wrote the *Principles* he was strongly supportive of workers' cooperatives. The key text, here, is Mill's famous chapter "On the Probable Futurity of the Labouring Classes" from Book IV of the *Principles*. It is a strikingly radical essay.[6]

6. It should be noted that in his autobiography Mill gave generous credit for this chapter to his wife Harriet Taylor (Mill [1873] 1981, 255).

Mill started by drawing a contrast between paternalist protection and independence. He explicitly rejected the efforts by Carlyle and others to romanticize the past. If there ever was a time that the upper classes offered meaningful protection to the masses, that time had long past. Looking forward to a new set of social relations to replace the highly unsatisfactory relation of worker and capitalist employer, progress demands not "dependence" but "self-dependence" ([1848] 1965, 759).

Despite his conviction on this matter, Mill was surprisingly gentle, and even eloquent, in his requiem for the virtues of feudal society. Asserting that the facts of history can't support the romantic idealization of such a society, he noted that the "feelings" surrounding that idealization are real and powerful. They form a "seductive" alternative to the "repulsive idea" of a society dominated only by the weak relations of the market place. The protective ideal generates feelings of "strong personal attachments and disinterested self-devotion."

> [I]n an age of lawless violence and general hardness and roughness of manners, in which life is beset with dangers and sufferings at every step . . .—a generous giving of protection, and a grateful receiving of it, are the strongest ties which connect human beings; the feelings arising from that relation are their warmest feelings; all the enthusiasm and tenderness of the most sensitive natures gather round it; loyalty on the one part and chivalry on the other are principles exalted into passions. (760).

But as deep as these feelings run, they lose their base in a society where violence has been checked and where civil protections are the rule. Ironically, in the modern world the worst threats to individuals arise precisely from the most dependent relations, such as wife battery and child abuse.

Again, Mill denied that the idealization ever held widely. In a condemnation worthy of Marx or Engels, Mill asserted: "All privileged and powerful classes, as such, have used their power in the interest of their own selfishness, and have indulged their self-importance in despising, and not in lovingly caring for, those who were, in their estimation, degraded, by being under the necessity of working for their benefit." While men can change, the softening of the ruling classes toward their charges will not likely be accomplished before the lower classes will achieve the capacity to govern themselves (760).

The readiness of the working classes to take control of their own lives had come about as they achieved a modicum of literacy, began to read "newspapers and political tracts," heard the preachings of dissenters, moved ever more freely from place to place, sought political representation and been "brought together in numbers, to work socially under the same roof" (762). It was too late to turn around the direction of progress in favor of dependency and protection.

Mill explored at least three alternatives to the traditional relationship between capital and labor: independent proprietors, profitsharing, and cooperatives. He strongly felt that cooperatives were the most likely to succeed, the most productive, and the most appropriate to the general welfare. The radical argument builds on a materialist understanding of progress.

Independent Proprietors

Mill starts with the possibilities of independent proprietorship. He acknowledges that only a few chapters earlier in the *Principles* he had supported just such institutions as a fundamental and useful reform in the context of the Irish agrarian economy.[7] But that economy was rude and backward. In the modern economy of Britain the advantages of large-scale production were obvious. Nowhere does Mill apply the utilitarian argument more forcefully. Nowhere does he mix utilitarianism and materialism more explicitly. Nowhere is the promise of accumulation and progress more clear.

> [A] people who have once adopted the large system of production, either in manufactures or in agriculture, are not likely to recede from it; and when population is kept in due proportion to the means of support, it is not desirable that they should. Labour is unquestionably more productive on the system of large industrial enterprises; the produce, if not greater absolutely, is greater in proportion to the labour employed: the same number of persons can be supported equally well with less toil and greater leisure; which will be wholly an advantage, as soon as civilization and improvement have so far advanced, that what is a benefit to the whole shall be a benefit to each individual composing it. (768)

It would be a grave mistake, counter to the underlying direction of progress, to give up these major gains of "the large system of production."

Mill adds to this economic argument two "moral" arguments. First, petty proprietorships are likely to be patriarchal. The welfare of women argues strongly against enshrining the tyranny inherent in patriarchal forms. Second, if "true justice and equality are desired, association, not

7. We observed this support in Mill's discussion of land reform in chapter 5.

isolation, of interests is the school in which these excellences are nurtured." The goal is not "to place human beings in a condition in which they will be able to do without one another, but to enable them to work with or for one another in relations not involving dependence" (768). The vision borders on millennial: a world in which association in production brings forward individuals' best efforts in common pursuit. And Mill tells us that progress is making this vision a real possibility.

Profitsharing and Unions

In its weaker manifestation, association will take the form of profitsharing between workers and capitalists. Mill considers in some detail the subcontracting arrangements that Babbage had so glowingly described in mining and fishing enterprises. And he praised Babbage for suggesting that such systems could be applied productively to manufacturing. In the same vein, Mill praises various experiments undertaken in France by M. Leclaire.

Conceivably, profitsharing schemes might be advanced by the owners themselves either out of sympathy with the workers or for the purpose of building incentives. But Mill expresses no optimism on this score. Rather he argues that profit sharing, if and when it comes will be generated as a central demand of unionized workers. Largely for this reason Mill endorses unions and strongly opposes moves to criminalize them.

Mill includes his most extensive discussion of unions as part of his chapter on inappropriate overreaching of government. Mill for the most part reassures his readers that unions and strikes will generally be unsuccessful. But he argues that they should not be illegal since such legislation only convinces workers that futile activities might be useful if they were allowed. This conclusion strengthens the delusions of the working classes.

That said, Mill goes on to suggest that unions and strikes are the only practical way that workers can discover the true market price for their labor. Even if a united strike can only achieve the wage dictated by supply and demand, a worker on his or her own can hardly ever know the level of the true market-clearing wage. Harking back to Adam Smith's discussion of "higgling" in the market, Mill observes that poor workers dealing with rich employers will inevitably be paid less than "the demand for their labour would justify, unless, in vernacular phrase, they stood out for it." And he continues, "[H]ow can they stand out for terms without organized concert? What chance would any labourer have, who struck singly for an advance of wages? How could he even know whether the state of the market admitted of a rise, except by consultation with his fellows, naturally leading to concerted action?" (932). Trade unions are not "a hindrance to a free market for labour" but, rather, are "the necessary instrumentality of that free market."[8]

Mill does not stop with the argument that unions facilitate the determination of market wages. In what must have struck some of his readers as a major shift in position Mill introduces a more radical proposition. Citing Henry Fawcett as a source, Mill observes that in the "more intelligent trades" unions are capable of predicting in advance the likely success or failure of a strike for wages. "The workmen are now nearly as well informed as the master, of the state of the market for his commodities; they can calculate his gains and his expenses, they know when his trade is or is not prosperous, and only when it is, are they ever again likely to strike for higher wages." The employer understands these realities and hence will likely capitulate when the union is actually ready to strike. "The tendency, therefore, of this state of things is to make a rise of wages in any particular trade usually consequent upon a rise of profits, which, as Mr. Fawcett observes, is a commencement of that regular participation of the labourers in the profits derived from their labour, every tendency to which . . . it is so important to encourage, since to it we have chiefly to look for any radical improvement in the social and economical relations between labour and capital" (933). Intelligent unionism provides a path toward profitsharing.

The basic argument here can only make sense in the context of progress involving capital accumulation, population control, and an expanded demand for labor. In this version of the stationary state, trade unions act as a democratic institutional mechanism to channel workers' intelligence and energy into an effective partnership with capital.

Cooperatives

Mill sees profitsharing as an attractive improvement over the status quo. But profitsharing is essentially only a waystation toward fuller association. Profitsharing still leaves workers with no direct say or control over their workplace. It leaves the "capitalist as chief, and workpeople without a voice in the management." Mill declared that if progress was to continue, it must inevitably lead to full association in cooperatives, "on terms of

8. Again this position is consistent with Mill's general approach to the wage-fund theory both before and after his "recantation." See Chapter 5, note 14, above.

equality, collectively owning the capital with which they carry on their operation, and working under managers elected and removable by themselves" (1848 [1965] 775).

We have already seen in Mill's 1825 debates with Thompson that the young Mill was highly dubious of the possibilities of cooperatives. However, by 1834 he was acknowledging the logic, if not the practicability, of producer cooperatives. In particular, at that time, Mill looked positively on trade union experiments with cooperative production. Instead of investing laborers' savings in strike funds to support workers in idleness, Mill was encouraged that some unions directed their savings toward production. He asserted, "The doctrine of the Trades' Unions now is, that when they resolve upon a strike, their course must not be to cease working, but to work on their own account. . . . Possessing the necessary funds, the labourers mean to become capitalists, and to make actual trial of the difficulties of a joint management." Should these experiments succeed, they would achieve "one of the most important fruits of modern civilization, the demonstrated possibility of arrangements of society under which the whole produce of labour would belong exclusively to the labourers" ([1834] 1982, 190).

But Mill in 1834 wasn't optimistic that such cooperatives could succeed. At that time he suspected workers would discover "that the attempt to realize (otherwise than with the slow progress of human improvement) the cooperative principle as applied to the production of wealth, causes so much waste of labour in the intricate business of management and check, and such a relaxation of the intensity of individual exertion, that under the fairest possible distribution there is a smaller share for each, than falls or might fall to the lot even of the most scantily remunerated, under the present arrangements" (191).

Mill's understanding of the promise of cooperatives was turning. Very likely he was responding to arguments being made by Harriet Taylor, who from the early 1830s was becoming a major force in his life. But Mill's full shift toward seeing the cooperative as central to the future of the industrial economy waited on the French Revolution of 1848. In the *Principles,* he looked with great admiration on the French cooperative movement established in that turmoil. The French cooperatives sought to free workers "from the necessity of paying, out of the produce of their industry, a heavy tribute for the use of capital . . . not by robbing the capitalists of what they or their predecessors had acquired by labour and preserved by economy, but by honestly acquiring capital for themselves" ([1848] 1965, 775).

Mill took the experiences of 1848 as a significant test of the viability of cooperatives. Starting with the 1852 edition of the *Principles,* he drew heavily on the testimony of Henri Robert Feugueray, an editor of *La Revue Nationale* and a participant in the government efforts of the time. Mill noted that "excluding all the instances of failure, there exist, or existed a short time ago, upwards of a hundred successful, and many eminently prosperous, associations of operatives in Paris alone, besides a considerable number in the departments" (776).

Mill relates the experience of a number of workers' associations that struggled to accumulate their basic capital through discipline and privation. He takes their story as providing a working guide to the future of cooperatives. Small loans from other workers also provided support, but larger loans from the government, Mill thought, are potentially dangerous because they were less carefully managed. On occasion such loans can actually result in failure. When cooperatives are well run, accumulation becomes a regular claim on their incomes. While new members share in the profits generated from previous investments, those leaving the cooperative should be able to take no portion of its capital with them.

Mill moved on to consider the successes of the Rochdale consumer cooperatives and their backward integration into production. By the 1865 edition of the *Principles*, Mill claimed the cooperative movement to be "one of the recognized elements in the progressive movement of the age" (790). Consumer cooperatives promised higher productivity because they keep employment to the minimum needed to effectively distribute the products in question. The result is to free labor for other more directly productive tasks.

More generally, all cooperative enterprises benefit from setting free the workers' initiative and creativity. Instead of a hostile workplace marking the conflict between classes, a place where workers sought to provide the minimum required, the cooperative establishment presents a scene of healthy comradery and friendly rivalry focused on the common purpose. By the 1860s Mill was convinced that the productivity gains of cooperatives would allow them to compete with and best the private establishments. While in the short run the middle ground of profitsharing may demonstrate advantages derived from decisive centralized decision making, over time full-fledged cooperatives would win out. Over time workers will insist on these associations.

Eventually "owners of capital would gradually find it to their advantage . . . to lend their capital to the associations." Interest rates would continue to fall and in the end capitalists might well trade their capital for "terminable annuities." At such a point, "the existing accumulations of capital might honestly, and by a kind of spontaneous process, become . . . the joint property of all who participate in their productive employment." Still within a market context,[9] the cooperative form would thus replace existing capitalist enterprises. Here is the new society toward which the transitional period of laissez-faire capitalism was headed. The contemplated "transformation" will fully meet the utilitarian criterion for the greatest happiness of the greatest number. "[A]ssuming that both sexes participate equally in the rights and in the government of the association(s)," the new cooperatives "would be the nearest approach to social justice, and the most beneficial ordering of industrial affairs for the universal good, which it is possible at present to foresee." This is Mill's fullest statement of the radical program to refashion the institutions of production (793–794).

The projection of a system of workers' cooperatives makes coherent Mill's radical reform agenda. Establishing such a system requires substantial energy applied by workers just as the older system is reaching its limits. Against the background of capital accumulation and the coming of the stationary state, the key reforms in the franchise, population control, inheritance, land rights, and education prepare the working classes for their role in organizing a new mode of production. Ultimately, a productive system built around worker cooperatives constitutes the radical promise of progress, the greatest happiness of the greatest number.

A NOTE ON MILL AND SOCIALISM

Mill's radical endorsement of cooperatives as a progressive alternative to capitalist organization leads naturally to questions of his views on socialism more generally. The simplest and most obvious starting point for such an inquiry is the fact that in his *Autobiography* he flatly asserted that by the 1850s he and his new wife Harriet Taylor Mill were best described as "socialists." At that point they held an "ideal of ultimate improvement" that "went far beyond Democracy, and would class us decidedly under the general designation of Socialists" ([1873] 1981, 238).

There can be little doubt that Harriet Taylor had considerable influence on Mill starting in the 1830s. She was very much a supporter of Owen and presumably won Mill over to many of Owen's views on cooperatives. From even earlier, however, Mill had been drawn to the ideas of the French socialists, particularly those of Saint-Simon. His own reading of the first edition (1848) of his *Principles* was that in it "the difficulties of Socialism

9. Mill is explicit on this point. Once population is no longer outrunning accumulation, all forms of competition benefit workers. The alternative to competition is monopoly and monopoly is a tax of the indolent on the productive.

were stated so strongly, that the tone was on the whole that of opposition to it." But he continued: "In the year or two which followed, much time was given to the study of the best Socialistic writers on the Continent, and to meditation and discussion (240)." Presumably not a few of these discussions were with Harriet Taylor. "The result was that most of what had been written on the subject in the first edition was cancelled, and replaced by arguments and reflexions which represent a more advanced opinion." The "more advanced opinion" was his new socialism, shared now with his wife as he and Harriet Taylor were wed in 1851, two years after the death of her husband.

But of what exactly did Mill's socialism consist? Clearly he viewed his endorsement of workers' cooperatives as a component, perhaps the chief component, of his socialism. Referring to himself and his wife, Mill stated that they, "welcomed with the greatest pleasure and interest all socialistic experiments by select individuals (such as the Cooperative Societies), which, whether they succeeded or failed, could not but operate as a most useful education of those who took part in them" (241).

In 1879 Helen Taylor, Harriet Taylor's daughter brought forward in the *Fortnightly Review* a series of Mill's essays on socialism. These had been written in 1869 and presumably represented Mill's final thoughts on the subject. In these essays Mill continued the identification of cooperatives with socialism. In particular, he argued that the cooperative movement "has the great advantage that it can be brought into operation progressively, and can prove its capabilities by trial." Expanding on its successes as workers acquired greater education, "It need not, and in the natural order of things would not, become an engine of subversion until it had shown itself capable of being also a means of reconstruction" ([1879] 1967, 737).

At the same time, Mill was sure that he had no sympathy for "that tyranny of society over the individual which most Socialistic systems are supposed to involve," ([1873] 1981, 238). Mill contrasted the evolutionary character of cooperative socialism with what he called "revolutionary socialism." Comparing its advocates to Robespierre and Saint-Just, Mill observed that this form of socialism aiming to destroy the current system at a "single stroke" required a "serene confidence in their own wisdom on the one hand and a recklessness of other people's sufferings on the other." However, he acknowledged that revolutionary socialism had gained popularity at least on the continent because it promised to accomplish its aims not over an indefinite future, but at once in the lifetime of its followers. ([1879] 1967, 737).

At root, Mill identified revolutionary socialism as an effort to conduct "the whole industry of a country by direction from a single center." Such a goal he judged "obviously chimerical." No one had advanced any serious blueprint for centralized planning. Mill predicted that ad hoc efforts would result in a helter-skelter decentralization. Unlike carefully planned cooperatives, these units would not be made up of motivated participants, but would necessarily include "all the malefactors," "all the idlest and most vicious," "the most incapable of steady industry," and the "majority who . . . are profoundly demoralized." The result would inevitably be a "disastrous failure." Revolutionary socialists harbored a "very excusable hatred of existing evils." And they might succeed in destroying the old system. But that would provide little solace in the face of the ensuing chaos, a "state of nature where every man is enemy to every man" (749).

Bentham had asserted that under liberal capitalism the plight of the poorest was better than in a state of nature. Mill, however, accepted that the worst off in the current world are hardly better off than they would be under a state of nature. He was no defender of the status quo. Unlike Bentham, Mill was optimistic that ultimately progress can make, and historically is destined to make, fundamental changes. But these changes will necessarily take time. The chaos following on an immediate socialist revolution would undue all the work of progress and leave no hope for improvement.

These dire predictions for revolutionary socialism reinforced Mill's conviction that any new system must be approached over time through experimentation in a market context. The market provided an excellent environment for testing new institutions. An evolutionary approach also allowed time for the further education of the masses. Members of cooperatives must achieve "a high standard of both moral and intellectual education." The first is required "to qualify them for doing their part honestly and energetically . . . under no inducement but their share in the general interest of the association." The second follows from the need to estimate "distant interests . . . sufficiently at least to be able to discriminate good counsel from bad" (746). That said, Mill asserts that it is possible to achieve such a standard of "every person in the nation." But achieving such an endpoint is necessarily slow. Especially with respect to the moral education necessary for communal life, the capitalist system is highly demoralizing. Hence, the project of education is best carried out in cooperatives themselves as they expand over time. Mill was cautiously optimistic about the promise of this evolutionary process. But he was equally sure that "to force unprepared populations into Communist societies, even if a political revolution gave the power to make such an attempt, would end in disappointment" (746).

We know that Mill was quite hostile to notions of socialist central planning. However, it is less clear what his attitude would be to the type of social democratic/welfare states that emerged in northern Europe after the Second World War. The promise of cooperatives was precisely that the national government would not be required to engage in substantial direct redistribution. Mill was very cautious as to the use of taxation to achieve greater income equality. He hoped workers could reach both prosperity and security without requiring the coercive force of the central government. Thus, Mill was, on the one hand, more radical than the social democrats, since he looked forward to a genuinely new mode of production. Indeed, it is his commitment to worker cooperatives that makes Mill's reform agenda a coherent whole. But on the other hand, Mill's timidity with respect to using the taxing power, must strike social democrats as an unfortunate residue of his classical liberal origins.[10]

A social democratic critique can easily miss the radicalism of Mill's position. In this respect it borders on a mainstream view that sees Mill as genuinely concerned with the inequities generated by laissez-faire capitalism, but because of his deep mistrust of government, willing to endorse that system as a more or less permanent second-best solution.[11] Both of these views are at odds with the position being taken in this book—that is, that the mature Mill accepted laissez-faire capitalism only as a transitional mode of production.

Mill standing at the very beginnings of modern radicalism is hopeful with respect to the promise of progress. Wary of the evils of governmental regimentation he advanced a broad radical program for the working classes, a program of cooperative experimentation, education, population control, and emancipation for women. He anticipated that workers could begin to implement this program largely on their own. Government could be supportive in a number of ways, but is neither the center of the effort nor the driving force. In effect, Mill asserted that the freedom achieved and expanded through the political process is sufficient to begin a new transformation of the economy and society from the bottom up. Mill's mixture of political economy and direct action, drawing on Enlightenment notions, utilitarian standards and popular enthusiasms, marks the starting point of modern analytical radicalism.

10. A contrast with the recent writings of Thomas Piketty (2014) suggests itself. While Piketty is eager to tax capital, he fails to address Mill's (and Marx's) central concern with the alienation of the modern workplace.

11. See for example the treatment of Mill in Medema (2009).

PART III

Echoes

CHAPTER 10

Marx and Mill

Karl Marx and John Stuart Mill were contemporaries. Marx moved to Britain from the continent in 1849, one year after Mill published the first edition of his *Principles*. At that point Marx was thirty-one and Mill was forty-three. They would both live in London for the rest of their lives, overlapping for almost a quarter of a century.

It is perhaps understandable that Mill has little to say about Marx. Marx's chief classical economic work, *Capital*, volume I, wasn't published until 1867 and then in German. Mill did not read German. An English translation didn't appear until 1887, some fourteen years after Mill's death in 1873.[1] Still, Mill did seem at least peripherally aware of Marx. In particular, in a fragment of a letter he wrote to the general council of the International Working Men's Association (First International), Mill gave an enthusiastic endorsement to a speech Marx had made to the association on the Franco-Prussian War.[2] Mill also followed the general developments in the association, and knew personally several of the British representatives. However, he judged the representatives from the continent as too eager to use violence and to expand state power. These matters are briefly discussed in a letter to George Brandes, dated March 4, 1872. On the basis of this letter, Feuer (1949) suggests that Mill did not appreciate the deep

1. A French edition had appeared in 1873. Harris suggests that Mill might have been indirectly aware of Marx's thought through Mill's connections to "British trade unions leaders, e.g., George Odger and William Cremer," who had been involved with Marx in the International Working Men's Association (Harris 1956, 174).

2. The speech was given on July 23, 1870.

split between Marx and Bakunin.[3] And certainly Mill had no inkling of Marx's major writings in political economy.

It is far less clear why Marx had so little to say about Mill. And why what Marx did have to say is almost uniformly negative. Mill's responses to the revolutions of 1848–49 Marx considered an attempt "to harmonise the Political Economy of capital with the claims, no longer to be ignored, of the proletariat." The result was a "shallow syncretism" indicative of "bankruptcy by bourgeois economy" (Marx [1867] 1906, 19). While Marx acknowledged that Mill was not to be classified "with the herd of vulgar economic apologists" (669), he insisted that Mill's discussion of profit superficially confused capitalist categories with underlying material relations. He concluded this passage with his most biting indictment of Mill: "On the level plain, simple mounds look like hills; and the imbecile flatness of the present bourgeoisie is to be measured by the altitude of its great intellects" (568).

Marx is more than reluctant to acknowledge any debt or even sympathy for Mill. Yet Marx's political economy falls squarely in the classical tradition, and Mill was the major classical writer during the period in which Marx seriously took up the subject. And if they both had learned much from Ricardo, they both aspired to a broad, comprehensive social science of which Ricardo had never dreamed.

If it weren't for Marx's invective, the deep similarities between these two mid-nineteenth-century political economists might well have become foundational. I start with this argument. Only after appreciating the broad common themes in their work does it make sense to consider the genuine differences between Mill's and Marx's progressive visions. And only then can a plausible story be told as to why Marx was so vested in denying his deep connections to Mill.

COMMON THEMES

Human Nature

Marx and Mill start with what today appear as quite similar, if somewhat romantic, notions about human nature. Yet, Marx at several points

3. Later the same year, Mill wrote to Thomas Smith of the Nottingham branch of the association with respect to the branch's program: "In the principles of the Association as set forth in the Programme I find much that I warmly approve, & little, if anything from which I positively dissent though, from the generality with which those principles are laid down it is impossible for me to say to what extent I should concur in the practical measures which the association would propose in

accused Mill of treating human beings as if they at all times and places could be fully characterized by the social relations of production found in the bourgeois economy (Marx [1867] 1906, 568). Whatever the relevance of such criticisms for other classical economists, no charge could be more unfair with respect to Mill. Mill had laid out a blueprint for a science of ethology with the aim of explaining the origins of differences in national character in the differing material conditions faced around the world (Mill [1843] 1974). Looking forward, Mill saw the entire thrust of material improvement and progress as moving human beings to a point where the great mass of people might be able to explore their capacities through self-defining activity. The achievement of the greatest happiness of the greatest number was ultimately bound up with this self-generated process of search (Donner, 1991).

There is very little distance between Mill's emphasis on self-development and Marx's own discussion of "species being." Marx, like Mill, was convinced that almost all individuals are capable of defining their own goals. Indeed, it is precisely this conviction that motivates the struggle against alienation (Marx [1844] 1966.). Marx argued that the central element in the species being is an eagerness to productively struggle with nature.

Marx was not poaching on Mill. His philosophical background on these matters predated his familiarity with British political economy. But whatever Marx suggested about Mill's ideas on human nature, the two approaches are surprisingly similar.

A Science of History

Mill's reputation was established with the publication in 1843 of his *System of Logic, Ratiocinative and Inductive: Being a Connected View of the Principles of Evidence and the Method of Scientific Investigation*. This volume ends with Book VI, "On the Logic of the Moral Sciences." Here Mill attempted to extend the scientific method to the study of mankind. He begins with a quote from Condorcet: "If man can predict, almost with certainty, those appearances of which he understands the laws; if, even when the laws are unknown to him, experience or the past enables him to foresee, with considerable probability, future appearances; why should we suppose it a chimerical undertaking to delineate, with some degree of

order to bring the principles into operation" (Mill 1972, 1910–1912). The program, of course, had been heavily influenced by Marx.

truth, the picture of the future destiny of mankind from the results of its history?" (Mill [1843] 1974, 545; translation from the French reproduced from Condorcet [1794] 1802).

Mill fully embraced Condorcet's viewpoint. And like Condorcet he saw the long story of history as one of progress. At the critical point, then, he accepted Comte's fundamental explanation for that progress as pivoting on periods of intellectual speculation. To the expansion of knowledge, all other facets of progress must ultimately be traced. For Mill the "most obvious case" of this causal connection was the proposition that "the progress of industry must follow, and depend on, the progress of knowledge" (604).

Marx was, of course, a materialist. As such he was hostile to Hegelian notions of "a so-called general progress of the human mind," independent of material conditions (Marx [1859] 1904, 11). Marx along with Engels emphasized that the possibilities of material development were at first stimulated by and subsequently limited by the social relations to which a mode of production gave rise.

I am not convinced that this materialist view is that different from that of Mill's. At first glance Mill seems to have endorsed an idealistic notion of progress. But his theory might reasonably be described from a Marxist view as incomplete, rather than wrong.[4] For Mill gives us little or no clue as to an explanation for the periods of widened intellectual speculation that he saw as so central to progress. However, a hypothesis along these lines might be drawn from Marx's brief sketch. Creative speculation may be stimulated to a high pitch by just those broad social changes that follow on the decline of one mode and its replacement by a new mode. Surely Marx must have had something relatively simple like this in mind when he asserted: "Mankind always takes up only such problems as it can solve; since looking at the matter more closely, we will always find that the problem itself arises only when the material conditions necessary for its solution already exist or are at least in the process of formation" (Marx [1859] 1904, 13).

Mill might quite reasonably have accepted just this type of completion of his theory of history. Marx, for all his hostility toward Mill, can be seen here as filling out Mill's own sketch. There exist inadequate materials on either side to fully demonstrate the affinity claimed here. However, with respect to the crucial question of the likely evolution of capitalism, there

4. The dominant view does not accept this point. For discussions that explicitly reject an economic interpretation of Mill's understanding of progress in favor of an idealistic understanding, see Hamburger (1999, ch. 2), Duncan (1973, 212–217), and Harris (1956, 173).

can be little doubt that Mill anticipated a quite Marxian transition. The new economy of the stationary state, according to Mill, will lead to a flowering of the "industrial arts," but now these, "instead of serving no purpose but the increase of wealth," will "produce their legitimate effect, that of abridging labour." The technological change achieved before the middle of the nineteenth century had enabled "a greater population to live the same life of drudgery and imprisonment," they had "increased the comforts of the middle classes," but they had not yet "begun to effect those great changes in human destiny, which it is in their nature and in their futurity to accomplish" (Mill [1848] 1965, 757). While clearly Mill saw this flowering as occurring in a very different institutional context than did Marx, both economists can reasonably be taken as predicting a creative explosion following on major changes in social relations.

These speculations can be related to G. A. Cohen's definitions of "inclusive" and "restricted" historical materialism. The first, the inclusive version of historical materialism, holds: "History is, centrally, the systematic growth of human productive power, and forms of society rise and fall when and because they enable and promote, or frustrate and impede, that growth" (Cohen 2000, 367). The second, the restricted version of historical materialism, simply substitutes for "centrally" in the above sentence the expression *inter alia*. Cohen suspects Marx preferred the inclusive version. I suggest Mill could feel very comfortable with the restricted version.

Whatever one might conclude at this abstract level, it is hard to avoid the similarity in Marx's and Mill's judgments concerning the capitalism of the nineteenth century. Both saw the laissez-faire capitalism of their day as essentially transitional. Both saw it as laying the material basis for an economic system capable of addressing the broader needs and aspirations of the population as a whole.

Production and Distribution

Mill's entire system of political economy starts from a distinction between production and distribution. For Mill, "The laws and conditions of the Production of Wealth partake of the character of physical truths." He had in mind here the diminishing returns common in agriculture and the increasing returns achievable through cooperation. But "the Distribution of wealth . . . is a matter of human institutions solely." Over historical epochs and across nations, institutions vary dramatically. And these institutions strongly affect the distribution of the economy's rewards. The contrast between production and distribution is fundamental to Mill.

Now, Mill's distinction between production and distribution comes very close to Marx's own distinction between the material forces of production and the social relations of production. Yet again Marx was hesitant to acknowledge a theme common to him and Mill. No, he was more than hesitant. He was almost perverse in denying their deep similarity. As observed by G. A. Cohen, Marx accused Mill of presenting production "as governed by eternal natural laws which are independent of history, and at the same time *bourgeois* relations are clandestinely passed off as irrefutable natural laws of society in *abstracto*" (from Marx's *Grundrisse*, quoted by Cohen 2000, 109).

Cohen quite rightly finds no grounds for this indictment of Mill. What Cohen does find is that Mill used the term " 'capital' as Marx does not, to refer to material requisites of production per se. But he makes it clear that 'capital needs not necessarily be furnished by a person called a capitalist' " (Cohen 2000, 109). Indeed, Cohen quotes Mill to the effect that political economists must be careful not to "class the merely temporary truths of their subject among its permanent and universal laws" (Cohen 2000, 111).

It is precisely Mill's assertion of the pliability of what Marx would call the social relations of production that lies behind the claim made throughout this book that Mill was a radical in a modern sense—in a sense that embraces Marx as well. Of course, that hardly means that the two foresaw the same path for future progress, or that Mill was as ready as Marx to countenance the confiscation of capitalist property. But it does mean that as Marx read Mill, he could hardly have missed the claim that the institutions of the present order were open to question and potential objects of major reform.

Labor as the Source of Profit

Marx and Mill were both Ricardian classical economists. As such, they were both committed to a labor theory of value. Yet, Marx was almost fond of insisting that Mill had let go of the central tenet of Ricardianism and instead had substituted a version of "profit upon alienation"—that is, profit originating in selling as opposed to in production. Most notably, in commenting on Mill's treatment of profit in *Some Essays on Unsettled Questions in Political Economy* (Mill [1830] 1844), Marx claimed to see hints of "profit upon alienation" and concluded that Mill "has abandoned his basic concepts and fallen far behind Ricardo, Adam Smith and the Physiocrats" (Marx [1968] 1972, 202). Yet in his definitive treatment in the *Principles*, Mill couldn't have been more explicit in his rejection of "profit upon alienation."[5] Here is the definitive passage (from which a quote in chapter 5 was drawn):

> To popular apprehension it seems as if the profits of business depended upon prices. A producer or dealer seems to obtain his profits by selling his commodity for more than it cost him. Profit altogether, people are apt to think, is a consequence of purchase and sale. It is only (they suppose) because there are purchasers for a commodity, that the producer of it is able to make any profit. Demand—customers—a market for the commodity, are the cause of the gains of capitalists. . . .
>
> This, however, is looking only at the outside surface of the economical machinery of society. In no case, we find, is the mere money which passes from one person to another, the fundamental matter in any economical phenomenon. . . .
>
> The cause of profit is, that labour produces more than is required for its support. . . . [T]he reason why capital yields a profit, is because food, clothing, materials, and tools, last longer than the time which was required to produce them; so that if a capitalist supplies a party of labourers with these things, on condition of receiving all they produce, they will, in addition to reproducing their own necessaries and instruments, have a portion of their time remaining, to work for the capitalist. . . . We thus see that profit arises, not from the incident of exchange, but from the productive power of labour (Mill [1848] 1965, 410–411)

A more straightforward expression of the classical theory of the origins of profit could hardly be found. Indeed, Marx's own theory of surplus value could be largely derived from this statement alone.

Yet, rather than seeing in Mill a major ally in support of the labor theory of value, Marx insisted on attacking him. Most notably, Marx took considerable pride in identifying shortcomings in Mill's treatment of constant capital. Marx was almost gleeful in his criticism. And in fairness to Marx, Mill in the *Essays* was awkward and even inconsistent in his efforts to work out the mathematics of successive rounds of production. Cutting short the infinite regress of production, Mill confused matters rather than illuminating them. There is no doubt that Marx had a more steady

5. This passage first appeared in the 1857 edition of the *Principles*. Although Marx had obviously read Mill's *Principles*, it is not clear whether he saw only earlier editions. In any case, Marx insisted that Mill's *Essays* contained "all that is original in Mr. John Stuart Mill's writings about political economy (in contrast to his bulky compendium)" (190).

command over the mechanics of constant capital. Yet Mill, perhaps realizing his difficulties in the *Essays*, gave up this line of analysis in favor of the simpler statement suggested by the long quotation from the *Principles* just given.[6]

Reviewing Mill's position, Ladislaus Bortkiewicz, one of the first rigorous commentator on Marx, concludes there was "no doubt of the fact that Mill deduces profit from surplus value, just as Marx does." Bortkiewicz accuses Marx of essentially misrepresenting Mill's position on purpose. Bortkiewicz goes on to speculate "one will not go wrong if one connects the ill will which Marx displays towards Mill, with the circumstance that Mill had, basically, anticipated Marx's theory of surplus value" (quoted in Hollander 1985, 341–342).

Be that as it may, it is hard to avoid the conclusion that Mill and Marx had come to the same basic theory of the origin of profit. Moreover, this worldview made both men sympathetic to possible transitions that would leave the working classes less dependent on the capitalists. Indeed, both saw such possibilities as not just desirable but also essentially inevitable.

The Falling Rate of Profit

It is hard to read classical economists of any stripe without noticing their virtual obsession with some one or another theory of the falling rate of profit. Adam Smith established this pattern with his speculations on how the expansion of markets was likely to reduce opportunities for arbitrage and the accumulation of capital was likely to leave it less scarce. Ricardo, famously, derived his theory of falling profits from Malthusian rent theory, emphasizing that the growth of population and the resulting scarcity of land must leave a larger and larger share of the final product in the hands of the landlords. This rise in the landlords' share could only come at the expense of profits, since wages, limited by subsistence, could not fall.

So it is no surprise that both Mill and Marx advanced theories of falling profits. We have already explored Mill's approach in chapter 5. There, we observed that Mill actually advanced two alternative theories. The first, with population unchecked, was simply Ricardo's older theory. The second was quite different. If population growth could be controlled by the working classes, then accumulation would necessarily imply upward pressure

6. The shift is discussed in some detail by Hollander (1985, 340–343).

on wages and downward pressure on profit. This was Mill's optimistic and radical theory of the stationary state and progressive institutional change. Marx ignored Mill's second vision and accused him of maintaining only the old Ricardian rent theory.

In any case, Marx advanced a very different theory. Rather than a rise in rents or wages, Marx saw capitalists as forced to devote an increasing share of their outlays, not to labor that might be exploited, but to intermediate goods and machinery for which they must pay full value. The notion of a rising organic composition of capital matched well with the trends toward higher fixed capital everywhere evident in the mid-nineteenth century. Technological change was very much biased in favor of such developments. But, as a number of commentators have since observed, the incentive to introduce new technologies at fixed wages generally guarantees not a fall in the general profit rate but a rise in that rate.[7] Of course, the general rate will not rise as much as the transitory rate in the innovating industry. For the innovating industry, the rate will fall from the transitory rate to the new general rate. And this observation might have confused Marx. But the new general rate will not be lower than the old general rate. In this fundamental sense, we get a tendency for profits to rise, not fall. Ever since this point was appreciated there have been a number of efforts to alter basic assumptions or develop more complicated dynamics, with the purpose of restoring a downward tendency to the Marxian profit rate (Alberro and Persky 1981).

At this first comparison, Mill's argument looks more compelling than Marx's. But the point here is not to pick between Mill's and Marx's approaches to falling profit rates. The point is to emphasize the central role a theory of falling profits plays in both men's theories. As emphasized by Bernice Shoul, "Both Mill and Marx assert that the fall in the rate of profit is decisive for capitalist evolution" (1965, 281). For Mill, as we have seen, the falling profit rate approaches a minimum that ushers in the stationary state and sets the stage for the emergence of cooperative enterprises. For Marx, the falling profit rate brings on a capitalist breakdown, resulting in the proletariat's seizure of power and the transformation to socialism.

Both Marx and Mill, then, saw capitalism as a transitional mode of production, one that accelerates the accumulation of capital and the growth of output. Both saw the industrial revolution as a defining event, one that

7. The proposition keeps reappearing. For the earliest statement see Bortkiewicz (1907 [1952]). The defining article by Okishio (1961) generated what is often referred to as Okishio's theorem. Also see Robinson (1942 [1967]), Alberro and Persky (1979), and Roemer (1979).

made possible and ultimately demanded the construction of a new set of social relations. Both credit the capitalist class with accelerating the slow progress that had characterized earlier ages.

There is no reason to think Marx drew on Mill for his optimism about socialist progress. More reasonably, Marx, like Mill working within the classical framework and committed to a theory of falling profits, saw an opportunity for institutional experimentation. Yet Marx's famous discussion of counter-tendencies seems very much influenced by Mill's approach. For example, both men pointed to technological change and foreign trade. But the telling observation is not that the two classicists listed the same counter-tendencies.[8] Rather, it is that Marx, like Mill, sensed the resiliency of capitalism. For both men, the entire logic of capitalism implies an aggressive search for means to bolster the profit rate. This is a deep insight. Indeed, in light of the subsequent economic history of capitalism, it seems that far from overestimating these counter forces, Mill and Marx both underestimated their depth and power. Even major institutional changes, whether brought on by reform or by revolution, have faced a capitalist class commanding massive resources in its defining search for profit.

Cycles

By the middle of the nineteenth century the cyclical nature of the new industrial economy had become clear to any number of observers. Despite his commitment to Say's Law, Mill constructed a surprisingly modern theory of the business cycle. This theory hinged on overly optimistic financial speculation leading to a crash characterized by a high increase in the demand for money and liquidity (Mill [1848] 1965, 574–575). As noted earlier, Mill argued that such cycles actually helped to put off the decline in profits as they destroyed substantial amounts of savings and capital. This theme of creative destruction was to reappear in a number of places in Marx's writings, although Marx never gave Mill credit for it.

Marx put forward several alternative explanations of business cycles. The usual list included a disproportionality thesis reminiscent of Sismondi,

8. Their two lists overlap substantially, but are not identical. Marx listed six countervailing factors: raising the intensity of exploitation, depression of wages below their value, cheapening of the elements of constant capital, relative overpopulation, foreign trade, and the increase of stock capital. Mill listed four: the waste of capital in periods of commercial revulsion, improvements in production, new power of obtaining cheap commodities from foreign countries, and overflow of capital into colonies or foreign countries.

an underconsumption thesis anticipating some elements of Keynesian economics, and what appears as Marx's most favored, a wage cycle in which labor demand runs ahead of supply and undermines profits. While Marx never put financial speculation at the center of the business-cycle story, he famously described the financial panics that accompanied business cycles: "On the eve of crisis, the bourgeois, with the self-sufficiency that springs from intoxicating prosperity, declares money to be a vain imagination. Commodities alone are money," but as the crisis spreads, "now the cry is everywhere: money alone is a commodity!"(Marx [1867] 1906, ch. III, section 3b "Means of Payment"). This sounds a good deal like Mill, although again Marx didn't make a connection.

THE TENSION

Clearly Marx shared a number of important themes with Mill. One can imagine any number of ways Marx might have accepted those similarities, acknowledged Mill's contributions to classical political economy, and then moved on to his own fundamental innovations. Of course, Marx was not known for his graciousness. Marx read widely and was ungenerous to many writers. And that may be all that was going on in this case.

Yet there was something especially tense in his relation to Mill, something that goes beyond Marx's general crankiness. One possible explanation for this tension might be Marx's desire to paint bourgeois political economy as having entered a period of decay. While often critical of Ricardo, Marx saw him as making major improvements in Adam Smith's economics. And surely Marx accepted that his own formalization of value theory was deeply based on Ricardian thinking. The intellectual trajectory of classical political economy for Marx paralleled the history of capitalism more generally. Without forcing the point, one can suggest that for Marx, just as capitalism was entering a period of general crisis, so too its ideological superstructure was in decline. The reorganization of the mode of production from feudalism to capitalism had given rise to the intellectual energy of the physiocrats and the classical school. Now that capitalism was beginning to wane, its ideologues could offer only the same old insights. Bourgeois political economy, like the bourgeoisie itself, was destined for the dustbin of history.

The complement to the charge of a decaying bourgeois political economy was the assertion of a rising political economy fit for a new age. Marx might plausibly be expected to maintain that constructive ideas/ideologies were associated with rising classes as they struggled to generate a fuller worldview.

Bourgeois thinkers had already made their contribution. The future of political economy belonged to the working classes and their intellectual representatives. Not the least attractive in such a position might be how it allowed Marx to identify himself as the inheritor of classical political economy.

This speculation has an element of plausibility. It deserves more consideration than it will receive here. However, I think there is another story, a story with a richer, less formalized line. Although Marx always referred to Mill as a minor post-Ricardian, Mill was not just a classical economist. The mature Mill was a radical utilitarian, committed to the greatest happiness of the greatest number. Like Marx, he saw capitalism as a transitional system. But he predicted and hoped for a very different future than the one Marx predicted and hoped for. Where Marx saw revolution and planning, Mill saw reform and cooperation.

Throughout, Marx denied that there was any serious substance to the British utilitarians. He was absolutely merciless in his treatment of Jeremy Bentham, whom in his ineffable manner he described as "the arch-Philistine, that insipid, pedantic, leather-tongued oracle of the ordinary bourgeois intelligence of the 19th century." If this wasn't enough, Marx went on to assert, "Bentham is among philosophers what Martin Tupper is among poets" (Marx [1867] 1906, 668). Tupper was known as a hackneyed versifier and author of *Proverbial Philosophy*.[9] In a famous footnote to this passage, Marx expanded his views on British utilitarianism: "[I]n no time and in no country has the most homespun common-place ever strutted about in so self-satisfied a way. The principle of utility was no discovery of Bentham. He simply reproduced in his dull way what Helvetius and other Frenchmen had said with esprit in the 18th century." Marx concluded, "Had I the courage of my friend, Heinrich Heine, I should call Mr. Jeremy a genius in the way of bourgeois stupidity" (Marx [1867] 1906, 668).[10]

9. *Proverbial Philosophy* includes such gems as:

> The fierceness looking from the lynx's eye, and the dull
> stupor of the sloth;
> To these and to all, is there added each its USE, though man
> considereth it lightly;
> For Power hath ordained nothing which Economy
> saw not needful.
>
> (Tupper 1848, 19)

It is not clear whether Marx knew of Bentham's own low opinion of poetry as of no more value than the game of push-pin (see Bentham [1825] 1962, 253).

10. The poet Heinrich Heine was a close friend of Marx. Marx greatly respected Heine as a poet and was tolerant of his erratic leftist politics. The two shared a similar social/religious background, having been born into prosperous German Jewish families eager to assimilate.

Now, Marx always appreciated the radical French philosophes, and especially Helvetius, for their insistence on materialism and their promotion of the commonweal. Yet, Marx hardly needed to consider in any detail the actual proposals made by these philosophes for social reorganization. Bentham, standing closer in time, was a more immediate concern, but as is clear from the quotes given earlier, Marx could easily dismiss Bentham as not the inheritor of the Enlightenment but, rather, as the mouthpiece for bourgeois platitudes. But Mill was a very different matter. Mill's utilitarianism was not so easily dismissed. In Mill, Marx should have, by rights, seen a serious attempt to apply Enlightenment principles in combination with the insights of political economy to the new industrial economy of the mid-nineteenth century.

Marx would have nothing of it. Apart from his lengthy (and largely justified) criticisms of Mill's numerical examples, Marx insisted on a dismissive posture toward Mill. In the preface to the 1873 second edition of *Capital*, just a few months before Mill's death, Marx presented his rather opaque summary of Mill's reform agenda:

> The Continental revolution of 1848–9 also had its reaction in England. Men who still claimed some scientific standing and aspired to be something more than mere sophists and sycophants of the ruling-classes, tried to harmonise the Political Economy of capital with the claims, no longer to be ignored, of the proletariat. Hence a shallow syncretism, of which John Stuart Mill is the best representative. It is a declaration of bankruptcy by bourgeois economy, an event on which the great Russian scholar and critic, N. Tschernyschewsky, has thrown the light of a master mind in his "Outlines of Political Economy according to Mill." (Marx [1867] 1906, 19)

It is a little difficult from this passage to sense what Marx was getting at. On the next page he added the observation that John Stuart Mill had attempted "to reconcile irreconcilables." But Marx offered no further explanation. However, there can be little doubt that this is the one place Marx recognized Mill's broader program. In particular, the link to the "Continental revolution of 1848–9" points squarely to Mill's expanded treatment of cooperatives. As we have seen, that treatment was strongly influenced by the French efforts to establish cooperatives during the Revolution. Thus Marx's charge of "shallow syncretism" must be leveled primarily at Mill's endorsement of cooperatives.

Nowhere did Marx explicitly mention Mill in connection with cooperatives. However, in the *Civil War in France* (which incidentally began with the speech on which Mill had commented favorably), Marx would certainly be including Mill and his followers among "those members of the ruling classes who are intelligent enough to perceive the impossibility of continuing the present system—and they are many—[who] have become the obtrusive and full-mouthed apostles of co-operative production" (Marx [1871] 2009, 89).

Marx's message for these supporters of cooperatives was clear and sharp: "If co-operative production is not to remain a sham and a snare; if it is to supersede the capitalist system; if united co-operative societies are to regulate national production upon common plan, thus taking it under their own control, and putting an end to the constant anarchy and periodical convulsions which are the fatality of capitalist production—what else, gentlemen, would it be but communism, 'possible' communism?" (89–90).[11]

Marx was sharply critical of any form of cooperative movement not including some explicit system of centrally planned control. Mill, of course, took just the opposite view. In his preface to the 1852 third edition of *Principles*, Mill had made the point quite clearly. Summarizing the experience of the French Revolution of 1848, Mill wrote, "[T]he time is ripe for a larger and more rapid extension of association among labourers than could have been successfully attempted before the calumniated democratic movement in Europe. . . . I have endeavoured to designate more clearly the tendency of the social transformation, of which these associations are the initial step; and at the same time to disconnect the co-operative cause from the exaggerated or altogether mistaken declamations against competition, so largely indulged in by its supporters" (Mill [1848] 1965, xciii).

It would seem that in the first several years of the 1870s, with the recent events of the Paris Commune still fresh, Marx for a brief moment engaged with Mill's ideas concerning "the tendency of the social transformation." He did not choose to write a major critique of those ideas. But it could not have escaped Marx's notice that there was a powerful similarity between Mill's emphasis on voluntary cooperation and the voluntarism put forward by the various anarchist groupings within the International Working Men's Association. Marx was actively involved in fighting these tendencies. Far from accepting voluntary cooperatives as central to solving the problem of exploitation in capitalism, Marx saw such talk as hopelessly utopian whether it originated from the anarchists on his left or the radical reformers on his right. Marx saw Mill's understanding of progress, not as a genuine forerunner of his own but, rather, as an impossible attempt to reconcile irreconcilables.

11. I first became aware of this discussion by Marx from Hollander (2008, 392–393), where part of this passage is cited.

CHAPTER 11

The Fabians, Early and Late

If Marx stood unwilling to acknowledge his connections to John Stuart Mill, many of the early British socialists were eager to claim such connections. Mill's able stepdaughter Helen Taylor provided a self-conscious link between his work and the emerging British left of the late nineteenth century. More lasting was the radical reform position of the Fabians, who with some justification saw themselves as descendants of Mill. The Fabian Society, founded in 1884 a year after Marx's death, became the exemplary model for modern radical reform organizations. Middle class in origin and intellectual in approach, the Fabians provided ongoing and constructive support to the expanding political movement of the British working class and their trade unions. For the most part they fought against dogmatism, pseudo-science, and the romanticization of violence, all common failings of the socialist left. While most of them differed with Mill on the question of nationalization, they gave substance to Mill's radicalism, emphasizing utilitarian principles and economic analysis.

HELEN TAYLOR

Helen Taylor, Mill's stepdaughter, was strongly influenced by his worldview. Like her mother, Harriet, Helen Taylor saw Mill's movement toward radical reform as a major development. Helen Taylor did everything in her power to identify Mill with the rising socialist movement in Britain. After Harriet Mill's death, Helen Taylor had become her stepfather's secretary and confidant. She played a contributory role in producing *The Subjection of*

Women in 1869, and she facilitated the publication of Mill's *Autobiography* after his death. She also brought out Mill's *Chapters on Socialism* ([1879] 1967), underscoring his sympathy toward working-class movements.

Helen Taylor participated actively in radical reform activities. Once she had aspired to be an actress, so perhaps it is not surprising that she became a first-class public speaker, widely sought after to address radical meetings. Nor is it surprising that she supported a number of Millean causes, including universal suffrage, land reform, and public education (Baylen and Grossman 1988, 800–803).

Taylor's interest in extending the suffrage to women was part and parcel of her work with her stepfather. She had played a major role in bringing together the 1866 Ladies' Petition of the Kensington Society, to which she belonged. Mill, then an MP, presented the petition to Parliament and attempted to attach it to legislation. The next year Taylor wrote an article, "The Claim of Englishwomen to the Suffrage Constitutionally Considered" (H. Taylor 1867) for the *Westminster Review*. After Mill's death, Helen Taylor continued her participation in numerous activities of the suffrage movement. She addressed major rallies in London and elsewhere. In 1885 she engaged in a much-publicized campaign to run for Parliament, but was denied the right to submit her nominating materials (Crawford 1999, 681).

Helen Taylor became a major advocate of land reform, a member of the Land League and then the more radical English Land Nationalisation Society. She played the central role in connecting the two societies with Henry George, who came to England in 1882 (Wolfe 1975, 84). This visit was critical to the development of the British left, having a major formative influence on future members of the Fabian Society and many other radicals. Taylor became personally acquainted with Henry George. Although George advocated a more radical program than Mill, his focus on land reform clearly echoed Mill's longstanding concern with the inequality of land ownership. Helen Taylor brought Mill's mantle to the dynamic reformer from the United States.

In the area of public education, Helen Taylor continued to develop her stepfather's ideas. Mill had been reluctant to fully endorse free schools. In 1870 he had been asked to run for the London School Board representing Southwark, but declined. Six years later, Taylor accepted and held the position until 1884, when she pulled back because of her health. By all accounts she was an active educational reformer: "[S]he campaigned tirelessly for free and universal education, for the abolition of corporal punishment, for the community's right to the use of school facilities outside of school hours, and for the provision of free meals and clothing for needy children. . . . Taylor was also instrumental in the appointment of working-class parents as school managers" (Levine 2004). Like Mill, Taylor clearly put emphasis on the crucial task of educating the working classes, even if she went beyond her stepfather's cautious, Smithian position.

In her advocacy of radical land reform and free education Taylor started from Mill's concerns and pushed toward more aggressive programs. She saw this shift as the logical evolution of Mill's utilitarian principles and his concern for the greatest happiness of the greatest number. This pattern was most sharply played out in her early support for British socialism. Taylor was one of the first members of the Democratic Federation, which later became the Social Democratic Federation.

The federation was founded in 1881 by erstwhile Tory Henry Hyndman, who for many years tightly controlled its politics and publications. Hyndman put forward an explicitly Marxian position for his new organization, which attracted William Morris, Eleanor Marx, and Helen Taylor, "who, next to Hyndman was probably the most important personage in the infant Federation" (Wolfe 1975, 77). The point to be made here is not so much that Taylor joined a Marxist organization, but that in just a few years she split from it, outraged at Hyndman's advocacy of violent revolution. In 1884 she left the federation, denouncing Hyndman as irresponsible (105–106).

Willard Wolfe has argued that Taylor's "loyalties were still rooted in the Radical past, dominated by the beliefs of her sainted stepfather" (106). And surely there is a sense in which her thinking was out of step with the development of insurrectionary versions of Marxian socialism. But her positions were very much consistent with the emerging character of modern radicalism, a radicalism that eschews violent revolution, looking instead to progress and structural reform as the driving force of change.

THE WEBBS AND FABIAN ORIGINS

Helen Taylor was an activist, but like her stepfather she saw her activism as growing out of a political-economic analysis of the world. Taylor did not herself attempt to add to that analysis. She looked to others, such as Henry George, to expand the critique and to identify promising lines of radical reform. In 1885, Taylor withdrew from the radical stage, spending the last twenty-two years of her life in a surprisingly secluded retirement. Be that as it may, there were many others eager to take up the Millean version of modern radicalism. If in the emerging British socialist scene Hydman and his federation followed a dogmatic line, the radicalism of their major competitor, the Fabian Society, was Millean to the core.

The Fabians came together in 1884. From the first, and in contrast to the federation, they emphasized the need for research and debate. Committing themselves to educating middle- and working-class radicals, they saw change as a slow progressive process that must build on the expansion of solid knowledge. This cautious approach was signaled in the very choice of their name. Fabians sought to emulate the Roman consul, dictator, and general Fabius Maximus Cunctator, or Fabius the Delayer. "Delayer" was originally meant by Fabius's critics as a derogatory epithet, but became a mark of praise, as his careful, guerrilla-like approach to fighting the second Punic War proved more effective than frontal assaults on Hannibal. The first tract produced by the Fabians included the following quotation: "Wherefore it may not be gainsaid that the fruit of this man's long taking of counsel—and (by the many so deemed) untimeous delays—was the safe-holding for all men, his fellow citizens, of the Common Weal" (quoted in Pease 1916, 39).[1]

The theme of gradualism was elaborated by George Bernard Shaw, an early recruit and long-time Fabian. The establishment of a new economy would necessarily take time. As Shaw put it, "Demolishing a Bastille with seven prisoners in it is one thing: demolishing one with fourteen million prisoners is quite another." The reality of the situation should not generate a sense of "relief" but rather feelings of "disappointment and humiliation" (Shaw 1891, 226). Be that as it may, to prepare the ground required taking counsel, and taking counsel meant studying theory and assembling facts.

The early Fabians set about just such a course. From the start the group attracted an impressive set of intellects, including most famously George Bernard Shaw but most notably Sidney and Beatrice Webb. Sidney Webb had been a member of the Fabians almost from the start. His wife joined the society after their marriage in 1892. Together the two became the core of the Fabians' numerous forays into social sciences. Webb's father had been an active political worker in Mill's 1865 campaign for parliament. According to Norman Mackenzie, Sidney Webb, who went to work at fifteen, was "the epitome of the scholarship boy." He attended courses at

1. A second quote was also included: "For the right moment you must wait, as Fabius did most patiently, when warring against Hannibal, though many censured his delays; but when the time comes you must strike hard, as Fabius did, or your waiting will be in vain, and fruitless" (quoted in Pease 1916, 39). Edward Pease, long-time secretary of the Fabians, acknowledges that neither quotation was the work of any ancient historian; rather, they were both contrived by an early member of the society. As to the second quote, which would seem at odds with the Fabians generally peaceful policies, a prominent Fabian, H. G. Wells, dryly observed that Fabius never did strike (39).

the City of London College, where he scored first classes. He won numerous prizes. Moving from the private sector to the civil service, he again excelled in examinations, obtaining a position in the Colonial Office (Webb and Webb 1978, 74). He also studied law, but seems not to have practiced much (Bevir 2011, 175). Webb's wife, Beatrice Potter, came from a well-off family. After their marriage Sidney Webb devoted his full time to research and activism.

Sidney Webb's own formal training in political economy was limited. However, he always insisted on a direct connection running from John Stuart Mill to Fabian socialism. He had started his intellectual-political life in the Zetetical Society, "a small discussion society influenced by the ideas of John Stuart Mill" (Webb and Webb 1978, 75–76). There, he met Helen Taylor. He also began his long-run collaboration with George Bernard Shaw at the society. Together the two of them joined the Fabians in 1884.

Sidney Webb eagerly claimed the mantle of John Stuart Mill for the Fabians. Webb insisted that Mill had become a full-blown socialists. In particular, Webb argued that the 1848 publication of Mill's *Principles* had been a turning point, a break with the philosophic radicalism of Bentham:

> [A] new scientific conception of the social organism has put completely out of countenance the cherished principles of the political economist and the philosophic radical. We left them sailing gaily into anarchy on the stream of laissez faire. Since then the tide has turned. The publication of John Stuart Mill's *Political Economy* in 1848 marks conveniently the boundary of the old individualist economics. Every edition of Mill's book became more and more socialistic. After his death the world learnt the personal history, penned by his own hand, of his development from a mere political democrat to a convinced socialist. (S. Webb 1889a, 58)

Webb repeatedly returned to Mill's contributions to socialism. He quoted Mill on the size of the upper classes' share of national income and their ability to extract a surplus "without any merit or exertion of their own" (S. Webb 1887, 6). He credited Mill for making the land question a serious reform issue before Henry George. He favorably cited Mill's strategy of encouraging independent labor candidates (Webb and Webb 1896, 271). And he invoked Mill's political economy of progress as the very basis for the development of a serious British socialism:

> Mill tells us how, as he investigated more closely the history and structure of Society, he came to find a sure and certain hope in the Progress of Socialism, which he foresaw and energetically aided. We who call ourselves Socialists

> to-day in England, largely through Mill's teaching and example, find a confirmation of this hope in social history and economics. (S. Webb 1890, 11)[2]

Among intellectual historians, there is a lively debate as to how seriously to take these claims by Webb. One position accepts them largely at face value, identifying Webb as a latter-day utilitarian. On the other side, a number of quite different arguments have been advanced: the Webbs drew more heavily on a humanitarian strain of the ethical positivism of the 1870s than on Mill; the Webbs rejected Mill's deductive analytics in favor of an institutionalist approach; the Webbs' strong endorsement of nationalization was at odds with the gradualism of Mill's emphasis on voluntary cooperatives; and finally the Webbs' enthusiastic endorsement of totalitarian regime of the Soviet Union was diametrically opposed to Mill's concern with individual freedom.[3]

A number of rebuttal arguments suggest themselves. Positivism of any type drew heavily on Auguste Comte. Mill and Comte had much in common, and it was Mill who made Comte intellectually respectable in Britain. Mill's positions also had a strong moral/ethical component. A mixture of ethical positivism and Millean utilitarianism seems easy to imagine.

For all his deductive acumen, Mill was never hostile to serious historical and institutional research. He looked to such researches to obtain critical evidence—evidence that could be constructively used to adapt theory. The Webbs never rejected deductive analytical reasoning. They maintained a strong interest in the developments taking place in mainstream political economy. Sidney Webb and George Bernard Shaw both looked to the ongoing theoretical work of William Stanley Jevons, Philip Wicksteed, and Alfred Marshall to bolster their radical arguments, even when that work seemed at odds with Marx's value theory. Beatrice Webb turned to Marshall to critique her work on cooperatives. Most dramatically, the Webbs were responsible for founding the London School of Economics (LSE) in 1895 with moneys that had been left to the Fabian Society.[4]

2. In the same passage, Webb goes on to glimpse "the glad vision of a brighter day, when, practically, the whole product of labour will be the worker's and the worker's alone." Having invoked Mill in support of this aim, he also attributed it to "the Apostolic rule ignored by so many Christians, that if a man do not work, neither shall he eat" (S. Webb 1890, 11).

3. These are all discussed in Bevir (2011, ch. 9) and Wolfe (1975).

4. Some of their fellow Fabians were disconcerted at this move. See the discussion in MacKenzie and MacKenzie (1977, 214–217).

Sidney Webb looked to the new institution to provide both theory and evidence for the socialist cause.

Beatrice Webb wrote a monograph on the cooperative movement in Britain in 1891. She and Sidney Webb wrote a work on consumer cooperatives in 1921. They were strong supporters of consumer cooperatives, but had serious doubts about the practicality of producer cooperatives. Of course, Mill had written approvingly of both types of cooperatives. But it was to producer cooperatives that Mill had looked for a resolution of the alienation created by capitalist production.

As early as 1889, Sidney Webb asserted that producer cooperatives suggested themselves as a "seductive means of escape." As a result, "social reformers cannot refrain from keeping alive lingering hopes that some means of performing the impossible may be found." Corporations dominate cooperation. Without aggressive nationalization, the socialist ideals of the earliest founders of the cooperative movement cannot be realized (S. Webb 1889b, 50–51).

From a modern liberal perspective, the failure of producer cooperatives to meet Mill's expectations, however unfortunate, has been largely unavoidable. As a result there is not much that can be done to address the fundamental inequality of the relation between employer and worker. This is essentially the position of modern Millean liberals like Wendy Donner (1991, 208–217). But such a response is inconsistent with a radical reading of Mill's utilitarianism. If cooperatives cannot be made to work on a large scale, some other means must be found to achieve a fundamental restructuring of the relation of the mass of workers to their employment. It is this quandary that the Webbs confronted. Their solution was to look to the nationalization of industry coupled with active trade unions. But the upshot is not a rejection of Mill's basic utilitarian principles. Rather, the difference is one of judgment concerning the feasibility of voluntary producer cooperatives. The question becomes whether, given all his misgivings about state power, Mill would have turned toward some form of democratic nationalization had he been convinced of the impracticality of producer cooperatives. I doubt that a convincing answer can be given to such a hypothetical. What is clear is that a radical utilitarian could reasonably reach such a conclusion. In this sense, the Webbs and the Fabians were very much in the Millean tradition.

As to the Webbs' endorsement of the Soviet Union and the ease with which they were flattered and hoodwinked, even to the point of justifying the show trials of the 1930s, all that can be said is that their actions at the time were at best the product of magical thinking. There is no argument here. The Webbs clearly took a position in their last years diametrically opposed to the Fabian emphasis on caution and much of their own earlier writing.[5] Interestingly Beatrice Webb, in praising the Soviet Union, admitted "It is the invention of the religious order as the determining factor in the life of a great nation that is the magnet which attracts me to Russia." She went on to observe, "Practically that religion is Comteism—the religion of Humanity. Auguste Comte comes to his own" (diary entry for January 4, 1932, quoted in MacKenzie and MacKenzie 1977, 406–407). One is tempted to take this statement at face value. Of course, it was just this side of Comte that Mill ultimately found unacceptable. And perhaps it is the case that despite its constructive Millean character, modern radicalism has too often demonstrated a weakness for Comtean order.

The Webbs' endorsement of Stalin's show trials suggests a dark side to modern radicalism. But even accepting this at face value, making no excuses based on their age or the depressing economic and political realities of the 1930s, I find it reasonable to conclude that the Webbs and the early Fabians more generally were essentially Millean. Central to this assessment is not so much that they advanced Mill's specific concerns or programmatics. Rather, it follows from their adopting a fundamentally Millean outlook. Their radicalism, even as it embraced nationalization, drew on Mill's basic philosophic utilitarian coda, looked to political economy to explain the nature of the social world, emphasized the progressive but transitional character of capitalism, anticipated the development of the working class, and remained confident that democratic, nonviolent reform could provide a path to a more equal economy.

This Fabian perspective on Mill is well summarized in the short Fabian biographical tract that appeared in 1913, written by the Webbs' close colleague, Julius West. In West's view, Mill had seen "behind all the cloudiness of the Socialists of 1848 something substantial, something real. He was able to sketch something very near the actual line of the future evolution of Socialist thought." If Mill had lived another ten years, West conjectured, "he would almost certainly have been amongst the founders of the Fabian Society." Far from describing Mill as a figure of just historical interest, West puts him forth as the touchstone of evolutionary socialism. In

5. For example, Sidney Webb had spoken of the "inevitability of gradualness" (MacKenzie and MacKenzie 1977, 380). Early in her career, Beatrice Webb had praised Robert Owen for advocating a socialism "which discovers itself in works and not in words," a socialism which "has silently embodied itself in the Factory Acts," public health acts and a range of progressive legislation. She explicitly contrasted this home-grown English socialism with that "of foreign manufacture which cries for an Utopia of anarchy to be brought about by a murderous revolution" (B. Webb 1899, 16).

a passage entitled "Back to Mill," West speculates, "It appears well within the bounds of probability that the attitude of the evolutionary Socialist upon matters connected with society (granted some few exceptions) is approximating to that of Mill" (J. West 1913, 22).

A NOTE ON AMERICA

The Fabians expanded into much of the British Empire—Australia, India, and elsewhere. There was also a foray into the United States in the form of the American Fabian Society, founded in 1896. The American branch never achieved the prominence of its English model. But Fabians interacted with a number of radicals moving toward progressivism and socialism.

In 1888 Sidney Webb made a trip to the United States, where he was rather critical of what he saw, with the exception of MIT and Harvard (MacKenzie and MacKenzie 1977, 94–95). On the trip he met Richard Ely, then a professor at Johns Hopkins and one of the founders of the American Economic Association (AEA). Ely convinced Webb to write a short book, *Socialism in England*, which was one of the early monographs published by the AEA (E. Roberts 2003, 7). This book expanded Webb's earlier essays on socialism and emphasized to an American audience the importance of John Stuart Mill. Webb states, "The economic influence most potent among the Socialist Radicals is still that of John Stuart Mill" (S. Webb 1889b, 47).

After the founding of the Socialist Party of America in 1901, twentieth-century American radicals never formed the type of left thinktank/association represented by the Fabians. The ideas of radical reform were largely generated from the universities, where progressives such as Ely pursued a mixture of political economy and political action. As pointed out by Evan Roberts, the similarities between Ely and the Webbs are quite striking. In particular, they "emphasized the organic and evolutionary nature of society. . . . Because they believed industrial society was changing over time, they recommended improvement in social conditions through slowly evolving reforms" (E. Roberts 2003, 12). The new world was the product of democracy and the industrial revolution.

It is not hard to trace this similarity in outlook to the Millean character of their radicalism. The emphasis on evolution and slow changes comes directly from Mill's progressive radicalism. Starting with an analysis of capitalist tendencies in the nineteenth century, with the fact that these developments awakened the working classes, and with the possibilities for reform made realistic by the malleability of the social relations of production, the Fabians and American Progressives echoed the radical Mill.[6]

FABIANS IN THE TWENTIETH CENTURY

During the twentieth century, the influence of the Fabians waxed and waned. With the formation of the Labour Party, Fabians had a powerful audience for their reports and policy ideas. Countless MPs and all six Labour prime ministers had at one time or another been members of the Fabian Society. Fabians early in the thirties had a major influence on future leaders of the Third World, including Nehru.

Fabians have held a range of economic and political positions. In their radical thinking, many of the twentieth-century Fabians accepted a broad framework constructed very much in the Millean tradition, and they often returned to themes that occupied Mill's own efforts. Obviously such a thesis is not subject to any explicit proof. Indeed, for a number of Fabians it is far from true. Still, the plausibility of the proposition can be bolstered by examples. As a start along these lines, consider briefly two twentieth-century Fabians, Hugh Dalton and Nicholas Kaldor. Both were economists with Fabian roots; both were educated at LSE; both were active in the Labour Party; and both in their thinking reflected Mill's progressive approach to radicalism.

Hugh Dalton

Hugh Dalton (1887–1962) came from a long line of professionals and clergymen. His father achieved some notice as the tutor and subsequent friend to Queen Victoria's sons, Edward and George. His mother came from a rich landowning family. He attended Eton and went on to

6. Roberts identifies a second bond between the Webbs and Ely. They were strong believers in eugenics. In this case, where both groups deserted Mill, they most unfortunately went awry. British Fabians and American Progressives embraced the message of eugenics as advanced by any number of political tendencies at the turn of the twentieth century. While Mill as a pragmatic matter had looked to an extended period in which the middle class would educate and lead the emerging working class, he was at root an Enlightenment egalitarian. Eugenics was a product of post-Darwinian pseudo-science in both Britain and the United States. (For an extended discussion of the tension between classical egalitarianism and the pseudo-Darwinian program, see Peart and Levy 2005.) As such it made a particularly inappropriate partner for Millean radicalism.

Cambridge, where he was close friends with the poet Rupert Brooke. At Cambridge, the Tory Dalton converted quickly to the intellectually fashionable Fabianism. He established a connection with A. C. Pigou, who was then bringing out his work on welfare economics. He impressed Beatrice Webb, who became something of a patron. Moving from Cambridge to LSE, Dalton took up the study of inequality, a field in which he would earn distinction. Returning after World War I, he continued this work as LSE expanded under the leadership of William Beveridge.[7]

The point here is not to trace Dalton's career as a major figure in the Labour Party. Rather, the point is to suggest how Dalton rooted his approach to social issues in a clearly Millean context. These ties are most strong in Dalton's major monograph, *Some Aspects of the Inequality of Incomes in Modern Communities* (1920a). This volume was based on his M.A. thesis, which he wrote under Edwin Cannan, the chairman of the economics department at LSE. Cannan edged the department away from Fabianism toward a more centrist position that ultimately resulted in the conservative orientation of Lionel Robbins.[8] But Dalton's work followed Pigou's position more closely than Cannan's.[9]

Inequality of Incomes begins by invoking Mill's discussion of justice in *Utilitarianism*, where Mill argues, "Justice is no more than a name for certain moral requirements, which regarded collectively, stand higher in the scale of social utility, and are more paramount obligation than any others"

7. This brief sketched is based on Pimlott (1985).

8. There is a serious history to be written on how the LSE economics department moved from a radical experiment to a center of mainstream views. Robbins, a veteran of World War I, had been a socialist in his youth and had shown an interest in Guild Socialism. Enrolling as a student at LSE, he was impressed by Dalton, but soured on the incipient Marxism of Harold Laski, then the mainstay of the political science department. Allyn Young had been brought to LSE to head the economics department, but he died suddenly in 1929. Dalton at this time was in the government. With support from Dalton, Robbins was brought back to LSE as a junior professor. The search for a senior professor continued, but Robbins became the head of the department. Disillusioned with much of radicalism, especially fearful of the implications of collectivization, and influenced by the development of economics on the continent, Robbins became "an economic liberal." He was "considerably influenced" by Ludwig von Mises and recruited F. A. Hayek to LSE. Robbins is most famous for his definition of economics as the study of "human behavior as a relationship between given ends and scarce means which have alternative uses" and his insistence that economics must eschew interpersonal comparisons of utility. See Howson (2004, 2012) and Robbins (1971).

9. For example, Dalton accepted as a basic axiom the proposition that other things equal, a transfer from a rich person to a poorer person raises social welfare (1920b). This axiom, which Pigou had advanced in his *Wealth and Welfare* (1912), now is called the Pigou-Dalton principle. Notice that Robbins's position rules out such statements.

(Mill [1861] 1987, 337, quoted in Dalton 1920a, 18).[10] Questions of equality cannot be separated from questions of social welfare. Reforms must consider consequences. Dalton went on in a Millean fashion to focus on reform of inheritance laws as a major policy tool for reducing inequality.

Acknowledging the ideas of Bentham and Mill on the subject, Dalton pushed a bit further by proposing that "only the surviving spouse and the direct descendants" should be allowed to inherit from an intestate. He then argued for two taxes, the first on the estate and the second on any inheritor. The first tax would fall only on that portion of the estate that was inherited previously. This was a variation on the Rignano principle[11] aimed at eventually nationalizing wealth. For the second, he explicitly invokes Mill's plan for a minimum and asserts that over such a minimum, a graduated tax should eventually reach a 100 percent rate.

Dalton's plan went further. Much of the inheritance taxes collected would undoubtedly be in the form of securities. Government securities could be simply retired, but other securities could form the basis of a public fund, with the revenue reinvested. Dalton anticipated that this engine of accumulation, if protected from finance ministers eager to balance their budgets, would make possible the expansion of an efficient public mechanism for achieving socialist ends. Dalton went so far as to suggest the "Public Assets Commissioners" might perhaps be "fenced off" from "direct control and surveillance of Parliament" (Dalton 1920a, 341–343).

In this fashion, Dalton blended Mill's approach to inheritance with an ingenious plan for expanding national ownership. Ultimately, much of the national accumulation would be based on purchased capital, providing compensation to the owners, an idea that Mill, with his emphasis on the need for compensation, might well have seen as promising. Whatever one thinks of the merits of Dalton's Fabian proposals, one can easily see its Millean origins and utilitarian spirit. While later radical plans have generally had a less direct connection to Mill's own proposals, a concern to balance the achievement of greater equality and a peaceful democratic transition has characterized most all of them.

Nicholas Kaldor

Nicholas Kaldor (1908–1986) was born in Hungary, attended Humboldt University in Berlin, and went on to the London School of Economics.

10. On Mill's discussion of justice, see chapter 13.
11. On the Rignano principle and Dalton's championing of it, see Erreygers and Di Bartolomeo (2007).

Moving from student to lecturer, he was immersed in the rich intellectual life of LSE. He came to London a socialist, strongly influenced by the Fabian materials he had seen (King 2009, 89).[12] In the 1930s the economics departments of the Webbs' socialist school had taken on a distinctly conservative tack under Lionel Robbins and Friedrich von Hayek. For a while Kaldor took up their positions, leaving behind his youthful socialism. As one biographer puts it, he "had fallen, briefly, under Hayek's spell" (King 2009, 17). The spell didn't last long. He was soon pulled back to the left by an exciting younger generation of economists at LSE, including Abba Lerner. He became enamored with the Keynesian revolution and returned to a mild version of Fabian socialism. After World War II, Kaldor moved on to Cambridge.

Kaldor was a first-rate theorist and a policy activist in the Labour Party. He worked with Gunnar Myrdal to develop the notion of cumulative causation in opposition to development theories of equilibrium and convergence. He wrote on Keynesian economics. He made contributions to economics across any number of fields, demonstrating a breadth typical of nineteenth- more than twentieth-century economists. Toward the end of his life he became a major critic of the drift rightward in economics and politics, reasserting his conviction that capitalism was a transitional system.

Kaldor was a major contributor to the New Welfare Economics. The need for a new version of welfare economic had been generated by Lionel Robbins's famous *Essay on the Nature and Significance of Economic Science*. Robbins had attacked the Old Welfare Economics of Pigou and Dalton for its insistence on making interpersonal comparisons of utility and in particular for asserting that a dollar to a poor person generated more utility than a dollar to a rich one. Robbins argued that since utility is intrinsically a subjective matter, comparisons across individuals have no scientific basis. That is, we have no way of knowing that a Brahmin might not enjoy another dollar of income ten times more than an untouchable. And Robbins was not shy about identifying how economists had been misled. The problem resulted from "the accidental deposit of the historical association of English Economics with Utilitarianism." Robbins was sure that both utilitarianism and economics would be improved by a separation (Robbins 1932, 124–125).

Robbins's challenge struck a chord with economists struggling with the foundations of utility theory. More significant for the present discussion, those interested in policy feared that economists would effectively be removed from offering expert advice. Except in the highly unlikely

12. Apparently he had tea with Beatrice Webb when he first came to LSE in 1927 (King 2009, 89).

situation in which all persons saw their welfare improved by a public activity (i.e., the situation known as a Pareto improvement), economists would seem to have no way to determine whether a program represented a social gain.

In a concise article (Kaldor 1939), Kaldor offered a solution to Robbins's challenge. The basic idea is simple. If after a policy-driven change the gainers from the policy have enough winnings to compensate any losers from the policy, then the economist is in a position to advise this fact. This compensation test[13] effectively divided the welfare problem in two. First, determine if there is an efficiency gain to be achieved and then, consider the attractiveness of the new distribution of welfare. For an example, Kaldor offered the canonical policy intervention: the introduction of free trade in mid-nineteenth-century Britain. In that case, according to Kaldor, the economist could vouchsafe that the gains of free trade to manufacturers and workers exceeded by a considerable amount the losses to land holders.

Kaldor explicitly accepted Robbins's assertion that economists might have little to say about the second portion of the procedure. However, like A. C. Pigou, the major welfare economist of the time, he felt they might be able to help in the analysis of alternative ways of achieving the same distribution. What had Kaldor's argument achieved? It provided a strong commonsense endorsement of progressive applied economics. Kaldor's compensation test was fundamentally Millean, for Mill had always been a strong advocate of achieving reform with compensation.

In considering redistributive moves, Mill had consistently emphasized the wisdom of paying compensation. For example, he generally advocated compensation in the context of land reform. Perhaps, with less enthusiasm he accepted the political logic of compensation with respect to the emancipation of slaves. Similarly, he looked to producer cooperatives as compensating capitalists for their machinery. In each case, he was sure that the progress achievable on the base of reform would soon overshadow the costs of compensation. Peasant proprietors would be more productive than tenants, free labor would be more productive than slave labor, and cooperatives would be more productive than capitalist firms. This Millean optimism and faith in progress are very much reflected in Kaldor's test. The key to achieving equality was not through uncompensated appropriation but, rather, through demonstrating greater productivity.

13. The test became known as the Kaldor-Hicks compensation test or a potential-Pareto improvement.

Of course, Mill's empirical assumptions might prove wrong. In the modern period, many economists have accepted instead some version of Arthur Okun's leaky bucket, whereby distortions caused by direct redistribution can't be overcome and the result is a "big trade-off" between efficiency and equality (Okun 1975).[14] Such arguments assume a highly static economy—one which is largely unaffected by the reforms themselves. It is the very essence of modern Millean radicalism to assert the contrary and to uncover substantial gains achievable through egalitarian policies. (For examples, see the interesting treatment of this problem in Putterman, Roemer, and Silvestre [1998].)

In the end, Robbins had missed the significance of the marriage of radical utilitarianism with political economy. Yes, the joining suggested that a poor person could benefit more from direct redistribution than such redistribution would cost a rich person. *Pace* Robbins, that's not such a hard notion to accept. But the result of that joining had not been a wild-eyed argument for the improvement of the lot of the poor through direct redistribution. Rather, the utilitarian coda required of utilitarian radicals that they consider the entire range of consequences of policy. The point was to identify changes capable of generating major net gains, regardless of the compensation paid. Under such circumstances, it would be only politic to actually pay compensation. It was from such considerations that Mill had advised caution and encouraged compensation. Kaldor's emphasis on a compensation test was not just a clever means to avoid Robbins's solipsism. It was also a statement of faith in the Millean political economy of progress.

14. Notice that Okun himself was willing to accept considerable leakage in achieving redistribution in favor of the poor. The point here is not who is more "pro-poor" but, rather, the extent to which reducing inequality can be achieved through reforms that actually increase efficiency.

CHAPTER 12

Rawls and the Means of Production

The paradigmatic modern radical-liberal is the philosopher John Rawls. While in his early years Rawls advanced a utilitarian position, his hallmark work, *A Theory of Justice*, presents a contractual approach heavily influenced by Kantian ideas. Despite its contractual core, Rawls draws heavily on Mill. Rawls's theory, like those of most modern philosophers of distributive justice, can be seen as constructively addressing Mill's utilitarian challenge. I will develop that argument in the next chapter. The purpose here is to explore whether the modern Rawls makes progress vis-à-vis Mill in defining an appropriate institutional structure for realizing the radical vision. My claim is that like many modern radicals, and unlike Mill, Rawls fails to describe a coherent evolutionary path for radical reform.

What is missing from Rawls is any clear hope of progressive dynamics building on the development and agency of the working classes. Of course, Mill too had been a middle-class radical. But Mill had held out the promise of progress toward cooperative ownership. Mill had looked forward to the emergence of explicitly working-class institutions. In some fundamental way, Mill had seen such developments as both the means and the ends of his radicalism. Rawls, for all his emphasis on society's obligation to do well by the least advantaged, sees no explicit role for the development of institutions shaped by the least advantaged. Despite its deep sincerity, Rawls's radicalism, like much of modern radicalism, leaves little room for the working class as a progressive political and economic force.

After enunciating his two principles of justice, John Rawls explicitly turns to describing sets of institutions consistent with those principles and capable, he hopes, of providing an appropriate background for justice. He suggests that the selection of institutional structures is the payoff of the entire exercise. Rawls argues that two realizations, or "basic structures," are potentially acceptable. The first is a version of the institution of private property, a "property-owning democracy," borrowed from the work of the economist and one time Fabian James Meade. Rawls's discussion of this structure hardly constitutes a strong defense of private property. If it is a defense at all, it remains quite conditional. In this respect Rawls's position very much resembles that of the young John Stuart Mill. Rawls, like the young Mill, remains ambivalent with respect to private property. Like the young Mill, he hopes for a set of reforms in that system that will soften its harshness.

Rawls's second alternative, a lightly sketched "liberal (democratic) socialism," is even less fully developed. Indeed, Rawls offers no insights into the relation between his principles of justice and social ownership of the means of production under this mode of production. In this sense, his defense of socialism is also weak, suggesting only that such a system may not be hopelessly incompatible with justice. Here, as in his discussion of property-owning democracy, Rawls leaves little room for history or progress. In the end, Rawls seems almost casually indifferent, hovering between a weak defense of private property and a vague endorsement of liberal (democratic) socialism.

By contrast, the radical Mill provides a historical reading of accumulation coupled to an optimistic expansion of working-class power. In the context of the industrial revolution, private property played a key role in facilitating capital accumulation and the growth of per capita income. In the future Mill anticipated the decline of profit incentives, the emergence of a stationary state, and a widespread expansion of cooperative ownership. His was fundamentally a materialist reading of progress. Of course, more recent history might demonstrate Mill's radical vision as overly optimistic. Be that as it may, there is a coherence in Mill's radical counsel to patiently work for progress. Rawls's modern radicalism, whether played out in the context of a "property-owning democracy" or a "liberal (democratic) socialism," offers no such coherent rationale for patience and hard work. Instead, it hopes for a nebulous and largely ahistorical form of moral awakening.

RAWLS'S AGENDA

Not a few economists commenting on Rawls assumed he was talking about the optimal organization of a welfare state. Thus they have become used to treating John Rawls's notions about justice as a guide to taxation and income redistribution in a welfare state. In this vein, the Rawlsian social-welfare function, which judges states by the utility of the worst-off individual, is viewed as a dramatic alternative. The goal, then, is to maximize this minimum.[1] Such exercises undoubtedly lead to useful analysis. However, this interpretation of Rawls distorts considerably his basic concerns.[2] Rawls wasn't propounding some novel progressive income tax code. Indeed, his comments on the subject suggest that he favored a flat tax. Rawls explicitly introduced his principles with bigger game in mind. He advanced them as the basis for evaluating the basic institutional regimes of societies. For Rawls, the question is not whether we have set up a system of taxes and transfers to maximize the minimum utility in society, but whether the institutions of society are just. And among these institutions is that of private property.

Modern economists generally avoid questions of justice in favor of analyses of efficiency. Even when economists venture into questions of redistribution, they shun claims about justice. And yet the very foundations of the discipline in moral philosophy emerged out of discussions of justice. Rawls's efforts extend the work of J. S. Mill and David Hume. Mill and Hume were both eager to consider the question of justice in the context of their political economy. In evaluating the justice of his regimes, Rawls builds directly on their platform.

John Rawls begins with an extended search for "the most acceptable political conception of justice for specifying the fair terms of cooperation between citizens regarded as free and equal and as both reasonable and rational" (2001, 7–8).[3] Rawls dubs this search "the fundamental question of [democratic constitutional] political philosophy" (7). His efforts lead to his two now-famous principles of justice (2001, 42–43):

(a) Each person has the same indefeasible claim to a fully adequate scheme of equal basic liberties, which scheme is compatible with the same scheme of liberties for all.
(b) Social and economic inequalities are to satisfy two conditions: first, they are to be attached to offices and positions open to all under

1. See, for example, Gruber and Saez (2002).

2. Krouse and McPherson (1988) forcefully argue that Rawls's theory was hostile to the welfare state. Rawls subsequently endorsed their interpretation in his *Justice as Fairness: a Restatement* (2001).

3. Where possible I try to rely on Rawls's positions in their more or less final form as outlined in the *Restatement* (2001).

conditions of fair equality of opportunity; and second they are to be to the greatest benefit of the least-advantaged members of society (the difference principle).

It is not critical to our purposes here to recount Rawls's Kantian arguments in support of his principles. Rather, our concern focuses on the uses to which he puts this definition of justice. The entire exercise of deriving these principles is to serve as a basis for "regime" choice. Rawls's agenda is about such choice. His fundamental program is to identify one or more sets of social and political institutions, or "regimes," that satisfy his criterion of justice as fairness. This is the Rawlsian payoff.[4]

Presumably, regimes might differ in any number of characteristics. In practice, Rawls considers only five regimes: state socialism with a command economy, liberal (democratic) socialism, laissez-faire capitalism, welfare state capitalism, and property-owning democracies. As between the first two, the key question is the nature of the state's planning apparatus. As between the last three, the key question is the extent and character of the constraints placed on the institution of private property.

In analyzing each type of regime, Rawls acknowledges four questions that can be raised: the question of right, the question of design, the question of incentive compatibility, and the question of competence. The last three questions are largely practical ones: Can the regime design real-world institutions to do what it wants to do? Will those institutions win citizen compliance? Will officeholders actually be able to do what is expected of them? Rawls notes that much conservative thinking concerns these last three questions. He might have added much economic thinking, as well. But these are not arguments he wants to engage head-on. Such arguments are not relevant to his agenda. Instead, he asserts that his concerns are "largely limited" to the first question, the question of right. Assuming the other three questions can be reasonably addressed, he asks, Is a regime "right and just?" (2001, 136–137). Of course, some of us—conservatives, economists, or others—might have wished that Rawls had cast his net more broadly and explored these three other questions with respect to the regimes he considers.[5] But Rawls can reasonably respond that these

4. In his earlier work, *A Theory of Justice* (1971), Rawls hoped to achieve agreement on a "comprehensive moral doctrine." In his later works he advances his conception of "justice as fairness" as a "political conception." In either case, the purpose of constructing the principles of justice is to facilitate the choice among social institutions.

5. For example, Wylie Bradford (2000) suggests Rawls's property-owning democracy is likely to fail one or more of these requirements.

questions are simply not relevant to his undertaking. Rawls has explicitly constructed the grounds upon which he moves forward, and those grounds focus on the rightness and justice of institutions.

But that said, the entire point of developing the "principles of justice" is so that they can be used to pick among differing basic institutions and thus to serve as a defense for those basic institutions. And among these is the question of property rights. In his *Restatement*, immediately after making the arguments for his principles, Rawls begins his exploration of "institutions of a just basic structure" with a discussion of "property-owning democracy." Does such a regime answer the requirements of justice? Again, the relevant issue is not whether such a regime can exist but, rather, whether as described it meets and supports Rawls's two principles. To suggest an affirmative answer means we have enough information about such a regime and specifically about the role of private property in such a regime to comfortably conclude that (if everything works right) it will satisfy Rawls's principles. In this eventuality, we can interpret Rawls's endorsement of a property-owning democracy as a defense of private property based on the principles of justice.

By way of contrast, Rawls is clear that he judges centralized state socialism as violating "the equal basic rights and liberties, not to mention the fair value of these liberties" (2001, 138). However, he does not elaborate on how he reaches this conclusion, taking it instead as largely self-evident. Rawls is convinced that state socialism with a command economy cannot be defended as a just regime. But he also explicitly rejects laissez-faire capitalism and welfare-state capitalism, both of which build on conceptions of private property endowed with broad rights. Given his rejection of these familiar versions of private property regimes, one might begin to suspect that private ownership of the means of production, like centralized command planning, is simply not a defensible institution in terms of Rawlsian justice. But that is not Rawls's conclusion. Indeed, as noted above, he asserts that a property-owning democracy will meet his basic principles. In putting forth this argument, Rawls produces a highly conditional defense of private property.

RAWLS AND MEADE

Rawls's discussion of property-owning democracy draws directly on the work of the economist J. E. Meade, whom Paul Samuelson famously called "the last of the utilitarians." Meade in his early years had been a close friend of Hugh Dalton and an active Fabian. Like other Fabians of his generation, he was strongly influenced by John Maynard Keynes's macroeconomics. Like other prominent Fabians, Meade was a key economist in the Labour Party government after World War II.

Following hints in Mill's *Principles*, Meade wrestled with the possibilities for reforming the institution of private property so as to make it more compatible with a social commitment to equality. In 1964, Meade published a short set of lectures, *Efficiency, Equality and the Ownership of Property*. In *A Theory of Justice*, Rawls invokes Meade's work, but doesn't explore it in depth. In the *Restatement*, Rawls provides only a slightly expanded treatment. Does Meade construct a convincing defense of his property-owning democracy? Can Rawls rely on Meade's work to do the heavy lifting in his argument? Rawls seems to suggest this. But Meade's argument almost trivializes the role of property in the economy even as it ignores the deeper questions of justice that Rawls sees as so central.

Meade's short volume is fundamentally about automation.[6] Meade is worried that while the development of more and more sophisticated physical capital is likely to increase the average productivity of labor, it is also likely to reduce the productivity of labor at the margin. Since in a neoclassical world it is the marginal productivity that determines wages, the result will be a very large share of income in the hands of capital owners. We can note here that there is something rather odd in Meade's basic scenario. As capital-labor ratios rise, Meade expects the marginal product of labor to fall. That is, society is faced with a rising profit rate just as profit becomes most abundant. Meade envisions what is essentially a dual economy, one in which very high capital labor ratios are applied to some primary sectors, but not to other secondary sectors.

Asserting the probability of such predictions, Meade finds the resulting world nothing short of "hideous," a "Brave New Capitalists' Paradise" in which "the working population required to man the extremely profitable automated industries would be small." He anticipates, then, "a large expansion of the production of the labour-intensive goods and services which were in high demand by the few multi-multi-multi-millionaires." In the end "we would be back in a super-world of an immiserized proletariat and of butlers, footmen, kitchen maids, and other hangers-on" (Meade 1964, 33).

Meade's "solution" to this highly unattractive outcome is to take advantage of his very special assumption about the duality of the automated

6. Several writers, and especially Bradford (2000), have pointed out the rather special assumptions Meade makes with respect to automation.

economy. The primary economy has only a modest need for labor. The more widely and evenly spread is the ownership of private capital, the less compelling is the need to work. "[B]y the wave of some magic wand" Meade creates a society in which property is "equally distributed over the citizens in the community." Essentially it is a world of trust-fund babies who receive "a large part" of their incomes from property. In this economy, work has "become rather more a matter of personal choice," with a good deal more "play-acting, ballet-dancing, painting, writing, sporting activities" and the like, with much carried out on "a semi-professional semi-amateur basis" (Meade 1964, 41). The resulting economy is still dual in nature, but the hypothesized egalitarian distribution of property tames the beast. Meade's property-owning democracy sounds a good deal like a version of Mill's stationary state, but without cooperatives.

Meade trivializes the role of labor in his property-owning democracy. But in that construct he also trivializes the role of property ownership itself. Meade's property-owning democracy has largely wished away the investment-incentive problem. Meade is only mildly concerned that the erosion of capital's concentration could undermine the entrepreneurial incentives often seen as driving productivity growth and the application of technology. In Meade's world, property ownership acts as only a mild prod to accumulation. The almost universal class of small owners who work occasionally in community theaters leave much of the decision making in the economy to bureaucratic agents, the executives of corporations, and mutual funds.

What a bland sort of property, indeed. Meade acknowledges the existence of a problem, but he clearly considers it a minor one. Asserting the productiveness of private property, Meade expresses concern that in selecting among progressive tax measures to roughly maintain equality in property, ownership attention should be paid to minimizing the effect on "the incentives to work and take risks" (1964, 54). But, Meade is extremely vague on just what those incentives are, what they generate for the community, and what difference it makes if the state takes major steps to distribute property more evenly. What is clearly missing is an assessment of the size and distribution of the costs (and for that matter, the benefits) of taking the basic redistributive steps involved.

In Meade's tame private property, Rawls hopes to find an institution he can endorse as just—an institution that respects equal liberty and works to guarantee the highest welfare of the worst off. But neither Meade nor Rawls suggests a dynamic that will bring the property-owning democracy into existence. While Rawls's understanding of justice is truly profound, his analysis lacks a historical engine.

RAWLS AND MILL

For all his protestations, Rawls shares a great deal with Mill. At the very least, he sees utilitarians as his chief audience. Repeatedly he compares his own notions to those of various utilitarians. In many ways, Rawls's project can be viewed as an elaboration of John Stuart Mill's effort to reconcile equality and liberty. From this vantage point, both Rawls and Mill are responding to early nineteenth-century utilitarian claims about justice and the institution of private property.

The utilitarian creed as it came down to John Stuart Mill from Jeremy Bentham held that the institution of private property served the greatest good in at least two ways. Indirectly it gave rise to our sense of justice, while directly it contributed massively to the material welfare of prosperous and poor alike. It was to this triumphalist creed that Mill eventually took great exception. In particular, John Stuart Mill raised serious doubts about the justice of the institution of private property as it appeared in the real world. At root, the radical Mill rejected the all-or-nothing choice offered by the earlier utilitarians. He saw the economic world as far more malleable than the one they described. As a result, Mill cast laissez-faire capitalism as a transitional stage.

Mill could be a harsh critic. He asserted that in its then-present state, the institution of private property led to a situation in which the produce of labor was apportioned,

> almost in an inverse ratio to the labour—the largest portions to those who have never worked at all, the next largest to those whose work is almost nominal, and so in a descending scale, the remuneration dwindling as the work grows harder and more disagreeable, until the most fatiguing and exhausting bodily labour cannot count with certainty on being able to earn even the necessaries of life." (Mill [1848] 1965, 207)

If private property actually necessitated such a state of affairs, he made clear that he would prefer communism with all its "difficulties."

In effect Mill turned the earlier utilitarian position on its head. Rather than giving rise to and reaffirming our sense of justice, the real-world institution of private property continually runs afoul of that sense. For

Mill, as observed earlier, justice is defined as "the appropriate name for certain social utilities which are vastly more important, and therefore more absolute and imperative, than any others are as a class" (Mill [1861] 1987, 338).[7] The excesses of private property are unjust.

Mill argued that private property as then constituted did poorly by the least advantaged *and* failed to maximize the greatest happiness of the greatest number. Like earlier utilitarians, Mill saw the welfare of the worst-off member and the representative member of society moving largely in tandem. But unrestricted private property had done less than well by both. Justice for Mill required that society's institutions do well by both of these. For Mill, the institution of private property as he found it allowed far too much field for the baser, largely unproductive aspects of self-interest.

Like Rawls, Mill at times did imagine that the institution of private property might conceivably be salvaged. As discussed in chapter 4, Mill made a case for a "principle of private property [which] has never yet had a fair trial in any country." In place of a system that has "heaped impediments upon some, to give advantage to others"; that has "purposely fostered inequalities"; and has "prevented all from starting fair in the race," Mill hoped for a reformed private property that allows all to "start on perfectly equal terms"(Mill [1848] 1965, 209). In the end, however, we know that Mill put his faith in the development of cooperative ownership.

In effect, Mill anticipated much of Rawls's argument from justice. Both Mill and Rawls express uneasiness with the reality of private property and look to a dramatic overhaul of the institution. Justice requires more than private property, plain and simple.

Rawls embraces an ideal form of property with only passing suggestions (following Meade) of what types of legislation might help move an economy in that direction. What we really learn from Rawls's discussion is that the institution of private property is highly problematic in precisely the Millean sense. When left to laissez-faire mechanisms, it leads to powerful concentrations of wealth that violate Rawls's principles of justice and Mill's most important social utilities.

Rawls maintains that justice is consistent with a tamed form of private property, but that justice is at odds with the aggressive acquisitiveness often associated with the institution. Whereas the early utilitarian defense of private property is fundamentally linked to the abundance

7. Mill notes that he sees no conflict of this definition with Kant's approach to morality.

(Bentham's word) that private property was supposed to generate, Rawls is actually suspicious of great material wealth. And he certainly doesn't see material progress of an economy as central to justice: "It is a mistake to believe that a just and good society must wait upon a high material standard of life." And, he goes on to state "great wealth . . . beyond some point is more likely to be a positive hindrance, a meaningless distraction at best if not a temptation to indulgence and emptiness" (Rawls 1971, 290).

Rawls is explicit that the difference principle "does not require continual economic growth over generations to maximize upward indefinitely the expectations of the least advantaged measured in terms of income and wealth." And just at this spot, he invokes Mill. Rawls suggests, "We certainly do not want to rule out [John Stuart] Mill's idea of a society in a just stationary state where (real) capital accumulation may cease" (2001, 159). Yet Rawls's endorsement of that state lacks Mill's vision for the development of cooperative ownership of the means of production. If our reading of Mill is correct, the historical purpose of the stationary state is not just to dampen the worst aspects of greed, but also to set the stage for a new mode of production built on cooperation.

In the end, Rawls never gives an argument actually in favor of private property in the means of production. His discussion of property is almost always in terms of the constraints to be placed on it, not in terms of its positive role. The only exception to this observation is where Rawls considers "the right to hold and to have the exclusive use of personal property." Unlike ownership of the means of production, a right to personal property[8] is "basic" to the extent that it allows "a sufficient material basis for personal independence and a sense of self-respect, both of which are essential for the adequate development and exercise of the moral powers" (2001, 114). Personal property is central to Rawls's conception of self-respect. It forms an extension of one's personality. But ownership of the means of production plays no such role. In this respect, Rawls leaves no room for Mill's progressive vision of the expansion of cooperative ownership and its importance to the independence, competency, and self-image of the working classes.

Rawls is also willing to endorse liberal (democratic) socialism as meeting his basic requirements. Liberal socialism, Rawls argues (and perhaps Mill would agree), is also consistent with the demands of justice. Thus those principles don't fully determine the basic structure but, rather,

8. Rawls includes "dwellings" and "private grounds" in the category of "personal property" and apparently doesn't consider such capital as part of the means of production.

"set out in a schematic way the outlines of a just economic system that admits of several variations." While Rawls is vague, he does suggest that liberal socialism might well involve "a firm's direction and management [being] elected by, if not directly in the hands of, its own workforce" (2001, 138). He goes on to suggest that the choice between property-owning democracy and liberal (democratic) socialism depends on "the traditions, institutions, and social forces of each country, and its particular historical circumstances" (1971, 274). Exactly what those historical and social conditions might be is never squarely addressed. Here again, the concrete character of progress is left very much unspecified by Rawls.

Rawls's approach seems more than a bit cavalier. History is invoked, but the import of that history is left unclear. In particular, Rawls fails to address the frightening alienation of work so central to the history of laissez-faire capitalism. The meaning of that history for our institutions remains obscure. The mature Mill anchored his understanding of progress in that history of alienation and workers' efforts to escape it. His political economy of progress projected the gradual emergence of a set of institutions, including, in particular, producer cooperatives capable of generating a rich environment for the greatest number of the population.

Perhaps reasonably, Rawls has a low opinion of economic knowledge and certainly doesn't suggest that we know much about the relation between our economic institutions and the performance of the economy. "Often the best we can say of a law or policy is that it is at least not clearly unjust. The application of the difference principle in a precise way normally requires more information than we can expect to have" (1971, 199).[9] While it is relatively easy to assess when the first principle of equal liberty is violated, it is "comparatively rare" that we can determine whether the "social and economic policies regulated by the difference principle" are in fact just. Faced with such uncertainties, Rawls retreats to rather vague statements about historical conditions.

Mill certainly couldn't have claimed to know much more about the specific effects reforms would have on the economy, but he did assert the importance of cooperative principles in the development of the working classes. As of yet, cooperatives have failed to meet Mill's hopes. But Mill's identification of the problem of working-class agency remains fundamental. It is the theoretical and practical challenge facing modern radicalism. Rawls, unfortunately, sidesteps that challenge.

9. This seems almost like an admission of the impossibility of determining the justness of some subset of regimes.

RAWLS, MILL, AND THE LIBERALISM OF FREEDOM

If Rawls avoids expanding on Mill's understanding of producer cooperatives, at a more abstract level Rawls is very much eager to claim Mill as an advocate of "the liberalism of freedom" along with Kant and Hegel. Rawls sees his own work as anchored in this tradition (Rawls 2000, 330). By including Mill in his camp, Rawls claims to have won Mill over from the classical utilitarians—Jeremy Bentham, James Mill, and Henry Sidgewick—a camp he labels the "liberalism of happiness." While these utilitarians "confirm the liberal freedoms," they take as their first principle the greatest happiness summed over the greatest number (2000, 366).

Rawls's *A Theory of Justice* (at least as originally written) can be viewed as an elaborate attempt to solidify the claims of the liberalism of freedom vis-à-vis the liberalism of happiness.[10] In a sense, J. S. Mill is the crucial borderline figure in this contest. One can imagine Rawls as essentially attempting to convince (browbeat?) Mill into renouncing the classical position and more fully accepting his (i.e., Mill's) inner or deeper tendencies.

Rawls's understanding of the liberalism of freedom and its relation to private property is most clearly presented in his discussion of Hegel. In *Lectures on the History of Moral Philosophy*, Rawls considers at some length Hegel's approach to private property. For Hegel, the material, utilitarian consequences of the institution of private property are beside the point. The value of the institution is that it allows the free expression of individual will.

Mill was convinced that private property in the context of nineteenth-century Britain had generated a system in which contribution and reward were almost inversely correlated. The mature Mill was ready to accept laissez-faire capitalism only as a transitional system to something far better. He could hardly accept Hegel's idealistic interpretation of property. Indeed, Rawls himself balks at such an extreme defense of private property.

There is considerable truth that Mill saw as central the need to make freedom meaningful to the great mass of working people. But for the radical Mill, the liberalisms of happiness and freedom are not separable. A meaningful freedom for Mill was part and parcel of his radical

10. In later works, such as *Justice as Fairness: A Restatement*, the central concept is a somewhat scaled-down "political liberalism," which is meant as a base rather than a complete philosophy. However, it shares the general outlook of the liberalism of freedom.

liberalism of happiness. In his essay on utilitarianism, Mill argued that freedom and justice are best understood as the highest utilities. Mill concluded that to make freedom meaningful to the working classes, institutions driven by the agency of the working classes must address the goals of the working classes. This brings us back to the institutions of cooperation. For Mill they represent a synthesis of the liberalism of freedom and the liberalism of happiness. Perhaps Mill's solution has failed historically. But that in no way erases this central Millean insight. Indeed, the modern radical dilemma remains how to actualize the freedom of the working classes.

Rawls made a major intellectual clarification of the radical meaning of justice. But with respect to institutions, Rawls leaves us with neither a convincing defense of private property nor a full determination of the justice of alternative regimes. Rawls avoids the hardest questions raised by modern economic history and loses sight of the challenge facing the working classes. We require a clearer path forward. To be relevant, modern radicalism, the radicalism of Rawls, must come to grips with the Millean definition of progress that sees the development and empowerment of the working classes as its fundamental end.

A NOTE ON LABOR-MANAGED FIRMS AND MODERN RADICALISM

Admittedly, economists have themselves added only modestly to our understanding of the strengths and weaknesses of cooperatives. But in the last two decades modern radical political economy has made a start at seriously exploring the advantages and disadvantages of such institutions. The emerging consensus holds that while worker-managed firms are internally more efficient than capitalist firms, they have difficulty in raising capital and making convincing commitments to potential investors. For example, Bowles and Gintis (1993) have considered the logic of worker-managed firms as a solution to the perennial problem of labor shirking in the capitalist firm. Rather than a detail of labor-management relations, shirking motivates much of the structure of the capitalist firm, which must resort to a mixture of pay premiums, highly imperfect monitoring, and hierarchical discipline. These actions generate an equilibrium with substantial involuntary unemployment. The continuing presence of such an overhang in the labor market then gives employers power over their employees in the form of an ever-present threat of dismissal. According to Bowles and Gintis, it is this power that spawns the often-tyrannical hierarchy of the capitalist workplace. Whereas the traditional view of markets hinges on their private and voluntary nature, this new reading of the capitalist firm insists that, like government itself, the firm has a public character that can be too easily corrupted and hence requires democratic control.

Bowls and Gintis go on to assert that a democratic firm avoids the worst of the inefficiency created by the shirking problem as experienced by the capitalist firm. Workers in the democratic firm will share in the residual surplus, they will be motivated to monitor each other, and they will generally receive higher wages. Under the circumstances, the democratic firm should prove more internally efficient. On the other side, Bowls and Gintis, like a number of other researchers of cooperative enterprises, fear that worker-managed firms will be too risk-averse in their investment decisions, failing to develop real opportunities for improvement. They see this as a serious institutional problem.

Apart from the specifics of their theory, Bowls and Gintis invoke one of John Stuart Mill's basic arguments in favor of the cooperative firm: "democratic governance is a school for the formation of democratic citizens capable of self-rule" (1993, 88). Their overall conclusion has a radical tone that Mill would have appreciated. For Bowls and Gintis, the firm is the most immediate space in which the responsibilities and challenges of democracy must be faced.

In a similar manner, Gregory Dow begins his volume *Governing the Firm* (2003) with an epigraph from Mill, the famous quotation predicting the emergence of worker owned and managed firms reproduced in chapter 9. Dow makes a pragmatic argument that the standard political machinery of a democracy can be used to create legislation requiring "control referendums" not unlike union representation elections. Dow, very much like Mill, supports approaches that require workers to reimburse the former capitalist owners of firms. At a mechanical level, Dow suggests a number of proposals designed to aid labor-managed firms in making "credible commitments" to capital. In Dow's view, like that of Bowls and Gintis, cooperatives have advantages in internal efficiency, but have difficulty in assuring capital of their trustfulness in contracting. While hardly amounting to a full reconstruction of capitalism, blueprints such as Dow's can form the stuff of real-world experimentation.

Mill's basic list of options for restructuring the workplace is still quite relevant. As a group, modern radicals have only started to define a serious program for achieving democracy in the workplace. Interesting work has been done.[11] But for the most part the various approaches for realizing these fundamental reforms have been left the stuff of theoreticians. In the modern period, programs of worker management have failed to capture the full attention of the left. For all its Rawlsian subtlety, the left has remained almost nonchalant about the most central of reforms. It is difficult to understand the passiveness of this acceptance. As Mill early suggested, radicals must offer an increasingly educated and skilled labor force a realistic path toward democracy in the workplace. Such an agenda is the keystone of a coherent radical program.

11. For a review of the literature, again see Dow (2003). For a recent overview of profitsharing and other structures short of full democratic control, see Kruse, Freeman, and Blasi (2010).

CHAPTER 13

Radical Luck

A defining characteristic of modern radicalism is its insistence on taking luck seriously. Most notably, the "luck egalitarians" see justice as demanding aggressive efforts to reduce inequalities produced by luck broadly conceived. This clearly radical position has been challenged by the advocates of "democratic equality," who have a considerably more limited reading of traditional liberal political values.[1] Most of this debate, when not ignoring Mill's radical utilitarianism, has been openly hostile to that position. Be that as it may, the claim made here is that modern attitudes toward luck can be traced directly to Mill. More constructively, I also claim that Mill's theory of progress suggests an attractive radical reconciliation of the two camps of the modern philosophical debate on luck. This reconciliation provides a core understanding of what radicalism means in a modern context.

In *Utilitarianism*, Mill posited that the historical progress of justice works against all types of social expediency, thus reducing the role of luck in human affairs. In effect, Mill anticipated that justice would require a

1. The "luck egalitarians" and the proponents of "democratic equality" are both groupings of moral philosophers concerned with the problem of distributive justice. Richard Arneson wrote his key paper in 1995 putting forward the central position of luck egalitarians. His work was then critiqued by Elizabeth Anderson (1999), who can be viewed as defining the democratic-equality group. Both groups were strongly influenced by the writings of Rawls, and each can be seen as attempting to develop the logic of the Rawlsian position. It was Anderson who was responsible for providing the luck egalitarians with their name, a name described as "apt" by one of the school's major proponents, G. A. Cohen (2008, 8).

move from something like "democratic equality" to the achievement of something like "luck egalitarianism." Rather than viewing these as competing approaches to justice, a Millean radical can reasonably see them as succeeding stages in the conquest of poverty and the historical achievement of justice.

While the institutional mechanisms of the projected transformation remain vague, Mill's plot for the conquest of luck, and especially the bad luck of poverty, builds squarely on his utilitarian roots. The older J. S. Mill is sometimes viewed as disenchanted with his earlier utilitarianism, absorbed instead by the liberalism of freedom. But *Utilitarianism* does not stop with classical liberal arguments for personal freedom and growth. Justice progresses toward a broader equality. The greatest happiness of the greatest number is ultimately achieved in an egalitarian society that no longer requires the most egregious instruments of expediency. The virtues of those who achieve this transformation are personally rewarding, but not valued independently of the consequences they achieve. Mill's sincere call to participate in this transformation is directed squarely at those who (like the advocates of democratic equality) might otherwise be tempted to stop with a more limited definition of justice.

LUCK EGALITARIANISM AND ITS CRITICS

It is a commonplace that luck affects all of us. Luck favors some and encumbers others. Our health, personal characteristics, and class position are all largely a matter of luck. For luck egalitarians, distributive justice requires those with good luck to compensate those with bad luck. In their view, it is "the responsibility of society—all of us regarded collectively—to alter the distribution of goods and evils that arises from the jumble of lotteries that constitutes human life as we know it." In this redistribution, "the lucky should transfer some or all of their gains due to luck to the unlucky" (Arneson 2008, 80).[2]

Richard Arneson, one of the key advocates of the luck-egalitarian position, traces the basic concern with luck to the work of John Rawls (Arneson 2008). Rawls's emphasis on compensating for "deep inequalities" has a strong appeal to those on the left. And, not surprisingly, many of the luck egalitarians are drawn from the radical left. Their ranks include a number

2. This passage is quoted by Elizabeth Anderson (1999) in launching her defining attack on the luck egalitarians.

of prominent radical philosophers: G. A. Cohen, Richard Arneson, John Roemer, and Thomas Nagel. Indeed, it is not unreasonable to see luck egalitarianism as the response of the radical left to Rawls's effort to rebuild the philosophy of justice.

Several of the luck egalitarians, including Cohen and Roemer, had long worked on attempting a reconstruction of Marxism. While such efforts contributed to sharpening radical discourse, Marxist philosophy in the late twentieth century remained something of a specialized niche. In the same period, Rawls's reconsideration of justice stimulated a renaissance in political philosophy. His interchanges with the right, especially those with Robert Nozick, reestablished the field as central to modern intellectual activity. Rawls's approach, at least that of his *A Theory of Justice*, is perhaps best described as left liberal or radical liberal. Any effort to operationalize Rawls must consider fundamental institutional reforms. In effect, Rawls was inviting a discussion with the radical left. He offered them an entree into the very core of political philosophy. The radical left responded enthusiastically with the development of luck egalitarianism.[3]

Radical philosophers are very much taken with Rawls's acknowledgment of the centrality of luck. But their luck egalitarianism pushes beyond Rawls. From an economic perspective, the most important difference between Rawls and the luck egalitarians derives from Rawls's acceptance, almost his championing, of the claims of material incentives as part of his theory of justice. Thus Rawls allows for inequalities that can achieve an improvement in the position of the worse off.[4] The luck egalitarians and especially G. A. Cohen have argued that such inequalities undermine Rawls's own fundamental insight. Material incentives hold hostage the least lucky. According to Cohen a citizenry that has internalized the Rawlsian concern for the worst off and least lucky should have no business with such hostage taking. Justice requires a more egalitarian treatment of the least lucky.

Of course, even among the luck egalitarians there are a range of debates concerning the degree of sharing appropriate to a just society. Egalitarians differ as to whether individuals should be compensated for their fate (their genes, parents, and the like), their fortune (acquired advantages due

3. This paragraph develops a line of argument suggested by an anonymous referee to an earlier paper (Persky 2013). The point is not that the left embraced Rawls uncritically but, rather, that the left was eager to engage a serious liberal. For an overview of a range of early left criticisms of Rawls, see DiQuattro (1983). Cohen (2008) makes his respect for Rawls most clear.

4. For a useful introduction to the secondary literature on Rawls's "difference principle," see Van Parijs (2003).

either to effort or circumstances), and/or luck proper (pure chance).[5] In the extreme, luck egalitarians emphasize only the importance of individual responsibility against a background of full compensation. They stand ready to endorse only inequalities arising from individual choices once the larger equalization of fate and fortune have been achieved. In this context, responsibility is itself difficult to define.[6]

Not surprisingly, the luck egalitarians are associated with a number of radical political positions. For example, the philosopher G. A. Cohen strongly advocates a socialism based on sharing. For Cohen, the appropriate model for dealing with the inequalities of luck is the type of sharing typical of camping trips (Cohen 2009).[7] Roemer has charted out a version of market socialism (Roemer 1994), while Nagel has advocated a range of radical tax reforms (Murphy and Nagel 2004).

Arrayed against these luck egalitarians are the proponents of "democratic equality," who view the general approach of the luck egalitarians as motivated by envy, invasive in its disregard of privacy, and demeaning in its "contemptuous pity" for the less fortunate (Anderson 1999, 289). In effect, the "democratic egalitarians" level a charge of elitism against the luck egalitarians. The advocates of democratic equality acknowledge the need to guarantee individuals a resource base sufficient to allow participation in the broader society, but not much more. Theirs is the democracy of the (perhaps robust) safety net, but not the camping trip. As such they are close in spirit to traditional liberal concerns.

The term "democratic equality" appears as a chapter title in Rawls's *A Theory of Justice*. In this vein, Norman Daniels (2003) views the philosophy of democratic equality as the appropriate interpretation of John Rawls's version of liberalism. Thus both democratic equality and luck egalitarianism are strongly shaped by the Rawlsian reading of moral and political philosophy. Daniels argues that democratic equality, much like

5. The distinctions between fate, fortune, and luck proper are suggested by Rescher (1995). The last of these, luck proper, is increasingly identified as "option luck" as opposed to the first two, which are referred to as "brute" luck (Daniels 2003).

6. The question of responsibility is confounded by a related discourse concerned with the concept of "moral luck" (B. Williams 1981). Moral luck asserts that meaningful moral evaluations rest on consequences. Hence if my reckless driving choices fail to lead to a pedestrian fatality, I have been lucky and bear no moral culpability. If, however, I do hit a pedestrian, I am fully responsible. Much of the hostility to utilitarianism in the luck literature derives from claims that moral evaluations should be governed by intentions and not by consequences (Rescher 1995).

7. I'm not sure what to make of this in the context of Cohen's admission that he himself doesn't much care for camping (Cohen 2009).

Rawls's philosophy more broadly, is a synthesis of classical liberal concerns and a sensitivity to the unfairness of brute luck. Daniels sees democratic equality as advocating considerably more redistribution than we currently are accustomed to, but considerably less than envisioned by the luck egalitarians.[8]

Not all proponents of democratic equality seem willing to go quite this far. Elizabeth Anderson (1999) in her seminal piece is reluctant to claim Rawls as a supporter, although she doubts that Rawls was a luck egalitarian. Her version of democratic equality seems to envision considerably less redistribution than that of Daniels. She puts more emphasis on the immediate relevance of democratic equality for the extension of classical liberal concerns. Anderson (1999) draws particular attention to the intellectual support that democratic equality offers for the political struggles of gays, the disabled, and women as they seek broader opportunities.

Among luck egalitarians there are a range of positions, but they share the fundamental concern about addressing the unfairness of bad luck. The advocates of democratic equality focus on using redistribution primarily as a means for enabling opportunity and public participation. Whatever the disagreements within the two camps, the tensions between them have loomed much larger. In the ongoing debate over luck and justice, the positions of the luck egalitarians and the democratic egalitarians are advanced as if they were fundamentally at odds or even contradictory. For example, Anderson (1999) pokes fun at what she views as the more extreme proposals of the luck egalitarians: the subsidization of lazy surfers, bidding for mating rights, and compensating the gloomy. At the same time, the luck egalitarians see democratic equality as overly conservative, if not disingenuous.

In this fog, it is easy to miss the fact that the two theories are fundamentally descended from the same utilitarian sources. While both sides may eschew the utilitarian label, each draws heavily on aspects of the utilitarian position of John Stuart Mill. It is Mill's historical utilitarian approach to justice and luck that set the stage for this more recent debate over luck. Democratic equality echoes much of the early liberal Mill, while the luck egalitarians build on the vision of the more radical mature Mill. Admittedly, Mill (perhaps like Rawls?) was ambivalent about these two motifs in his own writings, unsure himself as to the just response to inequalities of luck. Yet, he does attempt to synthesize them. And almost inevitably, such attempts invoke the promise of progress.

8. Daniels (2003) is willing to endorse redistribution for extremely bad option luck if it endangers individuals participating actively in the society.

MILL ON LUCK

There can be little doubt Mill recognized that the greatest variance in human outcomes (happiness?) is due to factors largely outside the control of individuals. In *Utilitarianism*, Mill observed that an individual who might otherwise live an "enviable existence" can often be unable to escape "the positive evils of life, the great sources of physical and mental suffering." Chief among these Mill listed poverty and disease, to which he added "the unkindness, worthlessness, or premature loss of objects of affection." Life leaves individuals in a "contest with these calamities," a contest "from which it is a rare good fortune entirely to escape; which, as things now are, cannot be obviated, and often cannot be in any material degree mitigated" (Mill [1861] 1987, 286).

It is not surprising that Mill's list included disease, an element modern philosophers would categorize as "fate." But it is noteworthy, indeed fundamental, that Mill also included poverty or indigence on his list. Mill, then, was placing the most striking income differences outside individual effort or control.

Mill's understanding of the social character, causes, and consequences of poverty is closely bound up with his general intellectual development. Suffice it to say that Mill's sympathy for the poor seems to have deepened over time—in response, perhaps, to the influence of his wife, Harriet Taylor.[9] Still, as discussed in chapter 7, Mill's pronouncements on the immediate policy questions surrounding public aid for the poor and the Poor Laws continued to reflect an abiding commitment to elements of the classical position of Bentham, Malthus, and Ricardo. Robson (1968) emphasizes Mill's continuing concern (shared with most all classical economists) that any transfers leave recipients in a position less attractive than that achievable by the working poor. Berger (1984) concludes that Mill favored public support of a "baseline" for the poor. Berger reads Mill's support of the Poor Law reforms as evidence that Mill "held that the poor have a *right* to subsistence income to be provided through governmental channels" (Berger 1984, 184). While this interpretation does not necessarily contradict Robson's more traditional version, it is colored by Mill's developing hopes for the educational and moral advancement of the working classes. Perhaps a more faithful reading of Mill would

9. For a still serviceable overview of Mill's intellectual development with an emphasis on his social and political thought, see Robson (1968). Key in Robson's treatment is Mill's shift toward a sort of Fabian socialism encouraged by his relation with Harriet Taylor and continental influences. See also Berger (1984), Donner (1991), and Reeves (2007).

emphasize the enhancement of security achievable through worker cooperatives.

The key observation to be made is that throughout his life Mill emphasized that poverty was essentially a matter of birth and circumstances—that is, of luck. Mill found it outrageous and unjust that children should starve through no fault of their own (Mill [1834] 1982). It was not that the poor worked little and the prosperous worked much. Mill observed that the poor often worked longer hours and more intensively than the well off, again suggesting that poverty is in many ways a matter of bad personal luck (Mill [1848] 1965).

Mill, anticipating John Elliott Cairnes's theory of noncompeting groups,[10] saw this inversion as fundamentally inequitable. In his discussion of wage differentials in the 1852 edition of the *Principles*, Mill expanded on the lack of compensating differences and noted "the inequalities of wages are generally in an opposite direction to the equitable principle of compensation erroneously represented by Adam Smith as the general law of the remuneration of labour. The hardships and the earnings, instead of being directly proportional, as in any just arrangements of society they would be, are generally in an inverse ratio to one another." It is those who "have no choice," who are left with the worst employments (Mill [1848] 1965, 383).

And where the character of the poor intensified their poverty, Mill attributed that character to the institutions of the broader society and government. Mill's plans for developing a science of ethology—that is, the study of the formation of character—were in large part motivated by his observation of the role of institutional influences in maintaining poverty (Mill [1843] 1974, book VI:ch. 5).[11] In this vein, we have already seen that Mill was hostile to institutions of inheritance and landed property, both of which he argued were deeply involved in perpetuating substantial inequalities based only on luck at birth.

Mill's understanding of the relation of luck and poverty is reiterated in his posthumous *Chapters on Socialism*. The introduction to those writings is very much an extension of Mill's position in *Utilitarianism*. Thus Mill observed:

> No longer enslaved or made dependent by force of law, the great majority are so by force of poverty; they are still chained to a place, to an occupation, and

10. On Mill and Cairns on noncompeting groups, see Brown (1977, 16).
11. For a discussion of the role of ethology in Mill's larger understanding of moral sciences, see Donner (1991, ch. 6).

> to conformity with the will of an employer, and debarred by the accident of birth both from the enjoyments, and from the mental and moral advantages, which others inherit without exertion and independently of desert. That this is an evil equal to almost any of those against which mankind have hitherto struggled, the poor are not wrong in believing. Is it a necessary evil? They are told so by those who do not feel it—by those who have gained the prizes in the *lottery* of life. But it was also said that slavery, that despotism, that all the privileges of oligarchy were necessary. (Mill [1879] 1967, 710)[12]

For the largest share of the population, for most of the working classes, luck and poverty stand in the way of meaningful individual development. Yet, as a growing body of Mill scholarship argues, Mill's central moral conclusion asserts the utilitarian good associated with the development of individuals' higher capacities (Berger [1984], Donner [1991], and O'Rourke [2001]). This argument is both convincing and basic to understanding Mill's utilitarianism. I will take its premises and conclusions as givens. Combining such a position with Mill's clear description of the ravages of poverty and much of working-class life, Mill clearly held a radical egalitarian position. (This is Donner's conclusion, also.) Making explicit the key role of luck in determining poverty, it would seem that Mill can also be classified as a luck egalitarian, or at least the major precursor of that view.

Yet Mill saw no speedy transition to the institutions required by luck egalitarianism. Rather, he looked to such a world as a goal, one that depends on the continuing contributions of progress. From a social-philosophical perspective, the path to that goal builds on Mill's understanding of the progressive and historical nature of justice. Such a reading places Mill's radical utopianism in the future while anchoring his tolerance of considerable inequality in the present. In addition to explicating Mill's theory of justice, such an approach allows a Millean diachronic synthesis of the two philosophies of luck.

12. In subsequent portions of these chapters Mill gave a series of socialist arguments and then went on to offer evaluations that were often critical of those arguments. At times it is difficult to tell exactly whose opinions are being put forth—those of Mill or those of the socialists. In any case, Mill's representation of the socialist position is powerfully crafted. The luck theme appears throughout. Mill compared the race of life to one conducted by a Nero or Domitian who demands that the last fifty racers be put to death. He maintained that it would not be "any diminution of the injustice that the strongest or nimblest would . . . be certain to escape." Sounding very much like G. A. Cohen, Mill asked "If the minds and feeling of the prosperous were in a right state, would they accept their prosperity if for the sake of it even one person near them was, for any other cause than voluntary fault, excluded from obtaining a desirable existence?" (Mill [1879] 1967, 713).

MILL ON THE PROGRESS OF JUSTICE

In a vein anticipatory of Rawls, Mill had an almost lexicographic commitment to justice before "pleasure or convenience." Again, consider his utilitarian definition of justice:

> Justice remains the appropriate name for certain social utilities which are vastly more important, and therefore more absolute and imperative, than any others are as a class (though not more so than others may be in particular cases); and which, therefore, ought to be, as well as naturally are, guarded by a sentiment not only different in degree, but also in kind; distinguished from the milder feeling which attaches to the mere idea of promoting human pleasure or convenience, at once by the more definite nature of its commands, and by the sterner character of its sanctions. (Mill [1861] 1987, 338)

Mill is clear that justice starts with the social utilities generated by equality. For all his criticisms and ambivalences over his mentor Jeremy Bentham, Mill anchored his approach to justice in Bentham's egalitarianism. This passage on justice continues to discuss Bentham's dictum: "everybody to count for one, nobody for more than one." From this dictum Mill inferred "The equal claim of everybody to happiness . . . involves an equal claim to all the means of happiness." This is a strong egalitarianism, indeed. However, Mill immediately qualified the radical conclusion by restricting such equal claims "in so far as the inevitable conditions of human life, and the general interest, in which that of every individual is included, set limits to the maxim; and those limits ought to be strictly construed" (336).

While recognizing social limits on egalitarianism, the key Millean-utilitarian insight into justice is that those social limits are themselves historical entities, subject to material and social progress. They are matters of "expediency" and not of principle. The principle rests on the egalitarian commitment of utilitarianism. Expediency is conditional on historically changing conditions.

Mill's general approach to progress was heavily influenced by continental thinkers, and in particular by Auguste Comte. Mill welcomed Comte's idea of an historical evolution of society from theological to metaphysical and then to a positive state. While Mill broke with Comte's elitism, he continued to see history as a progressive process. And he endorsed major elements of Comte's positive understanding of the fundamental direction of progress. Society was moving, however slowly, toward a point where people would "regard working for the benefit of others as a good in itself"

(Mill 1866, 148).[13] Mill associated this progressive development with the unfolding of justice for the greater number. At root, justice is a process deeply consistent with individuals' developing their higher potentials, a major theme of *Utilitarianism*. It is this movement that provides the hope of progress for the good of the greater number, but it is a historical process and must be seen in that light.

Thus, in *Utilitarianism*, Mill argued that the arc of history is one of removing the social inequalities established by custom and institutions. When inequalities are recognized as unnecessary, their continuation is quickly viewed as unjust: "And hence all social inequalities which have ceased to be considered expedient, assume the character not of simple inexpediency, but of injustice, and appear so tyrannical, that people are apt to wonder how they ever could have been tolerated." This had been the fate of the "distinctions of slaves and freemen, nobles and serfs, patricians and plebeians." Mill anticipated the same end for "the aristocracies of colour, race, and sex" (Mill [1861] 1987, 337). For Mill, then, justice consists in unraveling over time the web of customs and institutions that produce the great inequalities—inequalities that are, in effect, accidents of luck and birth.

One might argue that Mill in this passage was speaking only of the political justice of expanding civil rights. Such a reading would seem to put Mill in the liberal camp of democratic equality. Yet, his examples—slaves/freemen, nobles/serfs, patricians/plebians, and "the aristocracies of colour, race, and sex"—also invoke a wide range of economic inequalities rooted in the accidents of birth. Doesn't Mill here demand a fuller material equality in the name of justice? And, if so, how is he suggesting its achievement?

This question raises longstanding issues in interpreting Mill. Mill was surely impressed by the achievements of market economies, and he hesitated at the more extreme claims of socialists. Mill left murky the shape of the institutional changes on which progress is to develop. But he was clear that progress will include the reduction of material inequality. A central point of *Utilitarianism* is that over time progress will erode social and economic inequalities generated by fate and fortune. Perhaps most optimistically, Mill looked for the cooperative movement to play a transformative role in facilitating the material, intellectual, and moral development of the working classes.

Mill looked forward to the great narrowing of all the vicissitudes of life, including material poverty. He asserted, "most of the great positive evils of the world are in themselves removable, and will, if human affairs continue to improve, be in the end reduced within narrow limits. Poverty,

13. Comte's influence on Mill is discussed in Robson (1968).

in any sense implying suffering, may be completely extinguished by the wisdom of society, combined with the good sense and providence of individuals" (Mill [1861] 1987, 286).[14]

And if Mill was rather vague on details, he had a strong faith in the positive course of future events. In support of this faith, he repeatedly invoked the lessons of the past. For sure, these historical claims are only weakly researched in Mill's own writings. However, they give a distinctly progressive cast to both his conception of justice and his attitude toward the inequalities of luck.

Progress allows a temporal ordering in the historic movement toward the taming of luck. From this vantage point, Mill might reasonably be interpreted as expecting much of the program of democratic equality to be achieved prior to the program of luck egalitarians. Such an ordering fits well into the temporal priority Mill placed on the expansion of civil rights, including the franchise, education, and the cooperative movement.[15] Mill anticipated that these developments would be followed by a considerable widening in individual opportunities. Most notably, Mill emphasized just this ordering in his championing of women's rights. But only in the more distant future did Mill see the emergence of a society in which all (or almost all) individuals have a base to meaningfully pursue their own happiness, freed from the worst vagaries of birth and luck.

The proposition, then, is that Mill's framework of progressive justice, interpreted as a broad temporal move toward human development, equality, and the conquest of luck, provides a reasonable synthesis (or at least the sketch of such a synthesis) of the two major modern philosophic approaches to luck.

HUMAN NATURE AND LUCK

Modern participants in the luck debates might reasonably raise objection to the suggestion of a Millean synthesis based on the progress of

14. Mill's theme of progress here is strongly echoed in the optimism of John Maynard Keynes in his famous essay on "Economic Possibilities of Our Grandchildren" (Keynes 1931). For all their differences, Keynes like Mill saw the rapid accumulation of capital as the key economic prerequisite for a society that could place a greater emphasis on "the arts of life."

15. While a strong advocate of the expansion of the franchise, Mill did have doubts as to the appropriate pace of that expansion. He was very much concerned with the lack of education among the laboring classes and feared the emergence of demagoguery.

Utilitarianism. A central set of concerns might stem from differences between Mill's understanding of human nature and those more common in a post-Darwinian age.

As I've suggested in several passages, Mill's reading of human nature, like Adam Smith's, was fundamentally shaped by the thought of the Enlightenment. From that perspective individual differences had far more to do with nurture than nature. The Darwinian revolution has strongly asserted the significance of inherited characteristics. From a post-Darwinian vantage point, modern commentators on equality (whether philosophers or economists; radicals or conservatives) are likely to suppose a greater variation in inherited talents and abilities than that assumed by Mill.

In the mid-nineteenth century, Herbert Spencer's anticipations of social Darwinism still saw improvement of the species as achievable through the inheritance of acquired characteristics, a mechanism that leaves considerable room for nurture. By the turn of the century, advocates of eugenics like Francis Galton argued for selection based on Darwinian principles and saw little of value in the worst of us (criminal types, etc.). Economists followed a similar path. Economic thought shifted from the classical analytical egalitarianism of Smith and Mill to a more hierarchical view of human capacities (Peart and Leavy 2005). Indeed, eugenic solutions were advocated by many economists, both neoclassicals and institutionalists (Leonard 2005).

While such ideas lost popularity after the extremes of Nazi ideology discredited the eugenics movement, the continuing prestige of Darwinian biology, supported by the powerful metaphors of DNA, has worked to entrench beliefs in highly structured innate capabilities. The result is a modern emphasis on innate genetic characteristics that is shared by many on both sides to the debate over luck.

Assume Mill were to accept the interpretation of his thinking offered here. Then, given his classical egalitarianism, he would most likely expect that the luck-egalitarian position could be achieved with what, after the fact, would appear as only modest material redistributions from a starting position of democratic egalitarianism. Over time, education, nurture, and cooperation would achieve a major transformation of outcomes. Since people are not all that different, luck-egalitarian outcomes don't ultimately demand that much more than democratic-egalitarian outcomes. In such a world, substantial continuing redistribution is the exception rather than the rule. An advocate of the Millean synthesis might argue that proponents of democratic equality need not see such extensions of their egalitarianism as demanding a fundamental change in principles. Once progress has done its work equalizing the most blatant aspects of social luck (as opposed to genetic luck), the rest of the luck-egalitarian program will be achievable with only minor redistributions.

However, these classical expectations might today be sharply challenged by many luck egalitarians and advocates of democratic equality. Luck egalitarians influenced by modern genetics certainly do not present their understanding of justice as only a modest extension of democratic equality. Rather, they describe their position as requiring a far deeper acceptance of others than that offered by classical liberalism. For modern luck egalitarians, it will take quite a bit to counter the luck of genes and innate talents.

Advocates of democratic equality, under the influence of the same geneticism, may well agree that the luck-egalitarian program requires far more than democratic-egalitarian logic suggests. With visions of highly determinate double helixes in their heads, proponents of democratic equality may assert that justice doesn't require and wisdom doesn't dictate attempts at such considerable sharing among the lucky and unlucky.

If genes loom large and account for a great part of individual differences, accepting the logic of the Millean progressive synthesis becomes more problematic for both groups. The luck-egalitarian goal requires far more than the institutional structure of democratic equality. The philosophers of democratic equality are more likely to worry about the invasive character of the proposed expansion of institutional mechanisms. Rather than a relatively easy progression through time, we may be left with a harsh and strenuous climb to move from democratic equality to luck egalitarianism. That said, the climb may still be very much worth the effort.

MILL AND UTILITARIAN COMMITMENT

It may be that the Millean roadmap for the progressive overcoming of the inequalities generated by luck requires amplification and elaboration. But it would be unfair to question Mill's sincerity in encouraging those around him to work toward achieving that progress. The goal of eradicating the major sources of human suffering is difficult; "their removal is grievously slow" and will require "a long succession of generations" who "will perish in the breach before the conquest is completed." Only then will "this world become all that, if will and knowledge were not wanting, it might easily be made." But Mill was confident of success since "every mind sufficiently intelligent and generous to bear a part, however small and unconspicuous, in the endeavour, will draw a noble enjoyment from the contest itself, which he would not for any bribe in the form of selfish indulgence consent to be without" (Mill [1861] 1987, 287).

Surely, Mill saw himself as devoting his own life to this noble struggle. He revered the reform efforts of his wife in just this manner. The progressive unfolding of justice required such commitments. And while few commentators have questioned Mill's earnestness, many have found this call at odds with basic utilitarian notions concerning motivation.

Philosophers of a number of stripes have seen Mill's call to commitment and related discussions of virtue in *Utilitarianism* as unanchored in basic utilitarian theory. In such readings, Mill's essay sets out to defend the essence of Bentham's calculus of felicity. Yet, it ends by denouncing selfishness and encouraging self-sacrifice. Making this observation, commentators have gone so far as to conclude Mill had abandoned the core utilitarian claim that people's primary motivation is the pursuit of happiness.[16]

In *Utilitarianism*, Mill anticipates this question at some length. The heart of his argument is that over time, virtue becomes internalized as an end in itself. This occurs precisely because virtue's relation to the happiness of the community is continually observed. The connection of virtue to the highest social utilities of justice wins over those ready to appreciate the deep satisfaction of virtuous actions.

The reading of Mill presented here situates the argument for virtue squarely in the context of the progressive utilitarian conquest over the tyranny of luck. In effect Mill was claiming that those who can appreciate their own good fortune and the bad luck of others will be particularly susceptible to the attraction of virtue. This is part and parcel of the utilitarian progressive argument. The happiness of those participating in the transition rests on their appreciation of the broader utility they make possible.[17]

16. See discussion in Reeves (2007), but also Saunders (2010) for a recent treatment of Mill's conception of utility. The argument given here is consistent with Donner's (1991) discussion of Mill's utilitarianism of self-development, although we again place more emphasis on the progressive nature of the unfolding of justice.

17. Mill's emphasis on the need for active virtue in achieving the transition to a world freer from the constraints of luck can be compared to John Maynard Keynes's

Self-sacrifice apart from the expansion of justice contains no sweetness, and is abhorrent. The broader the domain of justice, the smaller and more limited the domain of luck and the less the happiness of virtue. Over time, the success of progress unbundles much of the appeal of virtue.

Mill was sure that the great mass of people, given the chance at education and unburdened from poverty, will echo his commitment to achieving justice. Progress works on both material conditions and on moral character. Mill was convinced of the ultimate success of this process, though he feared it would take a considerable time.[18] In his view, a commitment to facilitating this unfolding of justice will generate a "noble enjoyment." Of course, in this conviction Mill may have been projecting too easily his own preferences onto those of others. But he was surely not deserting the progressive utilitarian schema.

A case can be made that the conception of utility Mill presented here is not that far from Bentham's own. Bentham had included in his enumeration of pleasures and pains the pleasures of benevolence or sympathy as "pleasures resulting from the view of any pleasures supposed to be possessed by the beings who may be the objects of benevolence; to wit, the sensitive beings we are acquainted with" (Bentham [1780] 1987, 92). Perhaps, Mill attributed more weight to such sympathy than Bentham, but in doing so he was not violating some basic utilitarian principle. In essence, Mill was proposing that human development leads to a flattening of the sympathy gradient, as individuals extend their sympathetic understanding to those at greater distance. Mill was not endorsing some exaggerated Dickensian "telescopic philanthropy" but, rather, anticipating a broader sensitivity to the unfairness of luck.

Ultimately, the argument is founded in John Stuart Mill's understanding of his father's associationist psychology. In James Mill's *Analysis of the Phenomenon of Mind*, the development of sympathy is closely connected with pleasure children get from praise. Drawing on Smith's discussion in the *Theory of Moral Sentiments*, James Mill argued that as the experience of praise is reinforced, the individual gets substantial pleasure from the very state of praiseworthiness, even when independent of actual praise.

anticipation of an almost automatic emergence of an age without an economic problem, described in his essay "Economic Possibilities for our Grandchildren" (Keynes 1931).

18. In comparison to his wife, Harriet Taylor, Mill was distinctly pessimistic about the timeline involved in these transformations of character. Taylor was optimistic on this score, estimating that in a few years people could change dramatically. Mill, however, thought that she "greatly overrate[d] the ease of making people unselfish" (letter to Harriet Taylor, March 1849, quoted in Reeves [2007, 314]).

J. S. Mill, in his notes, responded warmly to this idea (Mill [1869] 1989, 239). For John Stuart Mill, the encouragement and development of such sympathy was pure utilitarianism.

Rather than a weakly argued tract by a J. S. Mill already disenchanted with utilitarian doctrine, *Utilitarianism* is a call to action and commitment. It advocates a progressive utilitarian conception of justice based on egalitarian insights. It seeks to enlist us in a struggle against the dominion of luck. And it holds out the promise of a meaningful sense of accomplishment.

MILL AND LUCK EGALITARIANS

This call at the center of *Utilitarianism* anticipates a major argument made by G. A. Cohen and other luck egalitarians. In *Rescuing Justice and Equality* (2008), Cohen faults Rawls for giving too much away in his difference principle. Rawls had argued that inequalities that had the result of improving the absolute condition of the worst off are consistent with justice. But Cohen is concerned that allowing such incentives amounts to little more than a bribe of the talented. Were the talented and the least fortunate part of a real community, there would be no need to bribe the former in the interest of the latter. The commitment to the greater good would, rather, be internalized.

Whatever the real-world practicalities of achieving such a community, Mill clearly anticipated Cohen's point. Mill called for serious people to make the achievement of justice and the minimization of luck a fundamental part of their own life's work. And he promised them a personal enjoyment far in excess of "any bribe in the form of selfish indulgence."

It is not surprising, then, to find Cohen, the luck egalitarian, quoting Mill at length on the question of incentives. In contrasting incentive-payment schemes and equal-payment schemes in the *Principles of Political Economy*, Mill argued (and Cohen quotes):

> The proportioning of remuneration to work done is really just, only in so far as the more or less of the work is a matter of choice; when it depends on natural difference of strength or capacity, this principle of remuneration is in itself an injustice: it is giving to those who have; assigning most to those who are already most favoured by nature. Considered however, as a compromise with the selfish type of character formed by the present standard of morality, and fostered by the existing social institutions, it is highly expedient; and until education shall have been entirely regenerated, is far more likely to prove immediately successful, than an attempt at a higher ideal. (Mill [1848] 1965, 210)

Mill's point here makes his sympathy for luck egalitarianism quite clear.

Still, in a footnote, Cohen goes on to criticize Mill's treatment of similar issues in *Utilitarianism*. Cohen writes that in *Utilitarianism*, "Mill argues, at great length, that justice is a species of expediency. But here [i.e., the passage just quoted] the self-same principle of remuneration is, under the stated conditions, both 'highly expedient' and 'an injustice.' It is a nice question whether that conjunction of designations is compatible with everything that Mill says in *Utilitarianism*" (2008, 85). Cohen suggests a contradiction in Mill. But what he has missed is Mill's sense of historic and progressive justice. Justice for Mill is not a species of expediency. Justice at any historical time acknowledges expediency without raising expediency to a principle. As progress moves society forward, we recognize that older expediencies as essentially unjust. Cohen has identified a perfect example of this process in the quote from the *Principles*, but he has missed the progressive and historical nature of the context. Accepting the interpretation of Mill offered here goes far toward generating a reassuring answer to Cohen's question. Mill's position is surprisingly consistent if we see his theory of justice as built upon our progressing ability to escape from expediency and the dictates of luck.

The demands of justice in limiting the inequities of luck remain hotly contested. Luck egalitarians interpret luck in the broadest possible manner, require much of justice, and favor radical economic restructuring. Advocates of democratic equality focus more narrowly on political institutions, draw on a classic liberal interpretation of justice, and emphasize process.

Mill's analysis of justice in the context of social progress provides an attractive resolution of the conflicts between democratic equality and luck egalitarianism. Rather than two schools separated by principle, a Millean synthesis suggests two historic phases of justice separated only by our evolving notions of expediency. Just as Mill saw laissez-faire capitalism as a transitional stage to a more cooperative economy, he saw something like democratic equality as a transitional stage to luck egalitarianism.

While Mill remained elusive about the sequence of institutional structures that will in time achieve a triumph over luck, he saw that victory as the very essence of justice. Progress starts with the vanquishing of the most egregious and unjust misfortunes such as slavery and serfdom. It moves toward a liberalism of political participation, civil rights, and education. This plateau corresponds roughly to the morality of democratic equality. But progress will push further, toward a broader equality of material outcomes and the enjoyment of a richer individual liberty. Perhaps, this movement will be associated with the expansion of industrial cooperatives, socialism, and/or some form of the stationary state. Progress holds promise of realizing the justice of the luck egalitarians.

Individual participation in the progressive struggle offers meaningful and satisfying rewards in personal utility, although it may well require the sacrifice of less noble sources of pleasure. Progress is as much concerned with the development of our sensibilities as it is with the expansion of material wealth. Over time, those sensibilities become more and more aware of the injustices of luck, less and less tolerant of the arguments of expediency. Individuals move from a material selfishness toward a sense of democratic equality and on to a broader luck egalitarianism.

Both advocates of democratic equality and luck egalitarians should be able to appreciate their origins in Mill's themes. The significant issue remaining between them is not Mill's utilitarianism. For all their protestations and concerns, both schools share a secret softness for utilitarianism at least in its Millean form. Instead, the key issue hinges on the facts. If progress generates the expanded range of sympathy anticipated by Mill, proponents of democratic equality could hardly maintain their complaint against the broader justice of the luck egalitarians. If no such deep change occurs, the luck egalitarians have little choice other than to accept pragmatically the more limited justice offered by democratic equality. While we wait for progress to unravel the misfortunes of luck, the evolution of our social psychology weighs more heavily than the debates of philosophers.

MILL'S VISION

I have tried to make the argument for the coherence of John Stuart Mill's radical writings. The emphasis in the last sentence should be placed on the word *coherence*. Mill's radicalism is made of whole cloth. It has a philosophic base built on utilitarianism and is close in spirit to modern theories of justice. Anticipating key elements of the Marxian model, it has a political economy that makes sense of the process of accumulation. And it has an approach to history that roots progress in economic realities. Most dramatically, Mill's radicalism envisions a highly productive cooperative economy in which the workplace is democratic and work is meaningful.

For much of his own work life at the East India Company, Mill participated in Britain's imperialist project. At times Mill fell back on triumphalist liberal clichés. He has been accused of inconsistency. Skipping a number of pages, one can read his economic magnum opus (as Marx did) as a slow retelling of standard classical political economy. No one is asserting Mill's sainthood.

Yet when considered seriously, the mature Mill's radicalism presents a coherence lacking in much of the modern discourse on the left. Mill's reformist position builds on his political economy and moves purposively toward the empowerment of the greater proportion of the population. Whereas Marx conjured images of repressive discipline, Keynes suggested a well-meaning, paternalistic elitism, and Rawls struggled with the material conditions of history, Mill presented an agenda based on the vast opportunities opened by the industrial revolution, an agenda sensitive to the working classes' widening demand for independence.

Here are the major elements of Mill's radicalism deserving serious consideration by modern radicals:

The utilitarian base still stands as a plausible starting point for normative guidance. Despite an ever-expanding academic critique of utilitarian principles, a convincing radical program must make the universal claim of seeking the greatest happiness of the greatest number. Even Rawls's principles of justice and his liberalism of freedom can be reasonably encompassed by Mill's utilitarianism. The language of rights is inspiring. But ultimately, as Bentham first argued, society, not God, constructs those rights. The utilitarian credo still provides the most reasonable guide to how we should go about this central political task.

The driving force of capitalist accumulation has opened a wide range of possible institutional changes, even as it has stimulated the working classes to fight for political democracy. Capitalist accumulation is subject to a deep tendency for the profit rate to fall. Capitalists will inevitably resist this tendency with all the means at hand. But ultimately, laissez-faire capitalism is a transitional mode, useful for laying a foundation but unattractive for any number of reasons.

A direct and revolutionary attack on private property in the means of production fails to pass the utilitarian test. Such an attack threatens at best a deadening centralism and at worst an unproductive chaos. A utilitarian approach to the complexity of the modern economy requires not revolution but deliberate and fundamental reform. The rise of democracy makes possible key institutional reforms. At the top of the list comes a reshaping of the laws of inheritance. Society can also benefit mightily from new systems of land tenure, welfare, and education. If from a modern viewpoint we find the specifics of Mill's reform agenda too confining, the list remains highly relevant.

Reform cannot only reside in the public sphere, but must also reach into the very heart of that oldest of institutions, the family. Most immediately, Mill saw such reform as a fundamental answer to the Malthusian problem of population. But at a deeper level he saw such reform as key to liberating women from age-old repression and exploitation.

With the increasing competency of the working classes emerges the very real possibility that the workplace itself can become a democratic institution. The promise of producer cooperatives offers the deepest reform. Cooperatives suggest a meaningful answer to a series of connected radical questions: How can we spend our workday in an environment that responds to our understanding, makes possible our productive contributions, and addresses our material needs? More clearly than Marx or Keynes or Rawls, Mill offered an answer to those questions, an answer anchored in philosophy, history, and political economy. In Mill's scenario, the

> transformation to cooperative ownership was to emerge, if not easily, relatively directly from a capitalism undermined by falling profit rates. Low interest rates and increasing capacity would allow the working classes to take control of production.

This last and central element of Mill's political economy of progress stands as a challenge to modern radicalism. A serious reconsideration of the promise of cooperatives is overdue. If in their present form cooperatives are awkward or impractical, are there reasonable alternative institutional forms that complete Mill's reading of the economic history of the working classes? A consideration of Mill's radicalism encourages us to go back to fundamentals and to explore and develop a historically appropriate radical agenda on work. This agenda must be both feasible and broadly appealing to the greatest number. It might involve the reorganization of cooperatives. It might involve new structures for unions, profitsharing, and worker councils.

The claim is not that Mill had the full answer either for his time or for ours. If for no other reason, surely history changes circumstances. But from the perspective of modern radicalism, we can recognize the Millean vision as coherent and deep. The left today sorely needs just such a vision.

BIBLIOGRAPHY

Alberro, José, and Joseph Persky. 1979. The Simple Analytics of Okishio's Theorem. *The Review of Radical Political Economics* 11: 37–41.

Alberro, José, and Joseph Persky. 1981. The Dynamics of Fixed Capital Revaluation and Scrapping. *The Review of Radical Political Economics* 13: 32–37.

Anderson, Elizabeth. 1999. What Is the Point of Equality? *Ethics* 109: 287–337.

Arneson, Richard. 2008. Rawls, Responsibility, and Distributive Justice. In *Justice, Political Liberalism, and Utilitarianism: Themes from Harsanyi and Rawls*, ed. Marc Fleurbaey, Maurice Salles, and John A. Weymark (80–107). Cambridge: Cambridge University Press.

Babbage, Charles. [1835] 1963. *On the Economy of Machinery and Manufacturing*, 4th ed. New York: A.M. Kelley.

Bacon, Francis. [1601] 1985. Of Usurie. In *The Essayes or Councels, Civill and Morall*, ed. Michael Kiernan (124–129). Cambridge, MA: Harvard University Press.

Baylen, Joseph, and Norbert Gossman. 1988. *Biographical Dictionary of Modern British Radicals, 3, 1870–1914*. Hassocks: Harvester Press.

Beccaria, Cesare. 1767. An Essay on Crimes and Punishments. London: J. Almon. Accessed from Google Books: https://books.google.com/books?id=IVl3jgEACAAJ.

Becker, Gary. 1991. *A Treatise on the Family*, enlarged ed. Cambridge, MA: Harvard University Press.

Bentham, Jeremy. [1780] 1987. *An Introduction to the Principles of Morals and Legislation*. In *Utilitarianism and Other Essays*, ed. Alan Ryan (132–176). London: Penguin Books.

Bentham, Jeremy. [1787a] 1962. Defence of Usury; Shewing the Impolicy of the Present Legal Restraints on the Terms of Pecuniary Bargains. In *The Works of Jeremy Bentham*, ed. John Bowring (vol. 3). New York: Russell & Russell.

Bentham, Jeremy. [1787b] 1995. *Panopticon Letters*, edited by Miran Bozovic. London: Verso.

Bentham, Jeremy. [1795] 1962. *Supply without Burden*. In *The Works of Jeremy Bentham*, ed. John Bowring (vol. 2). New York: Russell & Russell.

Bentham, Jeremy. [1819] 1962. Radicalism Not Dangerous. In *The Works of Jeremy Bentham*, ed. John Bowring (vol. 3). New York: Russell & Russell.

Bentham, Jeremy. [1825] 1962. Rationale of Reward. In *The Works of Jeremy Bentham*, ed. John Bowring (vol. 2). New York: Russell & Russell.

Bentham, Jeremy. [1828] 1962. *A Fragment on Government*. In *The Works of Jeremy Bentham*, ed. John Bowring (vol. 1). New York: Russell & Russell.

Bentham, Jeremy. [1838] 1962. *Principles of the Civil Code*. In *The Works of Jeremy Bentham*, ed. John Bowring (vol. 1). New York: Russell & Russell.

Bentham, Jeremy. [1843] 1962. *A Manual of Political Economy*. In *The Works of Jeremy Bentham*, ed. John Bowring (vol. 3). New York: Russell & Russell.

Bentham, Jeremy. 1981. *Correspondence of Jeremy Bentham*, vol. 4, edited by Alexander Milne. London: Athlone Press.

Berger, Fred. 1984. *Happiness, Justice, and Freedom: The Moral and Political Philosophy of John Stuart Mill*. Berkeley: University of California Press.

Bevir, Mark. 2011. *The Making of British Socialism*. Princeton: Princeton University Press.

Blanc, Louis. [1840] 1911. *The Organization of Work*, translated by Marie Dickore. University of Cincinnati Studies series II, volume 7 (1–59). Cincinnati, OH: University of Cincinnati.

Blaug, Mark. 1963. The Myth of the Old Poor Law and the Making of the New. *Journal of Economic History* 23: 151–184.

Blaug, Mark. 1964. The Poor Law Report Reexamined. *Journal of Economic History* 24: 229–245.

Blaug, Mark. 1985. *Economic Theory in Retrospect*, 4th ed. Cambridge: Cambridge University Press.

Bonner, John. 1995. *Economic Efficiency and Social Justice: The Development of Utilitarian Ideas in Economics from Bentham to Edgeworth*. Aldershot, UK: Edward Elgar.

Bortkiewicz, Ladislaus von. [1907] 1952. *Value and Price in the Marxian System*. International Economic Papers 2, 5–60. London: Macmillan.

Bowles, Samuel, and Herbert Gintis. 1993. A Political and Economic Case for Democratic Enterprise. *Economics and Philosophy* 9: 75–100.

Boyer, George. 1990. *An Economic History of the English Poor Law, 1750–1850*. Cambridge: Cambridge University Press.

Bradford, Wylie. 2000. Rawls and Meade: Unfortunate Bedfellows? Accessed at http://www.econ.mq.edu.au/__data/assets/pdf_file/0015/15261/8-2000_Aug00.PDF.

Brink, David. 2013. *Mill's Progressive Principles*. Oxford: Oxford University Press.

Brown, Henry Phelps. 1977. *The Inequality of Pay*. Oxford: Oxford University Press.

Burmeister, Edwin. 1984. Sraffa, Labor Theories of Value, and the Economics of Real Wage Rate Determination. *Journal of Political Economy* 92: 508–526.

Burston, W. H., ed. 1969. Introduction. *James Mill on Education*. Cambridge: Cambridge University Press.

Bury, J. B. 1920. *The Idea of Progress: An Inquiry into its Origin and Growth*. London: Macmillan.

Cairns, John. 1985. Introduction. In *The Collected Works of John Stuart Mill: Volume XX—Essays on French History and Historians*, ed. John M. Robson (vii–xcii). Toronto: University of Toronto Press.

Caldwell, Bruce. 2008. Hayek on Mill. *History of Political Economy* 40: 689–704.

Calhoun, Craig. 2012. *The Roots of Radicalism: Tradition, the Public Sphere, and Early Nineteenth-Century Social Movements*. Chicago: University of Chicago Press.

Chesterton, G. K. 1933. *St. Thomas Aquinas*. New York: Sheed & Ward.

Christie, Ian. 1993. *The Benthams in Russia: 1780–1791*. Oxford: Berg Publishers.

Claeys, Gregory. 2013. *Mill and Paternalism*. Cambridge: Cambridge University Press.

Cohen, G. A. 2000. *Karl Marx's Theory of History: A Defence*, expanded ed. Princeton: Princeton University Press.

Cohen, G. A. 2009. *Why Not Socialism?* Princeton: Princeton University Press.

Cohen, G. A. 2008. *Rescuing Justice and Equality*. Cambridge, MA: Harvard University Press.

Condorcet, Nicolas de. [1794] 1802. *Outlines of an Historical View of the Progress of the Human Mind*. Baltimore: G. Fryer. Accessed from Google Books: https://books.google.com/books?id=K3RZAAAAcAAJ.

Cottrill, Allin. 1997. Keynes, Ricardo, Malthus and Say's Law. Accessed at http://www.wfu.edu/~cottrell/says_law.pdf.

Cowherd, Raymond. 1977. *Political Economists and the English Poor Laws*. Athens, OH: Ohio University Press.

Crawford, Elizabeth. 1999. *The Women's Suffrage Movement: A Reference Guide, 1866–1928*. London: UCL Press.

Crimmins, James. 1998. Political Economy and Projectors: Bentham's *Defence of Usury*. The Science of Morality, 250th anniversary of birth of Jeremy Bentham, St Petersburg Metaphysical Society, Russia, reproduced in *The Philosophical Age Almanac 9. The Science of Morality: J. Bentham and Russia*, ed. Tartiana V. Artemieva and Michael I. Mikeshin (58–72). St. Petersburg, Russia, 1999.

Crimmins, James. 2002. Bentham and Hobbes: An Issue of Influence. *Journal of the History of Ideas* 63: 677–696.

Cubberley, Ellwood. 1948. *The History of Education; Educational Practice and Progress Considered as a Phase of the Development and Spread of Western Civilization*. Boston: Houghton Mifflin.

Dalton, Hugh. 1920a. *Some Aspects of the Inequality of Incomes in Modern Communities*. London: George Routledge.

Dalton, Hugh. 1920b. The Measurement of the Inequality of Incomes. *The Economic Journal* 30: 348–361.

Daniels, Norman. 2003. Democratic Equality: Rawls's Complex Egalitarianism. In *The Cambridge Companion to Rawls*, ed. Samuel Freeman (241–276). Cambridge: Cambridge University Press.

Defoe, Daniel. 1697. *An Essay upon Projects*. Accessed from Project Guttenberg, at http://www.gutenberg.org/etext/4087.

Defoe, Daniel. [1704] 1970. *Giving Alms, No Charity*. London: S.R. Publishers.

De Marchi, N. 1987. Nassau William Senior. In *The New Palgrave: A Dictionary of Economics*, ed. John Eatwell, Murray Milgate, and Peter Newman (vol. 4). London: Macmillan.

DiQuattro, Arthur. 1983. Rawls and Left Criticism. *Political Theory* 11: 53–78.

Donner, Wendy. 1991. *The Liberal Self: John Stuart Mill's Moral and Political Philosophy*. Ithaca, NY: Cornell University Press.

Donner, Wendy, and Richard Fumerton. 2009. *Mill*. Chichester, West Sussex: Wiley-Blackwell.

Dow, Gregory. 2003. *Governing the Firm: Workers Control in Theory and Practice*. Cambridge: Cambridge University Press.

Driver, Felix. 1993. *Power and Pauperism: The Workhouse System, 1834–1884*. Cambridge: Cambridge University Press.

Duncan, Graeme. 1973. *Marx and Mill: Two Views of Social Conflict and Social Harmony*. Cambridge: Cambridge University Press.

Economist Intelligence Unit. 2015. *Democracy Index 2014*. Accessed at http://www.eiu.com/Handlers/WhitepaperHandler.ashx?fi=Democracy-index-2014.pdf&mode=wp&campaignid=Democracy0115.

Elster, Jon, and Karl Ove Moene. 1989. *Alternatives to Capitalism*. Cambridge: Cambridge University Press.

Erreygers, Guido, and Giovanni Di Bartolomeo. (2007). The Debates on Rignaro's Inheritance Tax Proposal. *History of Political Economy* 39: 605–637.

Evensky, Jerry. 2005. *Adam Smith's Moral Philosophy: A Historical and Contemporary Perspective on Markets, Law, Ethics, and Culture*. Cambridge: Cambridge University Press.

Everett, Charles. 1931. *The Education of Jeremy Bentham*. New York: Columbia University Press.

Feuer, Lewis. 1949. John Stuart Mill and Marxian Socialism. *Journal of the History of Ideas* 10: 297–303.

Fleischacker, Sam. 2016. Adam Smith and the Left. In *Adam Smith: His Life, Thought, and Legacy*, ed. Ryan Hanley (478–493). Princeton: Princeton University Press.

Fogel, Robert, and Stanley Engerman. 1974. *Time on the Cross: Vol. 1: The Economics of American Negro Slavery*. Boston: Little, Brown.

Foley, Duncan. 2006. *Adam's Fallacy: A Guide to Economic Theology*. Cambridge, MA: Belknap Press.

Friedman, Milton. 1976. Adam Smith's Relevance for 1976. Selected Papers No. 50, Graduate School of Business, University of Chicago. Accessed at https://www.chicagobooth.edu/~/media/9535E51706DF4136AB8ED7B59A873A57.PDF.

Geisst, Charles. 2013. *Beggar Thy Neighbor: A History of Usury and Debt*. Philadelphia: University of Pennsylvania Press.

George, Henry. [1879] 1886. *Progress and Poverty*. New York: D. Appleton.

Gibbon, Edward. [1776] 1932. *The Decline and Fall of the Roman Empire*. New York: Modern Library.

Glaeser, Edward L., and Jose Scheinkman. 1998. Neither a Borrower nor a Lender Be: An Economic Analysis of Interest Restrictions and Usury Laws. *Journal of Law & Economics* 41: 1–36.

Gray, John. 1831. *The Social System: A Treatise on the Principle of Exchange*. Edinburgh: William Tait.

Gray, John. 1989. *Liberalisms: Essays in Political Philosophy*. London: Routledge.

Gruber, J., and E. Saez. 2002. The Elasticity of Taxable Income: Evidence and Implications. *Journal of Public Economics* 84: 1–32.

Halevy, Elie. 1955. *The Growth of Philosophical Radicalism*. Boston: Beacon Press.

Hamburger, Joseph. 1965. *Intellectuals in Politics: John Stuart Mill and the Philosophic Radicals*. New Haven: Yale University Press.

Hamburger, Joseph. 1999. *John Stuart Mill on Liberty and Control*. Princeton: Princeton University Press.

Hansen, Alvin. 1938. *Full Recovery or Stagnation?* New York: W.W. Norton.

Harris, Abram. 1956. John Stuart Mill's Theory of Progress. *Ethics* 66: 157–175.

Harris, Abram. 1964. John Stuart Mill: Servant of the East India Company. *The Canadian Journal of Economics and Political Science* 30: 185–202.

Hare, R. M. 1981. *Moral Thinking: Its Levels, Method and Point*. New York: Oxford University Press.

Helvetius, Claude Adrien. [1758] 1807. De l'Esprit or Essays on the Mind and Its Several Faculties. London: M. Jones. Accessed from Google Books: https://books.google.com/books?id=5UAAAAAAQAAJ.

Helvetius, Claude Adrien. [1772] 1969. *A Treatise on Man*, translated by W. Hooper. New York: Burt Franklin.

Hicks, John. 1941. The Rehabilitation of Consumers' Surplus. *Review of Economic Studies* 8: 108–116.

Hill, Christopher. 1972. *The World Turned Upside Down: Radical Ideas During the English Revolution, 1642–1660*. London: Temple Smith.

Himmelfarb, Gertrude. 1974. *On Liberty and Liberalism: The Case of John Stuart Mill*. New York: Alfred Knopf.

Hirschman, Albert. 1991. *The Rhetoric of Reaction: Perversity, Futility, Jeopardy.* Cambridge, MA: Belknap Press.
Hobbes, Thomas. [1660] 1996. *Leviathan*, edited by Richard Tuck. Cambridge: Cambridge University Press.
Hodgskin, Thomas. [1825] 1963. *Labour Defended against the Claims of Capital or the Unproductiveness of Capital proved with Reference to the Present Combinations amongst Journeymen*. New York: A.M. Kelley.
Hollander, Samuel. 1985. *The Economics of John Stuart Mill.* Toronto: University of Toronto Press.
Hollander, Samuel. 1999. Jeremy Bentham and Adam Smith on the Usury Laws: A 'Smithian' Reply to Bentham and a New Problem. *European Journal of History of Economic Thought* 6: 523–551.
Hont, Istvan. 2005. *Jealousy of Trade.* Cambridge, MA: Harvard University Press.
Howson, Susan. 2004. The Origins of Lionel Robbins's Essay on the Nature and Significance of Economic Science. *History of Political Economy* 36: 413–443.
Howson, Susan. 2012. *Lionel Robbins.* Cambridge: Cambridge University Press.
Hume, David. [1740] 1978. *A Treatise of Human Nature*, edited by L. A. Selby-Bigge. New York: Oxford University Press.
Hume, David. [1748] 1826. Of the Original Contract. From *Essays Moral Political and Literary*, in *The Philosophical Works of David Hume*, vol. 3. Edinburgh: Adam Black and William Tait. Accessed at http://oll.libertyfund.org/title/1483 on 2008-04-01.
Hume, David. 1751. *An Enquiry Concerning the Principles of Morals.* Accessed at http://www.gutenberg.org/dirs/etext03/nqpmr10.txt.
Hume, David. [1778] 1983. *The History of England from the Invasion of Julius Caesar to the Revolution in 1688.* Indianapolis: Liberty Fund. Accessed from Online Library of Liberty: http://oll.libertyfund.org/titles/hume-the-history-of-england-6-vols.
Hutcheson, Francis. [1725] 2004. *An Inquiry into the Original of our Ideas of Beauty and Virtue.* Indianapolis: Liberty Fund.
Iggers, George, ed. 1958. *The Doctrine of Saint-Simon: An Exposition; First Year, 1828–1829.* Boston: Beacon Press.
Israel, Jonathan. 2011a. *Democratic Enlightenment: Philosophy, Revolution, and Human Rights, 1750–1790.* Oxford: Oxford University Press.
Israel, Jonathan. 2011b. *A Revolution of the Mind.* Princeton: Princeton University Press.
Kaldor, Nicholas. 1939. Welfare Propositions of Economics and Interpersonal Comparisons of Utility. *Economic Journal* 49: 549–552.
Kay-Shuttleworth, James. 1853. *Public Education.* London: Longman, Brown, Green, and Longmans. Accessed from Google Books: https://books.google.com/books?id=stRJAAAAMAAJ.
Kay-Shuttleworth, James. [1862] 1973. *Four Periods of Public Education.* Brighton: Harvester Press.
Kelly, Paul. 1990. *Utilitarianism and Distributive Justice.* Oxford: Oxford University Press.
Kelly, Paul. 2000. Bentham and Smith on Projectors: The Moral Psychology of Economic Liberalism. Political Studies Association-UK 50th Annual Conference. Accessed at http://www.psa.ac.uk/cps/2000/Kelly%20Paul1.pdf.
Keynes, John Maynard. 1931. *Essays in Persuasion.* London: Macmillan.

Keynes, John Maynard. 1936. *The General Theory of Employment, Interest, and Money.* New York: Harcourt, Brace & World.

King, John. 2009. *Nicholas Kaldor.* Basingstoke, England: Palgrave Macmillan.

Korenman, Sanders, and David Neumark. 1991. Does Marriage Really Make Men More Productive? *Journal of Human Resources* 26: 282–307.

Krouse, Richard, and Michael McPherson. 1988. Capitalism, "Property-Owning Democracy," and the Welfare State. In *Democracy and the Welfare State,* ed. A. Gutman (79–106). Princeton: Princeton University Press.

Kruse, Douglas, Richard Freeman, and Joseph Blasi (eds). 2010. *Shared Capitalism at Work: Employee Ownership, Profit and Gain Sharing, and Broad-Based Stock Options*, National Bureau of Economic Research Conference Report. Chicago: University of Chicago Press.

Kurer, Oscar. 1998. Mill's Recantation of the Wages-Fund Doctrine: Was Mill Right After All? *History of Political Economy* 30: 515–536.

Légé, Philippe. 2008. Hayek's Readings of Mill. *Journal of the History of Economic Thought* 30: 199–215.

Leonard, E. M. [1900] 1965. *The Early History of English poor Law Relief.* Cambridge: Cambridge University Press, reprinted New York: Barnes and Noble.

Leonard, Thomas. 2005. Retrospectives: Eugenics and Economics in the Progressive Era. *Journal of Economic Perspectives* 19: 207–224.

Levine, Phillipa. 2004. Taylor, Helen, 1831–1907. *Oxford Dictionary of National Biography.* Oxford: Oxford University Press.

Lindert, Peter. 1986. Unequal English Wealth since 1670. *Journal of Political Economy* 94: 1127–1162.

Locke, John. [1690] 1988. *Two Treatises of Government*, edited by Peter Laslett. Cambridge: Cambridge University Press.

Locke, John. [1691] 1824. "Some Considerations of the Consequences of the Lowering of Interest, and Raising the Value of Money." In *Works of John Locke, Volume 4* (1–117). London: C. and J. Rivington, et al. Accessed from Google Books: https://books.google.com/books?id=_EM1AAAAIAAJ.

Lowenthal, Esther. [1911] 1972. *The Ricardian Socialists.* Clifton, NJ: A.M. Kelley.

MacKenzie, Norman, and Jeanne MacKenzie. 1977. *The Fabians.* New York: Simon & Schuster.

Macpherson, C. B. 1980. *The Life and Times of Liberal Democracy.* Oxford: Oxford University Press.

Malthus, Thomas Robert. [1798] 1970. *An Essay on the Principle of Population.* Baltimore: Penguin Books.

Malthus, Thomas Robert. 1826. *An Essay on the Principle of Population, or a View of its Past and Present Effects on Human Happiness; with an Inquiry into our Prospects respecting the Future Removal or Mitigation of the Evils which it Occasions*, 6th ed. London: John Murray. Accessed at http://oll.libertyfund.org/title/1945.

Mandeville, Bernard. 1924 [1732]. *The Fable of the Bees or Private Vices, Publick Benefits,* vol. 1., edited by F.B. Kaye. Oxford: Clarendon Press.

Mandeville, Bernard. 1924 [1729]. *The Fable of the Bees or Private Vices, Publick Benefits,* vol. 2, edited by F. B. Kaye. Oxford: Clarendon Press.

Marx, Karl. [1844] 1966. *The Economic and Philosophic Manuscripts of 1844.* In *Marx's Conception of Man,* ed. T. Bottomore (75–152). New York: F. Unger.

Marx, Karl. [1859] 1904. *A Contribution to the Critique of Political Economy.* Chicago: Charles Kerr.

Marx, Karl. [1867] 1906. *Capital: A Critique of Political Economy.* New York: Modern Library.

Marx, Karl. [1871] 2009. *The Civil War in France*. Gloucester: Dodo Press.

Marx, Karl. [1968] 1972. Theories of Surplus Value. In *Capital* Part III, ed. S. Ryazanskaya and R. Dixon (vol. 4). London: Lawrence and Wishart.

McCloskey, Deirdre. 1998. *The Rhetoric of Economics*, 2nd ed. Madison, WI: University of Wisconsin Press.

Meade, J. 1964. *Efficiency, Equality and the Ownership of Property*. London: G. Allen & Unwin.

Medema, Steven. 2009. *The Hesitant Hand: Taming Self-Interest in the History of Economic Ideas*. Princeton: Princeton University Press.

Meek, Ronald. 1963. The Economics of Physiocracy. Cambridge, MA: Harvard University Press.

Miles, Dudley. 1988. *Francis Place: The Life of a Remarkable Radical, 1771–1854*. Sussex: Harvester Press.

Mill, James. 1813. Education of the Poor. *Edinburgh Review* 21: 207–219.

Mill, James. [1815] 1969. Education. In *James Mill on Education*, ed. W. H. Burston (41–119). Cambridge: Cambridge University Press.

Mill, James. 1825. Government. *Supplement to the Encyclopedia Britannica*. London: J. Innes. Accessed from Online Library of Liberty: http://oll.libertyfund.org/titles/mill-government.

Mill, John Stuart. [1830] 1844. Of Profits, and Interest. In *Essays on Some Unsettled Questions of Political Economy*. London: Longmans, Green, Reader, and Dyer.

Mill, John Stuart. [1834] 1982. Notes on the Newspapers, 1834. In *The Collected Works of John Stuart Mill,—Essays on England, Ireland, and the Empire*, ed. John Robson (vol. 6). Toronto: University of Toronto Press.

Mill, John Stuart. [1836] 1977. *Civilization*. In *The Collected Works of John Stuart Mill—Essays on Politics and Society Part I*, ed. John M. Robson (vol. 18). Toronto: University of Toronto Press.

Mill, John Stuart. [1843] 1974. *A System of Logic Ratiocinative and Inductive, Being a Connected View of the Principles of Evidence and the Methods of Scientific Investigation*. In *The Collected Works of John Stuart Mill*, ed. John M. Robson (vol. 8). Toronto: University of Toronto Press.

Mill, John Stuart. [1848] 1965. *The Principles of Political Economy with Some of Their Applications to Social Philosophy*. In *The Collected Works of John Stuart Mill*, ed. John M. Robson (vols. 2–3). Toronto: University of Toronto Press.

Mill, John Stuart. [1849] 1985. *Vindication of the French Revolution of February 1848*. In *The Collected Works of John Stuart Mill—Essays on French History and Historians*, ed. John M. Robson (vol. 20). Toronto: University of Toronto Press.

Mill, John Stuart. [1859] 1977. *On Liberty*. In *Collected Works of John Stuart Mill—Essays on Politics and Society Part I*, ed. John M. Robson (vol. 18). Toronto: University of Toronto Press.

Mill, John Stuart. [1861] 1987. *Utilitarianism* (1871 edition). In *Utilitarianism and Other Essays*, ed. Alan Ryan (272–338). London: Penguin Classics.

Mill, John Stuart. 1866. *Auguste Comte and Positivism*. London: N. Trubner.

Mill, John Stuart. [1867] 1987. Bentham. In *Utilitarianism and other Essays*, ed. Alan Ryan (132–176). London: Penguin Classics.

Mill, John Stuart. [1869] 1984. *The Subjection of Women*. In *The Collected Works of John Stuart Mill—Essays on Equality, Law and Education*, ed. John M. Robson (vol. 21). Toronto: University of Toronto Press.

Mill, John Stuart. [1869] 1967. Thornton on Labour and Its Claims. In *The Collected Works of John Stuart Mill—Essays on Economics and Society Part II*, ed. John M. Robson (vol. 5). Toronto: University of Toronto Press.

Mill, John Stuart. [1869] 1989. Notes on James Mill's Analysis of the Phenomena of the Human Mind. In *The Collected Works of John Stuart Mill—Miscellaneous Writings*, ed. John M. Robson (vol. 31). Toronto: University of Toronto Press.

Mill, John Stuart. [1871] 1967. *Land Tenure Reform*. In *The Collected Works of John Stuart Mill—Essays on Economics and Society Part II*, ed. John Robson (vol. 5). Toronto: University of Toronto Press.

Mill, John Stuart. [1873] 1981. *Autobiography*. In *The Collected Works of John Stuart Mill*, ed. John Robson and Jack Stillinger (vol. 1). Toronto: University of Toronto Press.

Mill, John Stuart. [1879] 1967. *Chapters on Socialism*. In *The Collected Works of John Stuart Mill—Essays on Economics and Society Part II*, ed. John Robson (vol. 5). Toronto: University of Toronto.

Mill, John Stuart. 1963. *The Earlier Letters of John Stuart Mill: 1812–1848 Part II*, edited by Francis Mineka. In *The Collected Works of John Stuart Mill*, ed. John Robson (vol. 13.). Toronto: University of Toronto Press.

Mill, John Stuart. 1972. *The Later Letters of John Stuart Mill: 1849–1873 Part IV*, edited by Francis Mineka and Dwight Lindley. In *The Collected Works of John Stuart Mill*, ed. John Robson (vol. 17). Toronto: University of Toronto Press.

Mill, John Stuart. 1988. Debating Speeches, 1823–29. In *The Collected Works of John Stuart Mill—Journals and Debating Speeches Part I*, ed. John Robson (vol. 26). Toronto: University of Toronto Press.

Miller, William. 1966. The Economics of Education in English Classical Economics. *Southern Economic Journal* 32: 294–309.

Morishima, Michio. 1973. *Marx's Economics: A Dual Theory of Value and Growth*. Cambridge: Cambridge University Press.

Morley, John. 1886. *Diderot and the Encyclopaedists*, vol. 2. New York: Macmillan.

Mueller, Iris Wessel. 1956. *John Stuart Mill and French Thought*. Urbana: University of Illinois Press.

Murphy, Liam, and Thomas Nagel. 2004. *The Myth of Ownership: Taxes and Justice*. Oxford: Oxford University Press.

Noonan, John. 1957. *The Scholastic Analysis of Usury*. Cambridge, MA: Harvard University Press.

Okishio, Nobuo. 1961. Technical Change and the Rate of Profit. *Kobe University Economic Review* 7: 85–99.

Okun, Arthur. 1975. *Equality and Efficiency: The Big Trade-off*. Washington, DC: Brookings Institution.

O'Rourke, K. C. 2001. *John Stuart Mill and Freedom of Expression*. London: Routledge.

Owen, Robert. 1817. *A New View of Society: Essays on the Formation of Human Character, Preparatory to the Development of a Plan for Gradually Ameliorating the Condition of Mankind*, 3rd ed. London: Longman et al. Accessed from Google Books.

Owen, Robert. [1821] 1825. Constitution, Laws, and Regulations of a Community, appended to *A New View of Society*, first American edition (161–178). New York: Bliss and White. Accessed from Google Books: https://books.google.com/books?id=t9BLAQAAIAAJ.

Owen, Robert. 1830. *Lectures on an Entire New State of Society*. London: J. Brooks.

Oxley, Geoffrey. 1974. *Poor Relief in England and Wales, 1601–1834*. London: David and Charles.

Paganelli, Maria. 2003. *In Medio Stat Virtus*: An Alternative View of Usury in Adam Smith's Thinking. *History of Political Economy* 35: 21–48.

Paine, Thomas. 1791. *The Rights of Man: Being an Answer to Mr. Burke's Attack on the French Revolution*, 2nd ed. London: J.S. Jordan. Accessed at http://oll.libertyfund.org/title/798.

Paley, William. [1785] 2002. *The Principles of Moral and Political Philosophy.* Foreword by D. L. Mahieu. Indianapolis: Liberty Fund.

Peart, Sandra, and David Levy. 2005. *The "Vanity of the Philosopher."* Ann Arbor: University of Michigan Press.

Pease, Edward. 1916. *The History of the Fabian Society.* New York: E.P. Dutton.

Persky, Joseph. 1989. Adam Smith's Invisible Hands. *Journal of Economic Perspectives*, 3: 195–201.

Persky, Joseph. 1998. Wage Slavery. *History of Political Economy* 30: 627–651.

Persky, Joseph. 2010a. On the Thinness of Utilitarian Defenses of Private Property. *Journal of the History of Economic Thought* 32: 63–83.

Persky, Joseph. 2010b. Rawls's Thin (Millean) Defense of Private Property. *Utilitas* 22: 134–147.

Persky, Joseph. 2013. Utilitarianism and Luck. *History of Political Economy* 45: 287–309.

Persky, Joseph. 2015. American Political Economy and the Common School Movement, 1820–1850. *Journal of the History of Economic Thought* 37: 247–262.

Pigou, A. C. 1912. *Wealth and Welfare.* London: Macmillan.

Piketty, Thomas. 2014. *Capital in the Twenty-First Century.* Cambridge, MA: Harvard University Press.

Pimlott, Ben. 1985. *Hugh Dalton.* London: Jonathan Cape.

Place, Francis. 1972. *The Autobiography of Francis Place (1771–1854)*, edited by Mary Thale. Cambridge: Cambridge University Press.

Poor Law Commissioners. 1833. *Extracts from the Information Received as to the Administration and Operation of the Poor Laws.* London: B. Fellowes.

Poor Law Commissioners. [1834] 1905. *Poor Law Commissioners' Report of 1834.* London: Darling and Sons.

Putterman, Louis, John Roemer, and Joaquim Silvestre. 1988. Does Egalitarianism Have a Future? *Journal of Economic Literature*, 36: 861–902.

Rae, John. 1895. *Life of Adam Smith.* London: Macmillan.

Rawls, John. 1971. *A Theory of Justice.* Cambridge, MA: Harvard University Press.

Rawls, John. 2000. *Lectures on the History of Political Philosophy.* Cambridge, MA: Harvard University Press.

Rawls, John. 2001. *Justice as Fairness: A Restatement*, edited by Erin Kelly. Cambridge, MA: Harvard University Press.

Reeves, Richard. 2007. *John Stuart Mill: Victorian Firebrand.* London: Atlantic Books.

Rescher, Nicholas. 1995. *Luck: The Brilliant Randomness of Everyday Life.* New York: Farrar Straus & Giroux.

Rhodes, Rosamond. 2002. Reading Rawls and Hearing Hobbes. *Philosophical Forum* 33: 393–412.

Robbins, Lionel. 1932. *Essay on the Nature and Significance of Economic Science.* London: Macmillan.

Robbins, Lionel. 1968. *The Theory of Economic Development in the History of Economic Thought.* London: Macmillan.

Robbins, Lionel. 1971. *Autobiography of an Economist.* London: Macmillan.

Roberts, Evan. 2003. Patient Social Reformers. Mimeo. Accessed at http://users.pop.umn.edu/~eroberts/elywebb.pdf.
Roberts, Matthew. 2009. *Political Movements in Urban England, 1832–1914*. New York: Palgrave Macmillan.
Robertson, William. [1777] 1847. *The History of America*. In *The Historical and Other Works*, ed. Dugald Stewart (1–387). Edinburgh: Thomas Nelson.
Robinson, Joan. [1942] 1967. *An Essay on Marxian Economics*, 2nd ed. London: Palgrave Macmillan.
Robson, John. 1968. *Improvement of Mankind: The Social and Political Thought of John Stuart Mill*. Toronto: University of Toronto Press.
Roemer, John. 1979. Continuing Controversies on the Falling Rate of Profit: Fixed Capital and Other Issues. *Cambridge Journal of Economics* 3: 379–398.
Roemer, John. 1994. *A Future for Socialism*. Cambridge, MA: Harvard University Press.
Rothschild, Emma. 2001. *Economic Sentiments: Adam Smith, Condorcet and the Enlightenment*. Cambridge, MA: Harvard University Press.
Ryan, Alan. 1984. *Property and Political Theory*. Oxford: Basil Blackwell.
Samuelson, Paul. 1978. The Canonical Classical Model of Political Economy. *Journal of Economic Literature*. 16: 1415–1434.
Saunders, Ben. 2010. J.S. Mill's Conception of Utility. *Utilitas* 22: 52–69.
Schwartz, Pedro. 1972. *The New Political Economy of J.S. Mill*. London: Weidenfeld and Nicolson.
Senior, Nassau. [1830] 1966. Three Lectures on the Rate of Wages. New York: Augustus M. Kelley.
Senior, Nassau. [1841] 1973. Poor Law Reform. *Edinburgh Review*. In *Poverty and the Victorian Age*, ed. A. W. Coats (vol. 2). Farnbourough: Gregg International.
Senior, Nassau. 1854. *Political Economy*, 3rd ed. London: Richard Griffin. Accessed from Online Library of Liberty: http://oll.libertyfund.org/titles/senior-political-economy-1850-ed.
Senior, Nassau. 1872. Journal. In *Correspondence and Conversations of Alexis de Tocqueville with Nassau Senior, 1834–1859*, ed. M. C. M. Simpson (220–280). London: Henry S. King. Accessed from the Online Library of Liberty: http://lf-oll.s3.amazonaws.com/titles/2444/Tocqueville_1603-02_Bk.pdf.
Shabas, Margaret. 2006. *The Natural Origins of Economics*. Chicago: University of Chicago Press.
Shackleton, Robert. 1972. The Greatest Happiness of the Greatest Number: The History of Bentham's Phrase. *Studies on Voltaire and the Eighteenth Century* 90: 1461–1482.
Shaw, George Bernard. 1891. *Fabian Essays in Socialism*, American edition edited by H. G. Wilshire. New York: Homboldt. Accessed from Online Library of Liberty: http://oll.libertyfund.org/titles/298.
Shoul, Bernice. 1965. Similarities in the Work of John Stuart Mill and Karl Marx. *Science and Society* 29: 270–295.
Singer, Peter. 1972. Famine, Affluence, and Morality. *Philosophy and Public Affairs* 1: 229–243.
Singleton, John. 2011. "Money Is a Sterile Thing": Martin Luther on the Immorality of Usury Reconsidered. *History of Political Economy* 43: 683–698.
Smith, Adam. [1759] 2002. *The Theory of Moral Sentiments*, edited by Knud Haakonssen. Cambridge: Cambridge University Press.
Smith, Adam. [1776] 1976. *An Inquiry into the Nature and Causes of the Wealth of Nations*, edited by R. H. Campbell and A. S. Skinner. Oxford: Clarendon Press.

Smith, Adam. 1987. *Correspondence of Adam Smith*, edited by Earnest Mossner and Ian Ross. Oxford: Clarendon Press.

Spadafora, David. 1990. *The Idea of Progress in Eighteenth Century Britain*. New Haven: Yale University Press.

Spence, Thomas. [1775] 1920. *The Real Rights of Man*. In *The Pioneers of Land Reform*, ed. M. Beer (5–34). London: G. Bell and Sons.

Sraffa, Piero. 1960. *Production of Commodities by Means of Commodities Prelude to a Critique of Economic Theory*. London and New York: Cambridge University Press.

Stango, Victor. 2012. Are Payday Lending Markets Competitive? *Regulation* 35 (Fall): 26–33.

Stegman, Michael, and Robert Faris. 2003. Payday Lending: A Business Model that Encourages Chronic Borrowing. *Economic Development Quarterly* 17: 8–32.

Stephen, Leslie. [1900] 1950. *The English Utilitarians*. London: London School of Economics and Political Science.

Stigler, George. 1988. *Memoirs of an Unregulated Economist*. New York: Basic Books.

Taylor, Helen. 1867. The Claim of Englishwomen to the Suffrage Constitutionally Considered. *Westminster Review*. Accessed from the Victorian Women Writers Project: http://webapp1.dlib.indiana.edu/vwwp/view?docId=VAB7170.xml.

Taylor, Joyce. 1996. *Joseph Lancaster: The Poor Child's Friend: Educating the Poor in the Early Nineteenth Century*. Kent: Campanile Press.

Thompson, Dorothy. 1984. *The Chartists: Popular Politics in the Industrial Revolution*. New York: Pantheon Books.

Thompson, William. [1824] 1963. *Inquiry into the Principles of the Distribution of Wealth*. New York: A. M. Kelley.

Thompson, William. [1825] 1970. *Appeal of One Half the Human Race, Women, against the Pretensions of the Other Half, Men*. New York: B. Franklin.

Thompson, William. [1827] 1969. *Labour Rewarded. The Claims of Labor and Capital Conciliated: or How to Secure to Labor the Whole Products of its Exertions*. New York: A. M. Kelley.

Tuck, Richard. 1996. Introductory essay. In *Leviathan* by Thomas Hobbes, ed. Richard Tuck. Cambridge: Cambridge University Press.

Tupper, Martin. 1848. *Proverbial Philosophy: A Book of Thoughts and Arguments*. Auburn: Alden and Markham.

Turnovsky, Geoffrey. 2010. *The Literary Market: Authorship and Modernity in the Old Regime*. Philadelphia: University of Pennsylvania Press.

Van Parijs Philippe. 2003. Difference Principles. In *The Cambridge Companion to Rawls*, ed. Samuel Freeman (200–240). Cambridge: Cambridge University Press.

Vardi, Liana. 2012. *The Physiocrats and the World of the Enlightenment*. Cambridge: Cambridge University Press.

Webb, Beatrice. 1899. *The Cooperative Movement in Great Britain*. London: Swan Sonnenschein.

Webb, Sidney. 1887. *Facts for Socialists from the Political Economists and Statisticians*. Fabian Tract No. 5. London: Fabian Society.

Webb, Sidney. 1889a. The Historic Basis of Socialism. In *Fabian Essays in Socialism*, ed. George Bernard Shaw. London: Fabian Society.

Webb, Sidney. 1889b. *Socialism in England*. Baltimore: American Economics Association.

Webb, Sidney. 1890. *English Progress Towards Social Democracy*. Fabian Tract No. 15. London: Fabian Society.

Webb, Sidney, and Beatrice Webb. 1896. *History of Trade Unionism*. London: Longmans, Green.

Webb, Sidney, and Beatrice Webb. [1927] 1963. *English Poor Law History Part I*. Hamden, CT: Archon Books.

Webb, Sidney, and Beatrice Webb. 1978. *Letters of Sidney and Beatrice Webb: Vol. 1, Apprenticeships*, edited by Norman Mackenzie. Cambridge: Cambridge University Press.

West, E. G. 1975. *Education and the Industrial Revolution*, 2nd ed. Indianapolis: Liberty Fund.

West, Julius. 1913. *John Stuart Mill*. Fabian Biographical Series, No. 4, Fabian Tract No. 168. London: Fabian Society. Accessed through London School of Economics' Fabian Society Online Archive: http://digital.library.lse.ac.uk/objects/lse:kor293lan.

Wiggins, David. 2006. *Ethics: Twelve Lectures on the Philosophy of Morality*. Cambridge, MA: Harvard University Press.

Williams, Bernard. 1981. *Moral Luck*. Cambridge: Cambridge University Press.

Williams, Karel. 1981. *From Pauperism to Poverty*. London: Routledge & Kegan Paul.

Williams, Raymond. 1985. *Keywords: A Vocabulary of Culture and Society*. New York: Oxford University Press.

Wilson, Thomas. [1572] 1925. *A Discourse Upon Usury*, edited by R. H. Tawney. London: G. Bell and Sons.

Winch, Donald. 1996. Malthus versus Condorcet Revisited. *The European Journal of the History of Economic Thought* 3: 44–60.

Winstanley, Gerrard. [1649a] 1951. *The True Levellers' Standard Advanced*. In *Puritanism and Liberty*, ed. Arthur Woodhouse (379–385). Chicago: University of Chicago Press. Accessed from the Online Library of Liberty: http://lf-oll.s3.amazonaws.com/titles/2183/Clarke_1346_Bk.pdf.

Winstanley, Gerrard. [1649b] 1894. To my Lord Generall and his Councell of Warr. In *The Clarke Papers, Volume 2*, ed. C. H. Firth (217–221). Westminster: Camden Society. Accessed from the Online Library of Liberty: http://lf-oll.s3.amazonaws.com/titles/1985/0617-02_Bk.pdf.

Wolfe, Willard. 1975. *From Radicalism to Socialism*. New Haven: Yale University Press.

Zastoupil, Lynn. 1994. *John Stuart Mill and India*. Stanford, CA: Stanford University Press.

INDEX

www.ingramcontent.com/pod-product-compliance
Ingram Content Group UK Ltd.
Pitfield, Milton Keynes, MK11 3LW, UK
UKHW041433160926
475595UK00019B/14